LIONHEARTS

Other Books by the Same Author

Israel and the Arabs (1984)
Great Military Disasters (1987)
Elizabeth I (1988)
Saladin and the Fall of Jerusalem (1988)
The Book of Military Blunders (1991)
The Book of Decisive Battles (1992)
SNAFU (1993)
Blue on Blue (1995)
Fight or Flight (1996)

LIONHEARTS

Saladin, Richard I, and the
Era of the Third Crusade

Geoffrey Regan

WALKER AND COMPANY

New York

Originally published in Great Britain in 1998; first published in the
United States of America in 1999 by Walker Publishing Company, Inc.

Library of Congress Cataloging-in-Publication Data
    Regan, Geoffrey.
    Lionhearts: Saladin, Richard I, and the Era of the Third Crusade/Geoffrey
Regan.
        p.   cm.
    Includes bibliographical references and index.
    ISBN 0-8027-1354-8 (hardcover)
    1. Crusades—third, 1189–1192.   2. Saladin, Sultan of Egypt and Syria,
1137–1193.   3. Richard I, King of England, 1157–1199.   4. Great Britain—
History—Richard I, 1189–1199.   I. Title.
    D163
    956'.014—dc21   98–53348
                                                                       CIP

Printed in the United States of America
2 4 6 8 10 9 7 5 3 1

For Di and Roger Sheffield

Contents

List of Illustrations

‹

between pages 134 and 135

Church of the Holy Sepulchre *(Israel Government Tourist Office)*
Dome of the Rock *(Israel Government Tourist Office)*
Castle of Kerak *(Royal Jordanian Airlines)*
Castle of Gisors *(J. Goodman)*
Church at Vézelay *(David Martyn Hughes)*
Château Gaillard *(Arthur Shepherd)*
Cloister at Fontevrault *(Gerry Cranham)*
Richard I *(Britain on View Photo Library/Stockwave)*

MAPS

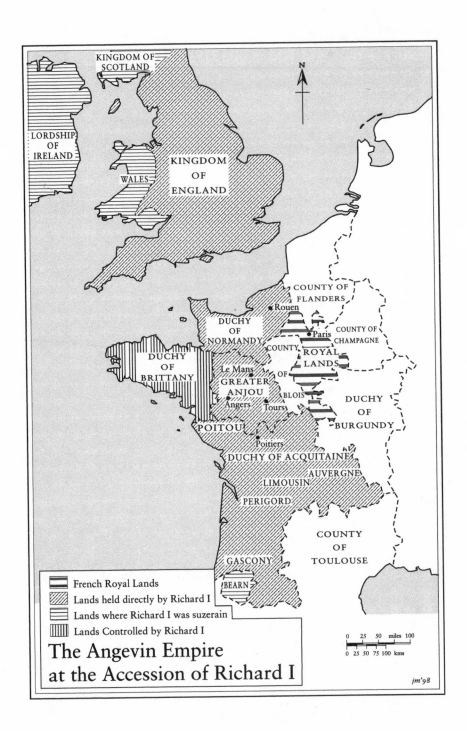

KINGDOM OF
SCOTLAND

N

LORDSHIP
OF
IRELAND

KINGDOM
OF
ENGLAND

WALES

COUNTY OF
FLANDERS

Rouen

DUCHY
OF
NORMANDY

Paris

COUNTY OF
CHAMPAGNE

DUCHY
OF
BRITTANY

COUNTY
ROYAL
LANDS

Le Mans
OF

GREATER
ANJOU

BLOIS

Angers

Tours

DUCHY
OF
BURGUNDY

POITOU

Poitiers

DUCHY OF ACQUITAINE

AUVERGNE

LIMOUSIN

PERIGORD

COUNTY
OF
TOULOUSE

GASCONY

BEARN

French Royal Lands
Lands held directly by Richard I
Lands where Richard I was suzerain
Lands Controlled by Richard I

0   25   50 miles 100

0 25 50 75 100 kms

The Angevin Empire
at the Accession of Richard I

jm'98

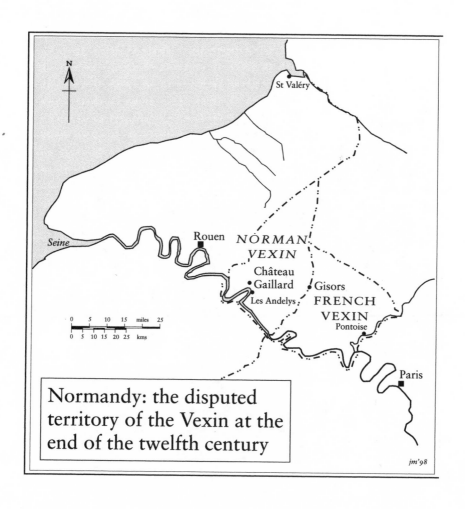

Normandy: the disputed territory of the Vexin at the end of the twelfth century

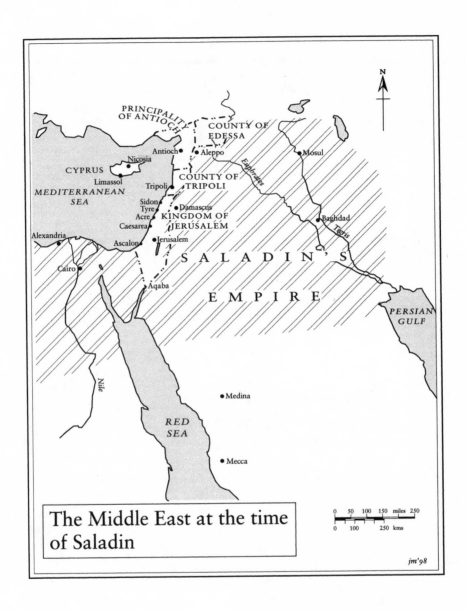

CYPRUS

MEDITERRANEAN
SEA

PRINCIPALITY
OF ANTIOCH

COUNTY OF
EDESSA

Antioch
Aleppo
Nicosia
Limassol

COUNTY OF
TRIPOLI

Tripoli

Sidon
Tyre
Acre
Caesarea
Ascalon

Damascus

KINGDOM OF
JERUSALEM

Alexandria

Jerusalem

Cairo

Mosul

Baghdad

Euphrates

Tigris

S A L A D I N ' S

E M P I R E

Āqaba

PERSIAN
GULF

Nile

Medina

RED
SEA

Mecca

N

**The Middle East at the time
of Saladin**

0   50   100   150   miles   250

0   100   250   kms

jm'98

The Kingdom of
Jerusalem

MEDITERRANEAN

SEA

Beirut

Litani

Sidon

Tyre
Toron
Banyas

Acre

Tiberias
Lake
Tiberias
Nazareth Hattin
1187
Yarmuk

Baisan

Caesarea

Nablus

Arsuf
Arsuf
1191
Jaffa
Ramla
Jerusalem
Jordan
Amman

Ibelin

Ascalon

Gaza
Dead
Darum
Sea

Kerak

Shaubak

jm'98

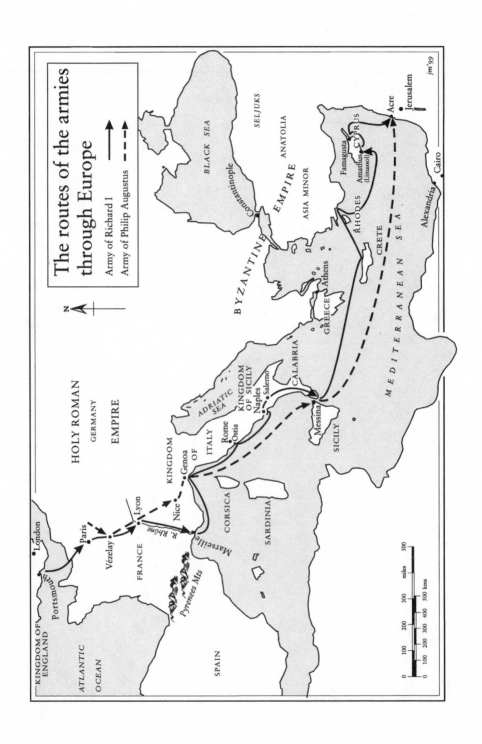

The routes of the armies through Europe

Army of Richard I
Army of Philip Augustus

N

HOLY ROMAN
GERMANY
EMPIRE

KINGDOM OF
ENGLAND

ATLANTIC

OCEAN

London

Portsmouth

Paris

Vézelay

FRANCE

Lyon

R. Rhone

Nice

Marseille

Pyrenees Mts

SPAIN

KINGDOM

OF

ITALY

Genoa

CORSICA

SARDINIA

Rome
Ostia

ADRIATIC
SEA

KINGDOM
OF SICILY
Naples
Salerno

CALABRIA

Messina

SICILY

MEDITERRANEAN SEA

GREECE
Athens

BLACK SEA

Constantinople

BYZANTINE

EMPIRE

SELJUKS

ANATOLIA

ASIA MINOR

RHODES

CRETE

CYPRUS
Famagusta
Amathus
(Limassol)

Acre
Jerusalem

Alexandria

Cairo

jm'99

miles   0   100   200   300   500

kms   0 100 200 300 400 500

Chronology

1174 Death of Nur al-Din and Saladin's father Ayyub; Saladin leaves Egypt and rides to Damascus

1175 Saladin defeats Mosulis at Hama

1176 Reginald of Chatillon released from prison, marries Stephanie of Milly and becomes Lord of Kerak

1177 Saladin suffers worst defeat at Montgisard at hands of King Baldwin IV of Jerusalem

1179 Richard establishes his military reputation by capturing Taillebourg

1180 Death of Louis VII and accession of Philip Augustus as King of France

1182 Reginald of Kerak's "Red Sea" operation threatens Muslim holy places

1183 Death of Henry the "Young King"; Saladin captures Aleppo; Egypt and Syria united under Saladin

1185 Death of Baldwin IV; accession of child king, Baldwin V

1186 Death of Baldwin V; Guy of Lusignan and Sibylla seize throne, Guy becoming King of Jerusalem

1187 Saladin invades kingdom of Jerusalem; battle of Hattin; Saladin captures Jerusalem and overthrows the kingdom; siege of Tyre; arrival of Conrad of Montferrat; Richard hears news of fall of Jerusalem and takes cross at Tours

1188 Siege of Acre

1189 Death of Henry II; accession of Richard I as King of England; German crusade sets out; Great battle of Acre—King Guy defeated by Saladin

1190 Anglo-French crusade leaves Vézelay; crusaders winter in Sicily

1191 Richard conquers Cyprus, marries Berengaria at Amathus; Richard arrives at Acre; fall of Acre; massacre of Muslim prisoners; Philip Augustus returns to France; crusaders march south to Jaffa; battle of Arsuf; Richard defeats Saladin; death of Taqi al-Din; William Longchamp overthrown by Prince John in England

1192 Assassination of Conrad of Montferrat; Richard fails to regain Jerusalem; battle of Jaffa; Richard defeats Saladin; three-year truce ends crusade; Richard leaves Holy Land; Richard imprisoned by Leopold of Austria

1193 Death of Saladin; Richard imprisoned in Vienna and Dürenstein; Philip Augustus invades Richard's territories; raising of Richard's ransom in England; Hubert Walter appointed Archbishop of Canterbury

1194 Richard released, returns to England and quells his brother John's rebellion; Richard declares war on Philip Augustus and begins regaining his lands

1195 Death of Leopold of Austria; Saladin's empire united under his brother al-Adil

1196–8 Richard builds castle of Château Gaillard

1198 Death of Henry VI, King of Germany and Holy Roman Emperor; succeeded by Richard's protégé Otto of Brunswick

1199 Death of Richard the Lionheart; buried at Fontevraud

Main Personalities

Henry II (1133–89). Son of Geoffrey Plantagenet, Count of Anjou, he married Eleanor of Aquitaine in 1152. They had eight children, including Richard the Lionheart. He ruled a vast Anglo-Norman domain known as the Angevin empire and became King of England in 1154.

Eleanor of Aquitaine (1122–1204). Having inherited the duchy of Aquitaine, in 1137 she married Louis VII of France, whom she accompanied on the Second Crusade. The fact that she bore him no sons contributed to the annulment of the marriage in 1152. She supported the sons of her second marriage in their rebellion against Henry II, who had her imprisoned between 1173 and 1189.

Henry (1155–83). Known as the "Young King" because he was crowned as his father's associate and successor in 1170, while Henry II was still alive.

Richard (1158–99). As Eleanor's favorite son, he became Count of Poitou and was due to inherit her lands in Aquitaine. Enthroned King of England in 1189.

Geoffrey (1158–86). Count of Brittany through his marriage to Constance of Brittany.

John (1167–1216). Known as "Lackland" and "Softsword," he was the youngest son and favorite of Henry II. He succeeded Richard as King of England in 1199.

Joanna (1165–99). She was Richard's favorite sister and married King William of Sicily. When the throne of Sicily was usurped by Tancred of Lecce after William's death, she was rescued by Richard and accompanied him to the Holy Land.

Geoffrey (1154–1212). Illegitimate son of the English woman Ykenai, who persuaded Henry II that he was the father. He was brought up by Eleanor with her own children. Richard appointed him Archbishop of York.

Alice. Daughter of Louis VII, betrothed to Richard the Lionheart but never married him. Stayed at English court and probably became mistress of Henry II.

PRINCIPAL CRUSADERS

Philip Augustus (1165–1223). Son of Louis VII, whom he succeeded as King of France in 1180. Known as "Dieu Donné," he was Richard's greatest rival, though no match for him militarily. One of the greatest of French kings, he regained Normandy and much of Anjou from John after Richard's death.

Hubert Walter (died 1205). The most able royal official of the Middle Ages, he was Richard's companion on the Third Crusade and was appointed Archbishop of Canterbury in 1193.

William Marshal (died 1219). The greatest knight of the age who came to symbolize chivalry, he served four kings from Henry II to Henry III. Richard rewarded his loyalty by heaping wealth and rank on him.

Robert of Leicester. One of Richard's most loyal supporters, he helped to save Rouen from the French while Richard was imprisoned in Germany.

William Longchamp (died 1197). Bishop of Ely. As Richard's most trusted civil servant, he was Chief Justiciar while Richard was on crusade. He was overthrown by Prince John in 1191.

Walter of Coutances (died 1207). Archbishop of Rouen. Richard sent him back to England from Messina to take over from Longchamp.

Mercadier. Mercenary captain. He served Richard during the crusades and was appointed commander of the Lionheart's armies in the wars against France.

Raymond III of Tripoli (1140–87). Lord of Galilee and opponent of

Guy of Lusignan. He served as regent of the Kingdom of Jerusalem, but his wise policies were set aside by such fanatics as Reginald of Kerak and Gerard of Ridefort.

Balian of Ibelin (died 1194). Lord of Nablus and supporter of Raymond III of Tripoli against Guy of Lusignan. On Raymond's death he rallied to Conrad of Montferrat.

Reginald of Chatillon (died 1187). Through his marriages he became Lord of Antioch in 1153 and Lord of Kerak in 1176. Greatest opponent Saladin faced before Richard. Executed by Saladin after the battle of Hattin.

Gerard of Ridefort (died 1191). Master of the Templars. As an enemy of Raymond III of Tripoli, he was the power behind Guy of Lusignan's seizure of the throne in 1186. Killed at the battle of Acre.

Conrad of Montferrat (died 1192). Savior of Tyre in 1187 and rival for the throne of Jerusalem to Guy of Lusignan. Assassinated by Old Man of the Mountain.

Guy of Lusignan (died 1195). Seized throne of Jerusalem with his wife Sibylla in 1186, but lost the kingdom at the battle of Hattin. He took part in the siege of Acre and was later rewarded with the throne of Cyprus by Richard.

LATIN KINGDOM OF JERUSALEM

Baldwin IV (1161–85). King of Jerusalem. Known as the "Leper King," he succeeded his father Amalric in 1174.

Baldwin V (1178–86). Son of William "Longsword" of Montferrat and Sibylla, sister of Baldwin IV, he was crowned during childhood in 1185, **Raymond III of Tripoli** serving as regent. His early death let **Guy of Lusignan** usurp the throne that Baldwin's uncle, **Conrad of Montferrat**, believed was rightly his. This dispute between Guy and Conrad split the Christian cause throughout the Third Crusade.

FAMILY OF SALADIN

Ayyub (died 1174). Father of Saladin and shrewd political adviser to Zangi and Nur al-Din.

Shirkuh (died 1169). Brother of Ayyub, uncle of Saladin and great warrior. Took Saladin on his expeditions to Egypt, which he eventually conquered and of which he became vizier.

al-Adil (died 1218). Brother of Saladin and second most able of the Ayyubids. Known to Westerners as Safadin, he spent much time ruling Egypt and became friendly with Richard during the Third Crusade.

Taqi al-Din (died 1191). Saladin's nephew and greatest general. His defection during the Third Crusade undermined Muslim military strength.

al-Afdal (1170–96). Saladin's heir and eldest son. Not as able as his father or his uncle, al-Adil.

OTHER MUSLIM LEADERS

al-Nasir, Caliph of Baghdad (died 1225). Abbasid ruler and spiritual ruler of Muslim world.

al-Adid, Caliph of Cairo (died 1171). Last Fatimid ruler of Egypt and leader of Shia cult.

Zangi (died 1146). Atabeg of Aleppo and Mosul. The first great opponent of the crusaders, he captured the county of Edessa in 1144.

Nur al-Din (1118–74). Son of Zangi and ruler of Syria. A great exponent of Holy War, he was an important patron of Saladin and Shirkuh.

Rashid al-Din Sinan. "The Old Man of the Mountain," leader of the Muslim sect known as the Assassins.

Imad al-Din Zangi. Nephew of Nur al-Din and Prince of Sinjar. Opponent of Saladin.

Saif al-Din Ghazi. Nephew of Nur al-Din and Prince of Mosul. Opponent of Saladin.

Introduction. Lionhearts

The fighting was over. The crusade had ended. Neither side had entirely achieved its objective, though neither side had failed by so much that it was eager to rejoin the struggle. Although the holy places of Jerusalem had Christian priests, and Latin ones at that, al-Quds, as the city was known in Arabic, was still a Muslim city. The coastal cities of Outremer were Christian once again, but the inland castles and fortresses were all held by the Muslims. Kerak was a place of ghosts. The "iron men" of Western Europe had returned home to rust in the damp atmosphere of their homelands, while the exuberant warriors of Islam rode their ponies on the desert plains armed only with polo sticks. "Coeur de Lion," mightiest of the Western Franks, had buried his collection of Muslim heads and was traveling to fresh battlefields, unaware that he was about to fall victim to treachery. The Lionheart was to be caged by Christians in a way no Muslim had ever managed to contain him. The Islamic "lionheart," Saladin, as cerebral and generous of spirit as the Frankish "Coeur de Lion" was physical and emotional, was facing death, not from the weapons of his foes but from the demands of his friends. The holy war known as the Third Crusade to Western historians but as the third barbarian invasion to the Muslims was now consigned to the chronicles.

Yet as the legends replaced the history one fact remained incontestable. The Third Crusade, however one viewed it, had seen a contest between two of the greatest figures of the twelfth century and, perhaps, even of the entire Middle Ages. Two men had risen to the challenge of holy war and, for all their inherent human failings, had triumphed over the intrinsic horror and cruelty of the struggle and inspired their followers to acts of sublime sacrifice.

Today we can challenge their motives; historians always do. Richard's enjoyment of war, his love of conquest, his territorial greed should all have consigned him to the category of conventional medieval warrior-kings, men of little learning and less understanding, but grim and strong and ruthless. Surely this description fits Richard, the man who blinded or drowned the garrison of Taillebourg and massacred the Muslims at Acre. But the cognomen of "Lionheart" that he brought with him to the crusade spoke of more than mere butchery and triumphalism. In the context of the kind of war Richard was conducting, an amphibious operation 2,000 miles from home, Richard's decision to massacre his prisoners, though eternally controversial, was a military one, requiring the greatest moral courage. The crusade could have ended at Acre, a victim of its own success, if Richard had employed a large part of his army to guard the Muslim garrison. It took a lionheart's courage to risk the opprobrium even of his own side.

Likewise, Saladin's killing of the Templar and Hospitaller prisoners after his victory at Hattin had revealed that for all his famed generosity of spirit he possessed the same kind of moral courage as his Frankish adversary in pursuit of victory in the holy war. Indeed, as revisionist historians will add, it was Saladin who arranged the murder of the Egyptian vizier Shawar, crucified a heretical poet, and, several times, arranged virtual auto-da-fés in which Christian prisoners were ritually slaughtered by Islamic men of religion. Yet this was the man who on countless occasions showed such kindness to the poor and helpless that he was admired by friend and foe alike. Historians must operate within the confines of their own subject. A man can only be judged, "warts and all," by the standards of the age in which he lived. In the context of the twelfth century and the crusades as a whole, both men rose above the limitations of their age, Richard as the military genius, Saladin as the noble "saint-king" of Islam.

The two lionhearts never met. Nevertheless, in the aftermath of the crusade, Christian and Muslim leaders were able to enjoy the fruits of peace together when Hubert Walter, Bishop of Salisbury, met Saladin in September 1192. The bishop described Richard in the usual effusive manner of a courtier as well as a cleric and one bred to flattery of the great:

As regards my lord the king, I may say that there is no knight in the world who can be considered his peer in military matters, or his equal in valour and generosity. He is distinguished by the full possession of every good quality. But why waste words? In my opinion—putting aside your sins—if anyone could give your noble qualities to King Richard and his to you so that each of you might be endowed with the faculties of the other then the whole world could not furnish two such princes.

Saladin and Richard shared the qualities of "Lionheart" to a greater or less extent: courage and nobility, pride and generosity, greatness of spirit and humility. Different as they were in personality, in their capacity to inspire their followers they were equals without peer.

1

|◆|◆|◆|

Richard of Poitou 1158–1189

WHATEVER WAS ENGLISH about Richard Plantagenet, nicknamed "Coeur de Lion," must have been passed to him through his wetnurse. Noble or royal ladies rarely if ever suckled their own offspring in the Middle Ages, so it was not the nipple of his mother, Queen Eleanor, that the newborn baby Richard first felt in his lips but that of Hodierna, an English woman of St. Albans, who had just given birth to her own son. It is possible that Richard spent most of his first two years in the family of Hodierna, whom he remembered with deep affection in later life. Her son, Richard's exact contemporary, was known as Alexander Neckham and later wrote a treatise on natural science, while Hodierna herself achieved a fame that few wetnurses ever have, being commemorated on the national map of England in the place-name of the Wiltshire parish of Knoyle Hodierne. When he became king, Richard showed his gratitude to Hodierna by granting her an annuity of £27 per annum from the royal domains at Chippenham.

Richard's parents, Henry of Anjou and Eleanor of Aquitaine, were two of the most formidable figures of the twelfth century. Their marriage, in 1152, brought together such an extensive territory that Henry overshadowed his overlord, Louis VII of France, by holding the entire western half of the country. Yet Henry of Anjou's elevation to such a position—in 1154 he became King of England as well—was dependent upon an astonishing blunder by the French king. In 1137 Louis VII had married Eleanor, the sixteen-year-old daughter of William X, Duke of Aquitaine.

As William had no sons, Eleanor was the heiress to the vast area of Aquitaine, being little less than all of France below the Loire to the Pyrenees and including Poitou, Auvergne, Périgord and Gascony. However, the marriage of Louis and Eleanor was unhappy: he found her flirty and trivial, she him saintly and monkish—and in fourteen years they had just two daughters and no sons. Desperate for a son, Louis divorced her and married Constance of Castile. Eleanor immediately married Henry of Anjou and in the first six years of marriage bore him five children, including three sons. In an instant the strategic situation in France had changed. Louis VII's lands had shrunk while those of Henry of Anjou had swelled enormously, and when he succeeded to the throne of England he had become in a matter of a few years the most powerful ruler in Europe and lord of the new Angevin empire.

Richard was born on September 8, 1158, at Beaumont Palace in Oxford. In spite of his becoming one of the most famous of all English kings, there was nothing English in the blood he inherited from either parent, nor any particular feeling for the island kingdom. In every respect he was a Poitevin and was brought up to love every aspect of life in his mother's duchy of Aquitaine. In view of the high infant mortality in medieval times, Richard presented an investment in an uncertain future for his parents. Already, the royal couple had lost one son, William, a sickly child who had died before Richard was born. Inured to the grief of losing a proportion of all the children she bore, Eleanor, like all mothers of the time, conserved her love for later, after a child had passed the dangerous early years. Yet, she always had special affection for this her third son, making it clear to her husband that it was Richard who would be heir to her lands and would be designated Duke of Aquitaine and Count of Poitou.

In his early childhood Richard cannot have seen much of either of his parents: during the 1160s Henry II was constantly on the move throughout England and at first Eleanor frequently rode with him and his courtiers. In the first year of Richard's life, 1159, it has been estimated that the two traveled over 3,500 miles, on horseback, averaging nearly 10 miles every day. This peripatetic way of life was quite unsuited to young children and hardly less so to the queen, who was frequently pregnant and longed for the elegant court life of her distant Poitiers. Moreover, during the decade of the 1160s the great struggle between Henry and Thomas Becket, Archbishop of Canterbury, took up much of the king's time, leaving him tired and irritable. The king frequently gave vent to the famed "Angevin temper" or "black bile" which was eventually to cost Becket his life. During Henry's tantrums he shrieked and screamed, rolled on the ground, spat and dribbled, gnawed at mats, bit blankets, smashed furniture, and tried to strike anyone or anything in range, sometimes with his hands, sometimes even with his sword. He used these displays partly to release tension but more often to get his own way; they were a product of the childhood frustrations he must have suffered. Of all his sons, none of whom inherited a temper quite like his own, Richard came closest to sharing the "black bile." As a role model, admittedly a distant one in Richard's early childhood, Henry set a poor example.

Eleanor found life in England with her boorish husband a drab experience compared with the gay and artistic life of Aquitaine. As Richard grew older Eleanor took him with her from England and brought him up at her court at Poitiers, capital of the county of Poitou. In view of the fact that he was the second living son, Richard could not expect to become king himself, although with medieval life being something of a lottery, particularly for those who lived by war, he needed to be ready at any moment to succeed a father or elder brother who died unexpectedly.

In view of the legends that surround the adult, it is surprising that none of the surviving chronicles give details of Richard as a child. Starved of anecdote, one is forced to presume that his upbringing resembled that of any young boy of noble or royal blood in the twelfth century. What may have marked Richard out from his fellows, besides his skills in war games, was his poetic and musical ability, which was cultivated to a high level at the court of Eleanor of Aquitaine. In addition, Richard was well educated, speaking Latin to a level that apparently once embarrassed an Archbishop of Canterbury, and writing verse in French and even Provençal. His great-grandfather, William IX of Aquitaine, had been a poet of distinction and some of the literary accomplishments of the court undoubtedly rubbed off on the young man. In this respect his education may even be said to have exceeded that of his great rival, Saladin, but these matters are relative. In the twelfth century, education in Europe was primitive compared with that in the Islamic world and the Muslims, probably rightly, tended to see the Christian crusaders as barbarians. Moreover, those Christians who, like

Raymond of Tripoli or Reginald of Sidon, grew up in Outremer and learned the ways of the East, often shared the Muslim view of the crusaders from Western Europe. It was in the activities of war that the Franks excelled and so, in spite of the music and literature to which the young Richard was exposed, it was learning to be a knight that occupied much of the young boy's time. Many boys or young men of his class excelled in physical activity and the martial arts, but Richard combined physical strength with a talent for all things military, from the use of weapons to studies of siegecraft and strategy. Skills as a fighter were a vital part of any young nobleman's upbringing, as war was to play the major part in their lives. Life expectancy was literally based on ability with sword, spear, lance, and ax. In his use of weapons Richard was to exceed his companions so completely that had he not been a prince he might have earned his living by his victories at tournaments like his contemporary, William Marshal.

In trying to understand the man Richard the Lionheart was to become it is vital to know something about his father, a complex figure whose character was full of such strengths that they frequently acted as weaknesses. One, in particular, was that he was dynastic by mentality but at the same time miserly in his capacity to surrender or delegate power even to those for whom he claimed to be acting. It was power that he loved above his own sons. Although he allocated them vast expanses of territory over which to hold titles, he never granted them what they came to want most, the reality of their titles. Henry, his eldest son, may have been crowned "king" of England, but his father never failed to demonstrate how hollow the title was in practice. This habit infuriated all of his sons in turn, though none more severely than it did Richard of Poitou, ensuring that father and sons would forever be at loggerheads.

In 1169 Richard had acknowledged Louis as his liege lord for the duchy of Aquitaine, which his father planned him to rule. Part of Henry II's plan involved Richard being betrothed to Louis VII's younger daughter, the nine-year-old Alice, who was handed over to Queen Eleanor to be brought up at the Plantagenet court. The betrothals of Henry's eldest son to Alice's sister Margaret and of Richard to Alice were designed to win Henry important territorial advantages in the shape of the Vexin (a buffer zone between the Ile-de-France and Normandy, whose chief castle was Gisors) but the early death of the "Young King" and the failure of Richard to marry Alice meant that the ownership of the Vexin caused constant dispute between the Capetians and the Angevins in the 1190s.

Richard was installed as Duke of Aquitaine in 1172, and Eleanor turned the occasion into a celebration of all that the duchy had meant to her in her childhood. Her grim experiences of married life at the court of Henry of Anjou in England were replaced by something closer to a re-creation of the magical city of Camelot in Arthurian legends, with herself a hybrid Arthur–Guinevere figure, at once politically masterful and yet with a zest for life that breathed the airs of southern France. Richard was invested with the ducal privileges in the city of Limoges and contracted a symbolic marriage with Saint Valerie, patron saint of Limoges, placing her ring on his finger and thereby creating an insoluble link between Richard and the lands of Aquitaine. Those critics of Richard as King of England would do well to consider how much of a Poitevin he really was and how little of England he knew or even cared to know. The island kingdom was forever a reminder of his father, whom he feared and came to hate, rather than his mother, whom he had loved above all other women, and of his childhood at Poitiers.

The court at Poitiers became a kind of crèche for the royal children of Western Europe. As well as her sons Henry, Richard, and Geoffrey, and their sisters Eleanor and Joanna, Eleanor also had around her during the 1160s the sons' prospective wives, Margaret, Alice, and Constance, all daughters of Louis VII, and numerous other royal offspring. The future Emperor of Germany, Otto of Brunswick, for example, was brought up at Poitiers.

In addition to being a royal crèche, Poitiers has been called an "oasis" of feminism, unique in European history, a center where women felt confident to express themselves in what was believed to be a "new age" for the sex. The traditional view of women as "Eve the Temptress" was being replaced by that of "Our Lady, the Queen of Heaven." Some historians had attributed to Eleanor and her band of ladies the laying of the foundations of European chivalry and of courtly love. However, if it was a beginning it was a very small one, for even the knights of Aquitaine were rough and barbaric compared with the knights of the late fourteenth century. Henry II was often alarmed at the effect that this "feminism" might have on the upbringing of his sons and feared that his wife might prove to be subversive not only within his family but within his lands as well. The events of 1173 convinced him that he was right and provoked him into putting an end to Eleanor's brilliant experiment.

Richard became duke at what we today would consider the tender age of fourteen. But there was nothing tender about fourteen-year-old boys in the twelfth century. Once he bore the title for the lands of Aquitaine he would be required to defend them from avaricious neighbors eager to exploit any childish weakness. Nor did his family provide much help. On the contrary, his father and brothers were often on the side of those who troubled him and instead he found himself looking for help to his prospective father-in-law, his overlord, Louis VII.

In the atmosphere of the court at Poitiers Henry's three eldest sons enjoyed the comfort and intellectual stimulation that was unusual for boys, even princes, in the twelfth century. Yet as they moved into adolescence they often brooded on the wrongs their father had done them. Their mother encouraged such free thinking and their father knew to whom to attribute the rebelliousness of his sons.

The chronicles record a description of the teenage Richard: "He was tall of stature, graceful in figure; his hair between red and auburn, his limbs were straight and flexible; his arms rather long, and not to be matched for wielding the sword or for striking with it, and his long legs suited the rest of his frame." His physical strength was proverbial, as the casualty lists of those who succumbed to him in combat bear out, and he had a natural athleticism until he became increasingly overweight in his late thirties. In many ways he became the archetypal knight of medieval chivalry, skilled in music and composing verse for the ladies, yet at the same time a fierce warrior in battle who showed no quarter to his enemy. Being brought up in a court where the female element tended to dominate may have had the effect of demystifying women so that he saw them less as sex objects than as inferior versions of his own mother. Certainly he found no woman in his life to match his peerless mother or his much-loved sister, Joanna, and this may have given him ambivalent attitudes toward his own sexuality. Most historians have taken Richard to be homosexual, and it is only recently that something of a critical backlash has taken place. Unlike such famous homosexual monarchs as Edward II with his "lover" Piers Gaveston and James I, with his circle of willing page boys and courtiers, no name is recorded to show that Richard enjoyed a relationship with any man or boy in particular.

During Christmas 1172 there was a very serious family row that had been brewing for some time. King Henry summoned Eleanor to bring his sons to join him at Chinon for Christmas festivities, but, as usual, no sooner were they gathered together than disputes broke out. Henry was apparently furious that his eldest son, now eighteen years old and married, had not come to join them. Eleanor tried to explain that the "Young King," as the young Henry was known on account of his token coronation as King of England, wanted territory of his own, as Richard had Aquitaine and Geoffrey Brittany, but King Henry furiously berated her for spoiling the boy at her ridiculous court, full of troubadours and idlers. He warned her that he intended to put a stop to her harmful influence. While Eleanor went home to Poitiers with Richard and Geoffrey, Henry began trying to prepare his eldest son and namesake for the responsibilities of kingship by dismissing his friends and boon companions. The "Young King" was now kept virtually under house arrest at Chinon. On March 5, young Henry escaped under cover of darkness and fled to the only place he could be certain of protection, the court of his father-in-law, Louis VII. His father tried to recapture him and pursued him through the night from Le Mans to Alençon and right up to the borders of Capetian France, but he was too late.

The "devil's brood," for so historians have described Henry II's family, now gathered together: the "Young King" summoned his brothers, Richard and Geoffrey, to join him in France and the three of them agreed to ally with Louis VII against their father. Prominent in this plot was their mother. But in spite of their initial successes, it was not long before Henry II began to reassert himself, buying the services of thousands of Brabançon mercenaries and snuffing out his enemies one by one. Louis VII abandoned his three young Angevin allies and made peace with Henry II on September 25, 1173, under the shade of the great elm tree at Gisors, the site of many such occasions during the twelfth century until cut down by Louis's son Philip Augustus. King Henry also made peace with his sons, offering them castles and money instead of the power they wanted. This peace could be no more than a truce while Henry failed to understand the basic principles of fatherhood. Henry may have made peace with France and with his rebellious sons, but he had already decided that there could be no peace with the woman who had borne his children only to corrupt them at her court. Queen Eleanor was at Poitiers when she heard that her husband was advancing into Aquitaine with a large army of mercenaries, wreaking havoc on her lands as he passed. It was a condign punishment, intended for her; yet it was her people who would have to bear it, with wrecked harvests, vineyards, farms and flocks. Soon the whole region north of Poitiers was in flames. Her advisers pressed the queen to flee, but her pride scarcely allowed her to abandon her home to so barbaric a conqueror. When she did flee it was already too late. Disguised as a knight and riding astride her horse, she rode through the smoking countryside escorted by just a few knights. Unfortunately she was intercepted by Poitevins loyal to her husband and imprisoned at Chinon. For months her sons had no news of her whereabouts. It is not known whether Henry planned this imprisonment as a short-term solution, but Eleanor remained a prisoner for sixteen years, until Henry's death in 1189. With the main prize in his net, Henry marched on to Poitiers and scooped up the remaining minnows, in the shape of his female relations, most of whom had been sheltering at Eleanor's court, including his daughter Joanna and Richard's supposed future wife, Alice. Henry grimly cleansed the Augean stable, sweeping away the splendor and placing the government under sound and trustworthy men of his own choosing.

While awaiting his mother's arrival in Capetian territory, Richard received the honor of being knighted by Louis VII. Hearing that his mother had been taken, Richard returned to Aquitaine to persuade his barons to support him against King Henry. However, battles between father and son held few attractions for the local lords of the south who knew that, if he lost, Richard would be forgiven by his father while they, if they had helped him, would likely finish at a rope's end. Richard was determined to act, with or without the help of his barons, and in May 1174 he achieved his first victory over his father, capturing the town of Saintes, but it could not last long. As the tide of battle turned against the rebellious sons they fell to quarreling with each other and then with Louis VII. Now aged seventeen, Richard was tired of so unprofitable a conflict and met his father at Poitiers, falling at his feet and begging forgiveness. A general peace was signed within the family to put an end to the fighting. King Henry forgave his sons but reined in even further their individual authority. Each son in turn was reduced to just a couple of castles to replace their dukedoms, though John, the youngest (and the king's favorite), had such an increased portion that it made his cognomen of "Lackland" even more ironical than the circumstances that had driven the "Young King" to rebellion the previous year. Richard, like his brothers, was forced to swear that they would not challenge their father in the future. Although the three young men emerged virtually unscathed from their struggle with their father, their mother remained a prisoner, having been moved under heavy guard to Salisbury and being given the barest minimum for her maintenance. She was paying a heavy price for failure, not as a mother but as a rebel. Her thoughts in captivity must often have centered on her favorite child, Richard, most able and intelligent of her Angevin brood. His time would come, and until then she must be content to wait.

During 1175 and 1176 Richard was concerned with the affairs of Aquitaine, almost constantly in the saddle, fighting one rebellious vassal after another and honing his military skills to a fine edge. When, the following year, Richard moved up to join his father in Normandy, the question was again raised as to when Richard's marriage to Alice, daughter of Louis VII, should take place. Richard had been betrothed to Alice since 1169, when he had been twelve and she just nine. The girl had been living at Henry's court in England since he sacked Poitiers, and the English king was not apparently eager to see his second son tied down by this alliance. As a result the marriage question was allowed to lapse once again, adding fuel to the rumors that Henry had already taken the by now sixteen-year-old French princess as his mistress. Rumors spread that Henry planned to disinherit his three elder sons in favor of John, who would then be married to Alice. Some even spoke of Henry fathering a "secret" child on the French princess that was to be the first in a new progeny. So alarming were the stories that Louis, worried for his daughter, appealed to the pope to insist that the marriage between Alice and Richard should take place immediately.

Richard's military reputation received a great boost from his siege and capture of the powerful castle of Taillebourg, on the river Charente, near Cognac in 1179. The castle was renowned as impregnable, perched up high on a craggy rock and unapproachable from three sides. The castle was protected by three inner walls and the garrison was well equipped with supplies and with water. It was the sort of target that normally would resist everything but a royal army, equipped with the sort of siege equipment that only a king could afford. Instead of siege equipment Richard brought himself. As it turned out, he proved to be more terrible than any siege weapon: a leader of ruthlessness and unequaled willpower. Although the twelfth century was not short of such men, Henry II being one of them, it is doubtful whether there was any other general of the time who had more effect on the outcome of battle than did Richard. Saladin was neither the first nor the last enemy to learn this.

Faced by the cloud-tipped battlements of Taillebourg, Richard re-fused to be deterred. He began his siege by giving defenders pause to think about the consequences for them if he should take the castle: his men torched the surrounding villages and farms, killing any peasants who had remained in their homes, slaughtering all their animals and de-stroying their harvest. Morale within the castle slumped as the villagers who had fled for safety to the castle watched as their livelihoods were destroyed, aware all the time that even if they saved their lives they had nothing to return to. Richard had camped unusually close to Taille-bourg's walls in the hope that the garrison might make a sortie to take him by surprise, and that is exactly what they tried to do. Rushing into the fray, Richard led his men into the outer bailey of the castle as the garrison retreated into the citadel. For the next two days the garrison, now hopelessly trapped, had to watch as Richard's men burned and plundered everything but the stone walls of Taillebourg. Eventually, with nothing left to defend, the garrison surrendered. Richard now showed just how ruthless he could be. With victory in their hands, most com-manders would have been content to withdraw and leave the clearing up to their subordinates. Instead, Richard stayed and supervised the an-nihilation of the castle stone by stone, even lending a hand now and then to speed the operation. Before withdrawing, he had to have the "cloud-tipped" castle leveled to the ground. It was worth the effort, for word spread of how terrible an opponent was this Richard of Aquitaine. A neighboring rebel immediately surrendered rather than risk another such siege.

The next time Richard visited his father in England he found the at-mosphere different. Henry had heard the full story of what had hap-pened at Taillebourg and recognized in Richard a worthy son and an even more worthy adversary. He rewarded Richard with a free hand in the county of Poitou.

The death of Louis VII in 1180 and the accession of the fifteen-year-old Philip Augustus was to change the political equilibrium in Western Europe, previously dominated by Henry II of England and the Emperor Frederick Barbarossa of Germany. It was to be Philip's achievement to ensure that the House of Capet prevailed over those of Anjou and Ho-henstaufen, but all this was still in the future. At Philip's coronation at Rheims Cathedral, which took place in November 1179 while Louis VII was still alive, the House of Anjou was so well represented that it looked as if they were the royal family visiting a provincial relation. Henry the "Young King" carried the royal crown and was accompanied by a dazzling retinue of lords and knights bearing in their hands and on their persons every outward manifestation of the wealth of the Anjous. Richard came as Count of Poitou and Geoffrey as Count of Brittany. With their father, still de facto Duke of Aquitaine and Normandy, the Angevins ruled far more of France than the boy king and the splendor of their entourage completely overshadowed that of their overlord, Philip "Dieu Donné." Certainly the adolescent eye of the new king cannot fail to have been impressed by the sight of the mighty Count of Poitou, towering over his companions and splendid in his rich apparel. Yet what may have begun as adolescent hero-worship was eventually to turn to rivalry and bitter jealousy as he learned the measure of the man who had a far greater right to the cognomen "Dieu Donné."

At Christmas 1182 an Angevin family reunion took place at Caen, in Normandy, where the "Young King's" jealousy of Richard brought on a severe family crisis. Reputedly a crowd of a thousand guests gathered at court to celebrate with King Henry, including nobles from throughout France and parts of Germany. No sooner had the younger Henry arrived than he began complaining to his father that Richard had intruded on his territory by building a castle there. The king showed little concern, whereupon his heir flew into a fury of "black bile," claiming he would surrender all his empty titles and take up the cross and go to Jerusalem, there to serve his life in a noble cause. The king had been brooding for some while on the likely outcome if on his own death his powerful son Richard should refuse allegiance to his weaker elder son. The result would be the breakup of the Angevin empire that he had spent all his life building up. As a result he ordered Richard to pay homage to the "Young King." Richard at first refused on the grounds that he held his title from his mother not his father and, moreover, had done homage for it to his legal overlord, Louis of France. Once started, Richard found it difficult to stop, raising the bitter subject of his mother's imprisonment and defying his older brother, saying that if he wanted land let him fight for it, rather than ask his father to give it to him. Richard left court in a fury, while his father, no less angry at the topic of Eleanor having been raised, incited his eldest son to "curb Richard's pride" by helping the Aquitanian rebels against him. Richard took the threat literally and hurried back to Aquitaine to prepare his defenses against his brother. King Henry, however, alarmed at what he might have started, had ridden to Limoges, to persuade the "Young King" that he had not meant that he should fight his brother and that he had spoken in haste. But the young Henry was not listening and the king was met with a hail of arrows, one of which penetrated his cloak. The "Young King" and Geoffrey now set about trying to undermine Richard, by besieging the fortified church at Gorre. But his brothers were "playing" at war and Richard descended on them like a thunderbolt, overwhelming their army and massacring the prisoners he took. As an example to all rebels in his lands, Richard drowned some of his captives, blinded others, and cut the throats of the remainder. Had Sultan Saladin known his enemy better in 1191 he would not have delayed paying the ransom for the Acre garrison as he did. The shock of the disaster at Gorre caused the collapse of his brothers' conspiracy against Richard in Aquitaine.

The younger Henry and Geoffrey had never been a match for Richard, perhaps the most able military commander alive, and the humiliation of defeat seemed to damage young Henry's mind. Accompanied by the young William Marshal and a band of desperate mercenaries, he began spreading terror throughout central and southern France for no discernible reason other than to punish his father. Among his deliberate outrages was to raid the shrine of Rocamadour, in the Dordogne, looting precious items from the altar and riding off with church treasures. To the very superstitious people of the time God's hand was seen in what happened next. In the midsummer heat Henry complained of feeling ill and was taken to a house in the village of Martel, where he developed a fever followed by dysentery. The dying prince had himself laid naked on a bed of ashes on the floor and passed away before his father could reach him. When King Henry heard of his son's death he "threw himself upon the ground and greatly bewailed his son."

The death of his eldest son seemed to concentrate King Henry's mind. He found in Richard, now his eldest son and presumed heir, too much of his own pride and ambition to make relations between them easy. He therefore decided to impose himself on Richard as he had on the late "Young King." If Richard was to have England he must give up Aquitaine and Poitou and these would pass to his younger brother, John. If Richard was to become a king he must now learn the art that his father had tried but failed to teach the "Young King." But this idea was not what Richard was planning for himself. He was already looking for an independent role and intended to use his lands in southern France to allow him to pursue this aim. Both Eleanor and Richard himself completely misinterpreted the king's motives, which were dynastic rather than personal and did not at this stage indicate that he intended to disinherit Richard in favor of John. Richard's emotional nature was hurt at the thought of losing Aquitaine, and he was not prepared to see his father appropriate the beloved lands of his childhood.

The death of the "Young King" also presented Henry II with the problem of his widowed daughter-in-law's dowry, which included the Vexin. In December 1183 Henry met Philip Augustus and agreed to something that his pride had previously made impossible. He agreed to do formal homage for his French lands to Philip, emphasizing the new king's suzerainty over him. Henry made this concession in order to hold on to Margaret's dowry, thereby retaining control of Gisors and the Norman Vexin, which otherwise would have returned to French control on the death of his eldest son. Philip reasonably pressed for the marriage of his sister Alice to Richard to take place at last. After all, they had been engaged for fourteen years and he wanted to see his sister settled. The fact that Henry was evasive on this issue indicates that there may have been truth in the rumors mentioned above, namely that Alice was the king's mistress and indeed had borne him a child. Henry tried to play down the marriage, even suggesting that Alice should marry his youngest son, John, perhaps a more willing accomplice. Richard, on the other hand, had no feelings for the lady and was not prepared to pick up a cast-off mistress of his father's. The dispute over the future of Princess Alice continued to sour relations between Richard and Philip Augustus for years to come.

Content with his French negotiations, Henry II now tried to resolve his differences with his heir. He suggested to Richard that he should take control of Normandy and Anjou, under his father's supervision, while surrendering Aquitaine to John. But Richard saw the king's plan, reasonable no doubt in his own eyes, as nothing more than an attempt to hobble him to the old man's plans. The quarrelsome and tempestuous Angevins were soon at it again. Tempers flared, and Richard walked out of the meeting with his father boiling with rage and shouting threats after him. In his rage Henry made another of his unfortunate outbursts: he told John that if Richard would not give him Aquitaine willingly, then John should invade Aquitaine and take it by force. Assisted by his bastard

[13]

half brother Geoffrey (who later became Archbishop of York), John took his father at his word and raised troops. As soon as Henry crossed into England in June 1184, John and Geoffrey invaded Aquitaine, pillaging and plundering as they went. They were saved the consequences of their actions because before Richard could descend on them and, no doubt, annihilate their armies, envoys arrived from England demanding that the brothers should put down their arms.

Henry now tried a new angle of approach to wrest the southern French lands away from Richard. In 1184 he temporarily released Eleanor from Salisbury so that he could demand, in her name, that Richard should release her lands in Poitou. Should he refuse, an army raised in his mother's name would invade the region and take it from him by force. Surprisingly, Richard surrendered Poitou to envoys bearing his mother's seal and, showing an unprecedented sense of family responsibility, he returned to his father's court in Normandy and for a while played the dutiful son, no doubt relying on his mother to prevent the king from handing his duchy over to John. But there had been no metamorphosis of Richard the warrior to Richard the diplomat; it seems that these were but two sides of the same coin. Those who classified Richard as no more than a bull-headed knight failed to recognize the quiet diplomacy that went on. Both Richard and his mother realized that they were walking a tightrope with Henry and for the moment a cautious approach was undoubtedly the correct policy.

While Henry and Philip continued in March 1186 to negotiate over the lengthy and precarious betrothal of Richard and Alice, Richard himself was beginning the tentative but eventually successful negotiations with Sancho of Navarre, one of the most strategically important of Aquitaine's neighbors, for a marriage between Richard and Sancho's daughter Berengaria. Unaware of this, the kings of England and France seemed content with their own agreement that the wedding to Alice should go ahead. Henry, apparently reconciled to Richard by his son's recent behavior, now sent him back to Aquitaine to subdue the rebels who had flourished in his absence. Freed of the need to repress his natural love of war, Richard returned to Aquitaine with a vengeance. His main target was Count Raymond of Toulouse, who had seized part of Richard's duchy and expected Philip Augustus to come to his aid if the Angevins proved too much for him to handle. Richard soon turned the tide of the war against Count Raymond, and it was not long before

Philip was forced to intervene to save his ally from complete defeat. Briefly all the Angevins were on the same side, with Henry enjoying the experience of having Richard, John, and their half brother Geoffrey all with his army in France at the same time. But the intervention of the Papal Legate prevented a general war between England and France from breaking out at a time when the unity of Christendom was deemed essential. He organized a two-year truce, during which the merry-go-round of relationships within the Angevin world saw several turns.

The friendship between Philip Augustus, mentally adept but physically adolescent, and the powerfully built and handsome Richard has often been seen as homosexual, but the evidence for this is minimal, based mostly on a record of doubtful provenance that the two men shared a bed. This need not carry any sexual connotations at all. Henry was alarmed at the developing friendship between his son and the King of France, which he presumed presaged a political relationship that might be harmful to him. He summoned Richard to return to Normandy, but before he could do so, an event occurred that changed everything. In early November 1187 Richard was in Tours when word of the Christian disaster at Hattin three months before and the Muslim capture of Jerusalem arrived. It fell like a thunderbolt upon everyone, from high to low, clerical and secular. The fall of the holy city of Jerusalem was felt as greatly as if the sun had fallen from the sky. Richard's response was typical of the man whose profound religious belief went hand in hand with a boyish sense of adventure. In an instant he decided that he must take the cross and reconquer the Holy Land for his faith. The word "crusade" was now on everyone's lips, with social divisions temporarily suspended in the shared affliction of the moment.

Henry was in Normandy when the news of the fall of Jerusalem reached him, accompanied by the even less palatable news that his son and heir had taken the cross. The double shock was hard for him to bear. In terms of both cost and Richard's time absent, a crusade would threaten the survival of the Angevin empire. If Richard was away for years in the Holy Land, who would defend Aquitaine from rapacious neighbors like Raymond of Toulouse or from overmighty subjects like Geoffrey of Lusignan? Besides Henry, another to regret Richard's decision was Philip Augustus, whose friendship might have been close but was not entirely altruistic. He expected something in return, and if Richard preferred to indulge in the worthy if ultimately unprofitable hobby of crusading he demanded compensation. Angrily, Philip demanded that either Richard marry Alice straightaway or else his father must return Gisors. If the Angevins refused then he would make war on them, devastating Normandy and supporting any rebels in Aquitaine.

Henry had to take this threat seriously. He hurried to Normandy and arranged a meeting with Philip at Gisors where, either by chance or by design (probably the latter), the Archbishop of Tyre happened to be preaching the crusade. It was the high point of the cleric's agenda, trapping the kings of both England and France in the same small town, and he was determined not to let them go without extorting the sort of commitment that could not be mistaken. The archbishop was a great orator, and on this vital occasion his words moved the masses of nobles and knights who had accompanied their kings to Gisors. Henry and Philip, their differences temporarily diminished, both agreed to take the cross. And they were joined by hundreds of the most important people present. It is reported that after the archbishop's service a cross appeared in the sky and was seen by all. Whether the vision was a product of the chroniclers' poetic license or the congregation's hysteria is irrelevant. All that mattered was that for a moment individual members of a massive crowd in a small French town forgot their petty differences and were joined as one in the idea of a crusade.

The Archbishop of Tyre had surpassed himself, inspiring with his words two notably reluctant crusaders in the kings of England and France. Swept up in the emotion of the moment, the two unlikely allies agreed to lead a crusade from France in a year's time, making the necessary preparations meanwhile. Even so, they and Philip, Count of Flanders, who took the cross at the same time maintained their national differences by using crosses of contrasting colors: red for the French, white for the Angevins, and green for the Flemings. While Richard needed nothing to persuade him to commit himself to fight for his faith, he benefited from the planning that his more earthbound father brought to bear, notably in financial terms. Henry devised an entirely novel scheme to raise what was known as the Saladin tithe, a direct tax of a tenth on both income and movable property for all subjects in the Angevin lands, including churchmen. The tithe was a great success, raising close to £60,000 for the crusade. The penalty for nonpayment was a severe one, being nothing less than excommunication. Self-assessment was the system used, which, in view of the fact that the tax was paid in

God's service, was not as unworkable as may have been the case in a more cynical age. Those who took the cross were exempt from the Saladin tithe, so those who were undecided about personal participation in the crusade had some incentive to be involved in a different way.

The initial passion for the crusade produced remarkable displays of self-sacrifice, some of which have a modern flavor to them, like the report that Archbishop Baldwin of Canterbury ordered his followers to dismount and lead their horses up steep slopes in Wales to condition them for the arduous journey ahead. At first Henry proposed to take the traditional land route to the Holy Land, through Hungary and the Byzantine lands. An Angevin agent, one Richard Barre, was even sent to the Balkans to negotiate with the rulers there for the safe passage of the Anglo-French forces and favorable rates at the markets. However, once it became clear that Frederick Barbarossa would be following the land route with an enormous army, Henry opted for the sea route instead, much to the scorn of the Germans, who referred to it as a short voyage "ideal for the lazy."

Richard's well-publicized decision to take the cross only served to encourage his rebellious vassals in the south to rise against him. Soon perennial troublemakers like Aimar of Angoulême and Geoffrey of Lusignan made common cause with Raymond of Toulouse in attacking Richard's lands. He retaliated with the sort of ruthless display characteristic of him, capturing one of Count Raymond's household and treating him so harshly that the count complained to Philip Augustus. The problem was that for men like Raymond and Geoffrey of Lusignan war seemed almost a sport. However, Richard took it very much more seriously and was not prepared to indulge in the kind of fighting in which only peasants and footsoldiers suffered. Frustrated at the way Count Raymond had plagued him in recent years, Richard decided to put an end to the frontier raids by annihilating his enemy. He invaded Toulouse, captured seventeen of the count's castles, and was preparing to assault Raymond's capital city when news reached him that Philip had done a volte-face and was preparing to attack Angevin lands in the north. In company with his kinsman, Philip, Bishop of Beauvais, the French king attacked Normandy, Touraine, and Berry, capturing Chateauroux in the process. This triggered off a general war between the three crusaders, who were supposed to have sunk their differences for the greater cause of regaining the Holy Land from Saladin. While the French ravaged

Normandy, Henry II with English and Welsh troops invaded Philip Augustus's lands, burning towns and villages as he cut his way south, while Richard, abandoning his struggle with the Count of Toulouse, turned on the King of France and advanced northward, threatening to catch Philip Augustus in the middle. Clearly seeing that he was overmatched, Philip called a halt, asking his Angevin foes to meet him at Gisors to settle their dispute. Traditionally disputes between the kings of France and the dukes of Normandy were settled by meetings under an ancient elm tree at Gisors, which had a trunk so vast that four men with arms outstretched could not encompass it and which was said to have roots both in France and Normandy. On this occasion—in August 1188—Henry II arrived first and sat under the shade of the tree while Philip Augustus was forced to sit in the heat of the sun. Henry unwisely told Philip that he would not give way to his overlord while the old tree stood. In a fit of pique Philip took him literally and ordered the tree cut down. And the fighting restarted, but not for long. The major nobles of France, most of whom had taken the cross, simply refused to support either side in the conflict. The war was brought to an end when Henry and Philip met at Bonmoulins, with Richard in attendance.

Richard's patience with his father, never very strong at the best of times, had run out. He constantly found himself wondering what his father had in mind for him and suspected that Henry intended replacing him as his heir with his brother John. The meeting at Bonmoulins took a dramatic turn when Richard confronted his father and asked to be confirmed as his heir. If Henry considered ending the charade, the moment was soon past. Richard publicly bent the knee to Philip and swore fealty to him for all the Angevin lands in France. Henry's policy was shattered; he had never believed that his son would betray him in this way and side with France against him, but he had driven Richard too far and this was the outcome. The Old King now bitterly proposed a new agreement with Philip, transferring all Richard's right to lands in France to John, but the French king refused and hostilities followed. At a time when the nobility of Western Europe was preparing for a crusade, the devil and his brood could not find time to subdue their family quarrels.

Richard and Philip Augustus now attacked Le Mans, Henry's birthplace, and drove the Old King out of his native city like King Lear onto the blasted heath. It was here that one of the most famous incidents of

Richard's life before he became king occurred. It involved William Marshal, the greatest and most famous knight of the age, a man whose loyalty and sense of duty personified all that was good and noble in the Age of Chivalry. Richard had played no part personally in the siege of his father's city, but when he heard that it was taken and that the Old King was in flight, he leaped on his horse, dressed only in doublet and wearing an iron helm, and led the chase. Unarmed and unarmored, he was, as so often in his career, risking his life among the heavily armored knights around him. It seems unlikely that he was pursuing his father in earnest, particularly as he knew the knights he was chasing and had been friends with many. However, several of his own men caught up the rearguard of Henry's army and began a skirmish. Just as Richard rode up, one of the king's knights unhorsed one of his, whereupon he called out, "William! you waste your time in folly; ride on!" Hearing and recognizing Richard's voice, another William suddenly entered the fray. It was William Marshal, and he charged straight at Richard with his lance set. Richard must have seen death approaching at the gallop and, showing the enormous physical strength he had, he managed to grasp William's lance and force it wide of its mark. He called out, "By God's Feet, Marshal, slay me not! It were an ill deed for I am totally unarmed." William had not been aiming at Richard. Having pulled his lance free from his grip, he drove it into Richard's horse, killing the beast and toppling Richard in the dust. As he did so William retorted, "Nay! May the devil slay you, for so will not I." With that he galloped off as Richard's knights rushed up and grouped around their shaken leader, who reproved them for seeking battle with the king's rearguard as they were fleeing. Richard petulantly stamped off, remarking, "You have spoiled everything; you are a set of distracted fools." In fact, Richard had looked deep within the abyss and he had not liked the sight. Many men would have learned from the lesson William Marshal administered, but Richard did not. As Saladin was later to remark, it was one of the Lionheart's gravest weaknesses, that he often seemed to risk his life where there was no need.

The Old King escaped on this occasion, but there was to be no escape from his declining health. Aware that he was dying, perhaps, Henry headed for Chinon, the castle of his ancestors. His enemies now ravaged his lands and he was helpless to intervene. With his loss of the city of Tours Henry called a halt to the fighting, painfully mounted a horse, and rode to meet Richard and Philip at Ballon, where he surrendered, pay-

ing the French king 20,000 marks and relinquishing Princess Alice to a
guardian, so that Richard would marry her on his return from the crusade. It was agreed that all Henry's subjects, French and English, must
swear allegiance to Richard as heir to his father's lands. Henry was required to give his son the kiss of peace but, as the chroniclers love to
record, he pretended to kiss his son and instead whispered, "God grant
that I may not die until I have had my revenge on you." On that note the
parties separated and Richard never saw his father alive again. Henry's
last hours were made even more bitter, so it is recorded, when he was
told that even his favorite son, John, had abandoned him and joined
forces with Richard and Philip. On July 6, 1189, Henry II of England
died and his monarchy passed to his son, until then Richard, Count of
Poitou, but soon to be throned as Richard I.

2

——————|◆|◆|◆|——————

Richard of England 1189–1190

RICHARD WAS PROBABLY at Tours when news arrived from William Marshal that his father had died at Chinon. He rode at once and arrived on July 7 at the abbey church where the night watch was being kept around the body. As usual legend surrounds every important event in Richard's life, not least his final parting from the father to whom he had been so disloyal and by whom he had been so taxed. It is reported that when he approached the body the two kings, one dead and cold, the other young and vibrant, seemed to greet each other. Richard gave an involuntary shudder, as if he glimpsed his own mortality in his father's features, while a sudden bleeding from the dead man's nostrils suggested to some onlookers that the Old King's temper was boiling at the sight of the son who he felt had betrayed him. After a moment, Richard knelt and prayed briefly. He was about to leave when he noticed two of the waiting knights, Maurice of Craon and William Marshal, loyal adherents of the dead king. In view of his recent meeting with the latter, Richard could not resist trying to score a point, or perhaps wipe the slate clean, with his great opponent. It is alleged that he remarked, "So, fair Sir Marshal, you were minded to slay me the other day! and slain I should have been of a surety had I not turned your lance aside by the strength of my arm. That would have been a bad day's work!" William, stung in his professional pride, replied that had he really intended to slay Richard nothing could have stopped him. His target had been the horse all along. Instead of growing angry at this proud response Richard showed a more likable side to his character by concluding, "Marshal, I will bear you no malice; you are forgiven." Richard did well to recognize William's loyalty for the great quality it was and Marshal served him as loyally as he had his father throughout his reign and during the next two reigns as well. From the Lionheart, William received the material rewards he had earned under Henry but had never received, gaining the wealth of the lordship of Leinster in Ireland, much of the county of Pembroke, and the hand of the heiress Isabel of Clare. It is reported that William was so eager to take up the riches and perhaps even the beauty of the young lady that in his haste to board a ship at Dieppe he fell off the gangplank and had his ardor doused by the cold water of the English Channel. Once in London, however, he wasted no time in marrying his lady. William Marshal also carried a royal message to England with him, ordering the release of the king's mother from imprisonment and requesting her to act as his representative until Richard could arrive in person.

Richard was now at last able to enter into his patrimony. Ruler of all the Angevin lands, in England and in France, he showed in his munificent gratitude something of the relief he must have felt now that his father was finally gone. His tour of his new territories started in Normandy, where the archbishops of Rouen and Canterbury were empowered by the Papal Legate to lift the excommunication that had been placed on him during preparations for the crusade. Richard was next installed as Duke of Normandy at Rouen Cathedral, receiving the fealty of his vassals. He then went on to meet Philip Augustus at Gisors, where the French royal chronicler took delight in recounting two minor mishaps: as Richard rode into Gisors a fire broke out; and the next day as he rode out, the wooden bridge broke beneath him and he and his horse fell into the ditch. In any case, at Richard's meeting with Philip, the two kings agreed to coordinate their preparations for the crusade and to set out together from Vézelay at Lent in 1190.

Richard now crossed the seas to his island kingdom, meeting his mother and the assembled notables of the realm at Winchester. Protocol had ensured that the Archbishop of Canterbury preceded the king from Normandy so that he could be ready for the coronation at Westminster Abbey. Richard, in fact, was in no hurry to be crowned and he concentrated his efforts in appeasing the English people, who, he felt, had suffered under his father. There was the usual general amnesty for wrongdoers, but Richard took it much further than was deemed wise. The contemporary historian William of Newburgh reflected, "At that time, the gaols were crowded with criminals awaiting trial or punishment, but through Richard's clemency these pests came forth from prison, perhaps to become bolder thieves in the future."

Richard's coronation on September 3, 1189, was one of the great ceremonial events of the Middle Ages in England. The chronicler Roger of Howden wrote a very full account of what took place, and as a result, this event set the pattern for all future royal coronations. Readers must remember that the crowning of a king was still very much a spiritual ceremony: the anointing of the monarch with holy water took precedence over the actual ceremony of crowning, which merely symbolized the ruler's authority on earth. In the twelfth century the service involved the anointing of a man, stripped of the earthly affectation of rich garments, wearing just a loincloth and shirt open at the breast.

Archbishop Baldwin of Canterbury, soon to be the king's fellow crusader in the Holy Land, presided and was assisted by the new Archbishop of York, Richard's half brother Geoffrey. The procession into the abbey was headed by Godfrey de Lucy, holding the royal cap on a cushion. Behind him walked other dignitaries, carrying a series of cushions bearing the king's golden spurs, the royal scepter topped with a gold cross and a second scepter emblazoned with a dove. Next came Prince John carrying a ceremonial sword flanked by the Earls of Huntingdon and Leicester, each carrying other ceremonial swords. Next in the procession were six barons and six earls holding a checkered board piled high with the royal vestments. They were followed by the Earl of Aumale, who carried the crown. Behind him came four barons holding up a silken canopy above Richard's head as he walked, flanked by the bishops of Durham and Bath.

Richard stood in front of the altar and began by taking three oaths, guaranteeing to maintain the decrees of the Church, justice for his subjects and good laws and customs for the kingdom. Once this was done he stripped off the robes he was wearing and was ceremonially dressed in the royal vestments. Then followed the crowning, the enthroning, and finally a celebratory mass.

In contrast with the rough-and-ready manners of his father's court, Richard was obviously a product of his mother's influence. Brought up in the artistic and literary atmosphere of Eleanor's court in Poitou,

Richard carried on her love of ostentation in his public and private life. The celebrations after his coronation lasted three days, during which the banqueting was truly splendid. Purchases of 1,770 pitchers, 900 cups, and 5,050 dishes were made for the occasion and give some idea of the numbers of guests involved. Unfortunately, the festivities revealed a much darker side of the medieval psyche: anti-Semitism. Women and Jews had been officially excluded from the event, and when some Jews tried to bring coronation gifts for the new monarch they were robbed and set on by the commonality. At first, what occurred seemed little more than the usual hostility toward Jews, but the incidents at the coronation seemed to spark off a pogrom. Waves of anti-Semitism swept London and hundreds of Jews were murdered and their homes ransacked. It was the crusading spirit of the times that fueled the prejudices of the young and hot-headed, filling them with anger at the words of their preachers that Christ had suffered death at the instigation of the Jews. Eager for revenge but as yet denied the opportunity to strike a blow against the Muslims who had seized Jerusalem, many turned their hatred on more local and defenseless victims. Richard was truly startled at the speed with which matters got out of hand. He sent orders that the Jews were not to be molested, but many had suffered already. Ironically, just three men were hanged for their atrocities and these for crimes committed in error against Christians. The coronation had been stained by this atrocity, which, in spite of the splendor of the official proceedings, conveys to modern readers the truly barbaric nature of medieval England.

In preparing for the crusade Richard was aware that the fundamental issue underpinning every Christian's hopes for success was the subject of money. A junior branch of the House of Anjou ruled in Jerusalem in the shape of Sibylla, queen and wife of Guy of Lusignan, and her sister Isabella. In a feudal sense Richard viewed the crusade of 1190 as his duty to restore the rights of Sibylla and Guy, which had been usurped by Saladin. To the Angevins Jerusalem was seen as a family inheritance. On the death of Sibylla Richard transferred his efforts to Isabella, who was eventually married to Henry of Champagne and placed on the throne. As King of England Richard was the head of the elder branch of the royal house of Jerusalem and, as such, viewed the coming crusade as peculiarly his own. As a result, he knew that the financial burden of the crusade, though officially borne by individual sovereigns and crusaders, may well devolve upon him. In this he showed prescience: without Richard's apparently bottomless purse the Third Crusade could neither have lasted as long as it did nor achieved its admittedly limited success. In raising funds for the crusade Richard revealed an understanding of crusader psychology that belies the notion that he was a man more of courage than intelligence. He knew that many men feel strong in company but weak alone, and that more feel ashamed not to match their fellows when, crowded together and hanging on the preacher's next word, the great cry of "Deus le volt" is raised. Large numbers of Englishmen—and, presumably, Frenchmen, Germans, and Italians—took the cross in the heat of the moment only to reflect that age, infirmity, family obligations or even nagging wives made the idea of a long and arduous journey to the Holy Land and probable martyrdom at the hands of the Turks a heavy price to pay for a moment's rash exaltation. How much easier it would be for them to stay at home and keep the ship steady while the younger, fitter men, with less to lose, carried the fight to the infidels. Richard, apparently, understood this feeling and decided to cash in on it. He therefore obtained from Pope Clement III letters patent releasing men from their vows on condition that they paid compensation to those crusaders who were going in their place.

In addition to the fines paid by fainthearts, Richard benefited from an even more lucrative source that was associated with the spoils of office. On the assumption that public officers held their positions not merely from a sense of duty to the crown but from a realistic appreciation of how much benefit they personally accrued, Richard decided to sack almost all of them and ask them to buy back their jobs if they wished. As one chronicler relates, Richard "deposed from their bailiwicks nearly all the sheriffs and their deputies, and held them to ransom to the uttermost farthing." He also auctioned royal offices and lands, leaving himself open to accusations that have been leveled at him of caring little for the welfare of England. This is probably unfair, yet there can be no doubt that the idea of the crusade had overtaken him completely, whether for personal or for spiritual reasons. Richard combined fund-raising with the payment of old political scores. One family, the Glanvilles, had grown rich and powerful through service to his father and he was eager to cut back their political influence. As a result, the ex-justiciar Ranulf of Glanville was stripped of the sheriffdom of Yorkshire and fined the enormous sum of £15,000, while his deputy, Reiner of Glanville, was fined 1,000 marks. As the Glanvilles were moved out they were replaced by kinsmen of Richard's allies, William Marshal and William Longchamp. Contrary to accusations that Richard weakened the government of England that his father had established, there is no evidence to suggest that the new men performed any less well than Henry's appointments. As Roger of Howden concluded, "The King put up for sale everything that he had." It is also recorded that Richard once admitted, "I would sell London if I could find a buyer for it." The treatment of the high officials was not unusual, and few of them protested. They knew when to keep quiet and when, once the king had gone abroad, to recoup their losses at the expense of the lower classes.

For the government of England during his absence Richard appointed two justiciars; one, William of Mandeville, was one of the late king's most trusted lieutenants and the other was Bishop Hugh of Durham, a man of immense wealth who bought his release from the crusade in order to fulfill his royal duties. Richard also filled five vacant bishoprics and filled the see of York with his half brother Geoffrey, who had previously been chancellor. This killed two birds with one stone. Richard was eager to see Geoffrey enthroned as archbishop, as it would end for all time any pretensions he might have to the throne. In addition, by making the chancellorship vacant Richard was able to hold an auction for the position among the most wealthy candidates. However, the transfer of Geoffrey to the see of York was a purely political decision, as he was no churchman by nature and preferred horses and dogs to spiritual affairs. Objections from clerics that Geoffrey was "conceived in adultery" and was "a man of blood" carried no weight at all and the new archbishop-elect actually played a part in his brother's coronation in Westminster Abbey.

For one person alone Richard laid out a huge fortune rather than draw it in, and that was his brother John. Richard's sense of loyalty to John showed that he wished to carry out his father's plans for the prince still ironically known as "Lackland." As Duke of Normandy Richard granted John the county of Mortain, while in England he extravagantly granted his brother the heritage of the late Earl of Gloucester as well as an additional six counties, with all the revenues that otherwise would have come to the Crown. It was an astonishing display of filial love, or perhaps guilt resulting from the way he had treated his father. Whatever the truth, Richard was guilty of imprudence that verged on irresponsibility. His brother's record for loyalty was hardly better than his own. Perhaps he hoped to soothe John's burning resentment by removing the cause. If this is true it was a misjudgment of extraordinary magnitude, as Richard was to learn in the next few years. He had given his brother power without responsibility, always a dangerous combination, and he should not have been surprised when someone with John's reputation misused it.

In November 1189 messengers brought Richard news from France that Philip Augustus and his nobles had sworn to be at Vézelay on April 1, 1190, ready to begin the crusade, and begged the English to join them there. Significantly, Frederick Barbarossa and the German crusaders would be so far ahead of them that by that date they would have crossed the Bosphorus and would be marching through Anatolia. However, Richard and Philip were to be saved from the embarrassment of arriving late by the German emperor's tragic but farcical death by drowning. The Anglo-French had their own agenda and it was based on Easter 1190, and no earlier. Much swearing of oaths now ensued, both by the French envoys "on the King of France's soul" and by William Marshal on Richard's that both sides would keep the appointment. Richard spent Christmas in Normandy, where he heard that his elderly chief justiciar, William of Mandeville, had died, and he therefore promoted the Bishop of Ely to fill the vacancy. He also reappointed as Seneschal of Normandy, William FitzRalf, a thoroughly reliable official who held the post for twenty years, from 1180 until 1200. In February he summoned his mother, brothers and justiciars to attend him in Normandy, where he made his final plans for the government of England in his absence. William Longchamp, Bishop of Ely, was to rule England as Richard's Chief Justiciar, assisted by Hugh of Durham, in the region north of the river Humber. Richard made his brothers John and Geoffrey swear that they would not enter England for three years without his permission. Longchamp was then sent back to England to "prepare things necessary for the king and for his journey."

The main requirements for the crusade, apart from money, were ships and horses, and these twin issues occupied Richard in the following months. Hundreds, probably thousands, of horses were shipped over to France for the use of the knights and nobles who were accompanying Richard to Vézelay, where they would meet the French contingent and travel south to Marseilles. Here the English fleet would be awaiting them, along with the bulk of the English forces. Once the problem of the horses was solved, the even more important one of raising a fleet of several hundred vessels had to be faced. All the seaports of England, Normandy, and western France were called upon to provide ships, and the Cinque Ports may have supplied as many as thirty-three of them. Apparently the king paid two-thirds of the cost of each ship as well as the wages of the crew, amounting to 2d a day for sailors and 4d for steersmen. Statistics indicate that Richard paid £5,000 or more to equip his fleet. Of the ships provided, some were donated to the English nobles who were traveling independently, like the late king's Chief Justiciar, Ranulf of Glanville, who traveled with Archbishop Baldwin of Canterbury and arrived in the Holy Land with his party seven months before King Richard.

Precise numbers for Richard's army and navy can never be known. They range from the extravagant figures of chroniclers whose work served as propaganda rather than history, to those of modern historians, whose statistical methods seem more suited to accountancy than to medieval history, where dragons and sea monsters still occupied unknown spaces on maps. From 600,000 as an estimate for Frederick Barbarossa's army of Germans to 6,000 as a modern assessment of that of the Angevins, the historian must learn to operate somewhere in between; it would seem safer to err on the side of the lower figures rather than the biblical proportions of the upper. There can be no doubt that Richard's Angevin force was enormous for his day, and when Richard of Devizes mentions 17,000 soldiers and sailors with the fleet he may not be far wrong. Naturally, quality is far more important than quantity and, in contrast to the numbers of poor pilgrims who traveled with the First Crusade, the Third contained mainly professional soldiers, both foot and horse, who were expected to finance themselves on the journey. The number of knights available to each king is again difficult to assess, but Richard may have had 4,000 of these elite fighting men, from England and from his French lands. The fleet that was supposed to meet Richard at Marseilles was carrying about 8,750 soldiers and sailors, while Richard had a large land army probably 6,000 strong with him at Vézelay, which was sufficient to cause the bridge across the Rhone at Lyons to collapse under their weight. This army divided at Marseilles, half going on ahead with Ranulf of Glanville, Hubert Walter, and Archbishop Baldwin and the other half remaining with Richard and taking ship eventually from Messina.

The English contribution to the crusade contained too many over-lords and not enough of the commonality. So great had been the response of the upper classes to the call to follow the cross that a high proportion of the political and administrative elite of the country was prepared to follow Richard. Eventually, however, the king had to persuade many would-be crusaders to put the interests of the country before that of their religion and leave the fighting to others, for fear that the government would be seriously weakened in the absence of so many able men. Richard, in fact, has been criticized for doing just this and undermining the strong government established by his father. This is unfair and, furthermore, inaccurate. The journey by sea between England and the Holy Land lasted no more than two months, and as there were so many senior spiritual and lay figures with him, he was able to keep a check on affairs in England so that matters never reached the alarming stage that the legends of Robin Hood relate.

The Angevin advance guard led by the Archbishop of Canterbury and the Glanville clan arrived at Acre in August 1190, imagining that they would soon be followed by the king and the main army. However, Richard was not entirely straight with them and his behavior in Sicily gives no impression that he felt any obligation to back them up with any urgency. Almost certainly Richard was using Archbishop Baldwin as a token of his power at Acre, while he himself held the reality in Sicily. If so, there were many good reasons for him to take this view. Somebody needed to take care of Angevin interests at the camp at Acre, which for the moment was the center of the crusading effort. Already it was apparent that Conrad of Montferrat was keen to take the throne of the defunct kingdom from Richard's vassal, Guy of Lusignan. Richard expected Archbishop Baldwin to prevent this happening before he, the king, could reach the Holy Land and settle the matter. Ironically, it was the Glanville clan, whom he had done so much to undermine, whom he was now using to back up his archbishop. Hostile though he might have been to the Glanvilles, he was not blind to the considerable ability of two of the younger kinsmen, so while the patriarchal Ranulf was ousted with his older generation, the younger Roger of Glanville did well in the crusade, while Ranulf's nephew, Hubert Walter, newly appointed Bishop of Salisbury, was probably the most successful of all the crusaders in the Third Crusade and rose to be Archbishop of Canterbury and one of England's greatest royal ministers.

Shakespeare would have enjoyed describing the composition of the English contingent of the Angevin army, containing as it did everyone from bishops and great magnates to ruffians like Falstaff and his motley crew. Just as men of national importance like Robert of Breteuil, Earl of Leicester, Andrew of Chauvigny, and the royal seneschal William FitzAldelin rode with Richard, so there were parochial groups like the men from the East Riding who rode together and other groups from Lincolnshire and a London group led by Geoffrey the Goldsmith and William FitzOsbert. Finally there were some few downright villains, like the "murderous" archers from St. Clear's and some notorious criminals from Usk, as described by Gerald of Wales. Overall, however, it was a very professional force, full of well-armed and well-trained soldiers, equipped with the finest weapons and armor. Even the large number of clerics who traveled with the crusade went well-armed, and several, notably Hubert Walter, proved to be able fighters and in Hubert's case no mean general. The Archdeacon of Colchester had his own moment of glory when, in June 1190, he rallied the crusaders after a Turkish attack and led them to victory in a major skirmish.

The equipping of the fleet was the final stage before the departure of the crusade, and this tested the efficiency of Richard's administrative skills to the full. The fact that he was able to launch such a huge amphibious operation, over a distance of thousands of miles, should never be underestimated. Those critics of Richard's government would do well to consider how far more efficiently the Angevin leader planned and put into operation the enormous requirements of the crusade than did his Capetian ally, Philip Augustus. Philip tried to crusade on "the cheap," hiring Italian ships to transport his troops and himself, trying to borrow some from Richard at Genoa and hoping to fund the expedition from money accrued from ransoms and despoiling conquests. Richard, on the other hand, planned everything in advance and ensured that he had adequate funds in the event of emergencies, as occurred several times on the crusade. Little was left to chance, and there is something very modern about the ruthless efficiency that went into the planning of the Angevin crusade. Richard was a hard taskmaster and accused his admirals of being sluggish when the fleet failed, by just a few days, to meet the rendezvous at Marseilles. However, by the time the king had reached the toe of Italy, the fleet was ready to sail into Messina harbor with all the splendor any twelfth-century ruler might have desired.

Preparing the fleet involved more than merely finding and paying the crews. The victualing of such an expedition was a truly enormous task, as Richard took responsibility for feeding everyone. From counties throughout England we read that huge supplies of food were collected and transported to the southern ports. From as far north as Lincolnshire came 14,000 cured carcasses of pigs, while from Hampshire came a charge for a hundredweight of cheese and from Kent and Essex masses of beans. In addition to victuals, Richard took responsibility for equipping as many as 4,000 knights with all the complex paraphernalia that went into furnishing these "iron men" for battle. Transport ships of the fleet each carried forty warhorses and armor and weapons for forty knights. The knights themselves were expected to pay for their own journey eastward, only earning the right to use the equipment when they arrived at Acre. Sixty thousand horseshoes came from the Forest of Dean, as well as millions of arrows and crossbow bolts for the archers.

With preparations for the crusade almost concluded, Richard made one last trip to Tours, where he received the traditional emblems of the pilgrim-crusader, the staff and purse, from Archbishop Bartholomew, though it is reported by Roger of Howden that as he leaned on his staff with all his weight it broke. What sort of omen this was taken to be is not clear to a twentieth-century reader. With the advantage of hindsight one feels entitled to see it as a symbol of Richard's interpretation of the crusade: he, as knight, would be dominant and the role of pilgrim subordinate. Richard went east as a conqueror, which the inhabitants of Sicily and Cyprus were soon to appreciate. Nevertheless, he saw himself as a holy conqueror in the tradition of the Byzantine emperor Heraclius, who had regained the True Cross from the Persians thirteen years after they had captured and sacked Jerusalem in 614. There can be no doubt that Richard dreamed of restoring the True Cross to Christians and, as a profoundly religious man, of serving God in the only way he knew, by smiting the infidel.

3

|◆|◆|◆|

Saladin the Apprentice 1138–1174

ONE NIGHT IN 1138 a group of muffled figures gathered in the darkness inside the main gate of the town of Takrit on the river Tigris, between Mosul and Baghdad. A baby's cry was the only sound in the group as they approached the guards. Strangled grunts followed as the guards fell forward and the main gate was hastily swung open, allowing a small party of riders to gallop out of the city. The newborn baby was Saladin, and with him rode his father Najm al-Din Ayyub and Ayyub's brother Shirkuh, escaping from present danger to a future that would bring each of the Kurdish brothers a degree of greatness and to the baby they carried with them immortality.

Ayyub and Shirkuh were able and ruthless men who cut their way through traditional Turkish prejudice against Kurds to rise to high rank in the state created by Zangi, Atabeg of Aleppo and Mosul, during the first half of the twelfth century. The few available sources on Saladin's antecedents suggest that his father and his uncle came from Dvin, in Armenia, and first found service with the Seljuk sultan, with Ayyub becoming the castellan of the town of Takrit. In 1132 a single action by Ayyub established the family's fortunes. Looking across the river one day from the battlements of Takrit, Ayyub saw the young Zangi fleeing for his life from his foes and sent a boat to help him to cross the river to safety. Zangi never forgot his debt to Ayyub. Six years later Ayyub and his family were forced to flee from Takrit when Shirkuh killed a man in a dispute. They were welcomed into Zangi's service, who repaid his debt to Ayyub by appointing him commander of the city of Baalbek.

Shirkuh, meanwhile, associated himself with Zangi's son, Nur al-Din, and when Zangi was murdered, in 1146, Shirkuh became the right-hand man of the new ruler of Aleppo. With Nur al-Din now the strongman of Syria, Ayyub and Shirkuh were established as his most powerful supporters, with Ayyub as governor of Damascus and Shirkuh, the power behind the throne, in Aleppo. The young Saladin grew up in Damascus, with his father. He was a serious boy, who apparently loved reading. His upbringing was conventional for a boy of his class and consisted in much learning by rote of genealogies, biographies, and the history of the Arab people, at which he excelled. His education was that of a gentleman, full of elegance and refinement as well as theological studies in which he showed an unusual interest. In his early teens he entered army service and left Damascus to work with his uncle Shirkuh at Aleppo, where he received an *iqta*, or military fief, in the service of Nur al-Din. His uncle was a great soldier and was just the man to forward his nephew's career. In 1149 the dwarfish but immensely powerful Shirkuh had won great fame at the battle of Inab by killing Raymond II of Antioch in single combat. Significantly, when Nur al-Din fell ill in 1157 he appointed Shirkuh his deputy, with full powers to protect his lands against any attacks from his Christian neighbors. With such a powerful sponsor, Saladin was secure in his future career: by the time he was eighteen he had become a liaison officer or ADC to Nur al-Din himself, never leaving his master's side whether at court or on campaign.

The First Crusade of 1096–9 had redrawn the map of the Middle East. The loose Seljuk polity was broken apart by the crusaders who established their control over the entire Mediterranean coastline from Antioch to Egypt. Four separate crusader states were created, the largest being the kingdom of Jerusalem in the south, stretching from Darum on the Egyptian border to Beirut in the north. Beyond that was the county of Tripoli and the principality of Antioch, while inland to the east of Antioch was the county of Edessa. These Western settlements were known collectively as Outremer, and separated the Fatimids of Egypt from their nearest Muslim neighbors in Syria. Here, during the twelfth century, a new political force developed under Zangi and Nur al-Din. Pivoted on the triangle of the great Syrian cities Damascus, Aleppo, and Mosul, the Zangids and later their protégé Saladin used the weapon of holy war to try to drive the

Christians of Outremer into the sea. While Egypt and Syria were disunited by religion and politics, the Muslims would never be strong
enough to defeat the crusader kingdoms, but if a single ruler—Nur al-
Din or Saladin—could unite Islam, then it would be possible.

The opportunities that the ambitious Shirkuh was eager to exploit
were opened up by events in Egypt. The Fatimid rulers of Egypt no
longer possessed the power that had once challenged their Abbasid rivals
in Baghdad for leadership of the Islamic world. As their military and
diplomatic powers diminished their wealth made them an attractive target for their acquisitive neighbors, in both Christian and Muslim lands.
In 1160 an eleven-year-old, al-Adid, became Caliph of Cairo, a position
of spiritual rather than temporal power. (The current schism within Islam was reflected in the Shia Muslims recognizing the Fatimid Caliph of
Cairo, while the Sunni Muslims recognized the Abbasid Caliph of Baghdad.) Al-Adid left the running of his affairs to his vizier, and three years
later there was a dispute over succession to this rank between two emirs,
Dirgam and Shawar. This purely internal squabble was soon to be ele-
vated to international importance when the ousted Shawar traveled to
Damascus to seek the help of Nur al-Din. Inside Egypt, Dirgam was
consolidating his position by a purge of army officers that was to weaken
the Egyptian army at the very time it was most threatened by its neighbors. Of these the most dangerous seemed to be the new Christian king,
the dynamic Amalric I, who planned an invasion of Egypt after Dirgam
foolishly withheld the annual tribute Egypt paid to the Christian kingdom of Jerusalem. Meanwhile, in Damascus, Shawar was bargaining for
Nur al-Din's help, so Egypt was facing invasion from two of her neighbors simultaneously.

Into the convoluted affairs of Egypt now stepped the man who, like
Alexander cutting the Gordian knot with a single blow of his sword, was
going to untangle the web: Shirkuh, brother of Ayyub and uncle of Saladin. In April 1164 Shirkuh led the first Syrian expedition to Egypt,
which succeeded in installing Shawar as vizier. Saladin almost certainly
went with his uncle and, at the age of twenty-six, probably held a command, though nothing is known of his achievements at this time. Shawar
now found that, like an unwelcome lodger, Shirkuh was in no hurry to
find a home of his own. As a result, Shawar decided to play off one enemy against the "friend" who was fast becoming an enemy. To get rid of
Shirkuh, Shawar approached Amalric of Jerusalem, who promptly in-

vaded Egypt and trapped Shirkuh in the fortress of Bilbais. Shirkuh was saved, however, by his master Nur al-Din, who won a great victory over the Christians near Antioch, forcing Amalric to withdraw his army from Egypt and hurry north to protect his borders against Nur al-Din.

Shirkuh returned to Damascus, presumably with Saladin, already planning to return to Egypt when he could convince Nur al-Din to support another expedition. Back in Syria, Shirkuh set about persuading the Sunni Caliph of Baghdad to declare a jihad, or holy war, against the Shi'ites of Egypt, and armed with this religious authorization and 2,000 elite Syrian warriors he set out once again, in January 1167, crossing the Sinai desert and defeating the combined Frankish-Fatimid army near Ahmunein. Saladin apparently commanded the Muslim center during this battle and acquitted himself well. There now began a period of complex warfare, during which the mobile Syrians led by Shirkuh outmaneuvered their enemy. While his uncle led the Franks and the Fatimids a merry dance Saladin was entrusted with the less glamorous but extremely difficult task of holding the Syrian base at Alexandria, with a garrison of just 1,000 men. For three months Saladin held the great port against besiegers many times his number, and by encouraging the Alexandrians to accept him and to help him resist Amalric's Franks he won the esteem not only of his uncle but of many of his emirs. Nevertheless, Saladin was close to defeat when Amalric suddenly called off the siege.

As was to be the case many times while Saladin was in Egypt, it was ultimately the actions of Nur al-Din in Syria that saved the day. Each time he raided the northern part of the Latin kingdom from Damascus, the Christians in the south had to call off their attacks on Egypt and return to defend their own land. It was a simple but effective strategy, and Saladin learned it from his master and used it himself in later years. Once Amalric heard that Nur al-Din was active on his frontiers he negotiated a truce with Shirkuh and withdrew northward. The success of Skirkuh's razzia had been minor, showing the old warrior that he was still far too weak to capture Egypt alone. Only the pressure from Nur al-Din in Galilee had saved Saladin and himself from eventual defeat. It was during the negotiations that ended this brief Egyptian war that Saladin first entered the stories of the crusades. It is related, probably apocryphally, that he was knighted by the Christian knight Humphrey of Toron. There are, however, well-accredited examples of such practices: Richard the Lionheart himself apparently "knighted" one of Saladin's nephews. Fraternization between Christian and Muslim knights was relatively common. Humphrey of Toron was highly regarded by Muslim writers as one of the greatest and noblest of Christian warriors: at his death in 1179, he used his own body to shield Baldwin IV from Muslim arrows, which brought him legendary status. A meeting between this peerless knight and the noble infidel must have whetted the journalistic appetite of chroniclers, both Christian and Muslim.

A diplomatic revolution now took place, bringing Shirkuh a change of fortune. Shawar was forced to make a fatal change of alliance. For too long he had been trying to play off one potential enemy against another, but when Amalric of Jerusalem married Maria Comnena, the great-niece of the Byzantine emperor Manuel Comnenus, Shawar found himself facing a Christian alliance aimed at Egypt. He had no alternative but to seek help from his previous enemy Nur al-Din. Yet he was almost too late. In October 1168, Amalric returned to Egypt, but this time not as an ally of Shawar but as a conqueror, carrying death and destruction with him. The Franks advanced on Cairo, overthrowing the Egyptian forces as they went. Only a desperate call to Damascus from al-Adid saved the country. He promised Nur al-Din a third of Egypt's wealth if he would save Egypt. Shirkuh was delighted at the prospect of returning to Egypt, but Saladin was not eager to go with him and had to be pressured by Nur al-Din himself. Saladin later explained to the chronicler ibn al-Athir how he was persuaded to go.

> I answered that I was not prepared to forget the sufferings endured in Alexandria. My uncle then said to Nur al-Din: "It is absolutely necessary that Yusuf go with me." And Nur al-Din thus repeated his orders. I tried to explain the state of financial embarrassment in which I found myself. He ordered that money be given to me and I had to go, like a man led off to his death.

Within days, Shirkuh was racing south at the head of 8,000 elite Syrian warriors, with the unwilling Saladin at his side. Saladin can hardly have guessed that he was on the brink of a greatness of which his ambition so far had not suggested he was capable.

Amalric tried to intercept Shirkuh's advance, but he was outmaneuvered by the skillful old warrior, who swiftly joined up with Shawar's forces so that the Christians were now heavily outnumbered. Spared a military debacle by withdrawing from Egypt, Amalric had nevertheless suffered a political defeat. He had driven Shawar into the camp of Shirkuh and the Syrians and moved the previously disunited Islamic world an important step on the road to unity under Nur al-Din or, if not him, of his successor. Shirkuh was at first willing to share power with Shawar, who had proved himself treacherous so often in the past. But on Saladin's advice Shirkuh was eventually convinced that there was no safety while Shawar lived. Revealing a ruthlessness that students of the later Saladin would have doubted he possessed, Saladin took action to dispose of the vizier. Shawar was apparently plotting to murder Shirkuh, and so, in a sense, what followed was inevitable. Shawar set out one morning to visit a mosque on the outskirts of Cairo but was arrested by Saladin and some of his Syrian troops, taken to his tent, and beheaded, apparently on the orders of al-Adid, who immediately appointed Shirkuh his new vizier.

When news of Shirkuh's success reached Damascus, Nur al-Din was furious, believing Shirkuh had betrayed him. Nor was the Abbasid Caliph of Baghdad any happier. What had begun as a holy war to overthrow heresy in Egypt had resulted in Shirkuh's using Nur al-Din's soldiers to seize power for himself and under a Shi'ite Caliph at that. What Shirkuh felt about his instant elevation will never be known as he did not live long enough to enjoy the power he had sought. On March 23, 1169, Shirkuh died, apparently from the results of overeating; the Syrian troops who had come with him to Egypt, including Saladin, were thus in a difficult position. Al-Adid, the Fatimid Caliph of Cairo, was advised by his Egyptian ministers to appoint Saladin as the new vizier, as he was the "weakest and most inexperienced of the Syrians" and, thus, probably the easiest to control. Saladin was summoned to the caliph's palace. For the occasion he dressed up as a flunkey, wearing a white turban stitched with gold and a scarlet-lined tunic, riding a chestnut mare with a golden saddle and carrying a golden sword. But if the Egyptian establishment thought they had reestablished their power now that Shirkuh was dead they were wrong. Saladin already had his mind set on sweeping away the archaic Fatimid regime, but first he had to establish his authority over the tough Syrian troops who had ridden with him from Damascus.

Without their commander the Syrians faced a real threat that a new

Egyptian strongman might rise up to seize power from them and drive them out on a wave of nationalist fervor. They needed a new commander, and quickly. But whom should they choose? Nur al-Din's army in Egypt was an elite force, made up of a mixture of nationalities, including Syrians, Kurds, and Turks, and it had been held together primarily by the strength of the late Shirkuh. Universal agreement on a successor was therefore impossible. Saladin had been his uncle's choice to succeed him, but the Turks, intensely loyal to Nur al-Din, would not support another Kurd. Saladin, however, had his friends even among the Syrians, of whom Isa al-Hakhari skillfully campaigned on his behalf to win him the army command, the natural companion to the viziership. Although many of Nur al-Din's troops promptly withdrew their support for Saladin and returned to Syria, enough remained to ensure a peaceful succession. Nur al-Din, however, could not reconcile himself to another act of treachery by the family of Ayyub and stripped Saladin of his lands in Syria.

Saladin's investiture as vizier, three days after Shirkuh's death, was the first tentative step on his rise to political supremacy. There was nothing premature about his elevation, nothing suggesting youthful precocity or Icarus-like overreaching. It was a rank that suited his ability as a thirty-year-old man, middle-aged by the standards of the time, who had much experience, both military and diplomatic, gained from his father and uncle. In fact, Saladin showed the caution necessary for a Kurd in a Turk-dominated society, appreciating the constant danger of the assassin's knife or the executioner's sword. There was no certainty that he could hold on to his position as vizier without first establishing himself securely in Egypt, for which he needed his relations around him in order to create an Ayyubid power base. To do this, however, he would face opposition not only from the local Egyptian establishment, which rightly viewed him as a foreign interloper, but also from those of his Syrian troops who remained loyal to Nur al-Din. To add to his difficulties, as a Sunni Muslim he owed allegiance to the Abbasid Caliph of Baghdad, while as vizier of Egypt he ruled with the authority of the Ishmaili Fatimid Caliph of Cairo. It was a political minefield that Saladin negotiated with consummate skill.

He faced the immediate problem that his uncle, Skirkuh, had taken power in Egypt with minimal military force, consisting mainly of his own personal followers and those he had been lent by Nur al-Din. In

Cairo alone the Fatimid armed forces comprised 40,000 cavalry and 30,000 "Black" (Sudanese) infantry. Saladin therefore set about creating his own military force, the Salahiyya, which was loyal to him alone. While he was engaged in strengthening his own position the opposition began to coalesce around a black eunuch called Mu'tamin al-Khilafa, who tried to gain help through an alliance with the Latin Christians of Jerusalem and eventually organized a rising against the new vizier among the Black troops. Saladin ruthlessly suppressed the revolt, hunting down and killing Mu'tamin al-Khilafa and scattering the Black troops, driving many to find refuge in Upper Egypt.

Nur al-Din now made a political blunder by allowing Saladin's brothers to join him in Egypt. In fact, it was Turan-Shah, Saladin's younger brother, who played the major role in suppressing the revolt against the new vizier. Nur al-Din must have known that he was taking a risk in allowing the other sons of Ayyub to join Saladin, yet he was already suspicious of the new vizier's ambitions and thought that the arrival of his brothers might drive Saladin immediately into open rebellion if that thought was in his mind. But this was a dangerous game to play. Nur al-Din respected Saladin's ability, while Saladin himself was torn between loyalty to his old master and ambition for his own family. In a situation where the two leaders had such ambivalent thoughts, sometimes no action was better than any particular action. Nur al-Din must have fretted at the idea that his young protégé was going to betray him. Eventually, he decided that if the presence of his brothers may have stoked the fires of Saladin's ambition, the presence of his father might douse them. He therefore asked the now elderly Ayyub to visit his son in Cairo. This was a masterly move that undoubtedly prevented the potential breach between Saladin and Nur al-Din. But in reality it was simply papering over the cracks. The price of preventing an open breach between Cairo and Damascus was to supply the final piece in Saladin's construction of an Ayyubid power base in Egypt. With his father and his brothers around him Saladin was truly master of Egypt de facto if not de jure. On the arrival of his father Saladin offered to surrender the viziership to him, but his father shrewdly refused, adding that God must have selected his son for so high a position and it was not for a mere man to interfere with God's will. Instead Ayyub accepted the job of treasurer.

The ending of the Fatimid caliphate revealed one of the first glimpses of the generosity of heart for which Saladin became renowned. With the suppression of the Black troops and their replacement with Mamelukes loyal to Saladin, the time had come for the religious revolution for which Nur al-Din had been waiting. He pressed Saladin to return Egypt to the Sunni fold by replacing the name of the Fatimid caliph with that of the Abbasid caliph in the prayer known as the *khutba*. As Saladin prepared the ground for this fundamental change the Fatimid caliph al-Adid fell mortally ill. In September 1171 the change took place and Egypt's population changed from Shi'ite to Sunnite at the moment that Sunnite prayers were spoken in Cairo's great mosque by a visiting priest from Mosul. As the change occurred al-Adid was on his deathbed and Saladin ordered that particular care should be taken to prevent the dying caliph from hearing what had occurred. As he said, "If he recovers he will learn soon enough. If he is to die let him die in peace." It was a sign of the sort of man Saladin was to become in later years.

At this time chroniclers report that Saladin gave up his youthful interests in earthly pleasures and "assumed the dress of religion." From this time onward Saladin makes a point of informing the Caliph of Baghdad at every opportunity of his commitment to the true religion and to the holy war, as if to combat any rumors that he had been sidetracked by the material pleasures of Egypt. Nobody would have blamed him much had he indulged himself in some earthly pleasures (as was common among successful men), but it seems as if Saladin had undergone a transformation. He had secured the base from which to launch the holy war, which had been his intention all along. Until he had a firm base in Egypt, he lacked the means—money and men—to unite the lands of Islam for an assault on the Christians who held Jerusalem.

Whether Nur al-Din recognized that this was Saladin's preferred path or whether he still saw him as merely an ambitious conqueror like so many of his race remains unknown. However, between 1171 and 1174 Egypt and Syria moved closer and closer to a war that both men knew was inevitable and yet both would have preferred to avoid. Saladin certainly tried to avoid betraying Nur al-Din, while recognizing that his old master was his master no more. On instructions from Damascus Saladin cooperated on a joint operation against the crusader castles of Oultre-jourdain, at Kerak and Shawbak, but at the last moment Saladin withdrew on the grounds that he was needed in Cairo, where there was a danger of a rising. It was a blatantly weak excuse, and Nur al-Din was very angry. Saladin did not wish these powerful castles to fall into Nur al-Din's hands, as they would provide the Syrians with a base to keep a close check on his own activities in Egypt. When a second expedition against the same targets had to be canceled two years later it was obvious to Nur al-Din that his protégé was acting deliberately and needed to be checked. He sent treasury officials from Damascus to inspect the Egyptian finances and set a high annual tribute for Saladin to pay. He did not expect Saladin to accept this and so he prepared his troops for war.

Saladin reacted by calling a meeting of his family and friends to determine how to react. The young hothead Taqi al-Din, Saladin's nephew, was all in favor of fighting the Syrians, but the patriarchal Ayyub slapped him down, realizing that spies would report back Saladin's reaction to Nur al-Din and that such reports might determine how severely he responded. Ayyub announced, "Know that should Nur al-Din come nothing would stop me or your uncle here from dismounting and kissing the ground at his feet." Ayyub then turned to Saladin and added, "Even if he ordered us to take your life we should do it. If we would act thus how do you think others would? For all the army and all your council here owe their homage to Nur al-Din should he come. This is his land, and if it pleased him to depose you we would immediately obey him. We are all Nur al-Din's Mamelukes and slaves and he may do with us as he chooses." Ayyub then advised his son to conciliate Nur al-Din by sending him a total submission along the lines: "News has reached us that you intend to lead an expedition to Egypt; but what need is there? My Lord need but send a courier on a camel to lead me back to Syria by a turban cloth about my neck—not one of my people would attempt to resist him."

After the meeting, Ayyub told Saladin that the sort of speech he had made at the council cost nothing. When facing a potentially greater power nothing provocative should be said of the kind that the young Taqi al-Din had given voice to. If Nur al-Din could be placated by mere words so much the better, but—and this was emphasized—if the Syrians did come to Egypt then he, Ayyub, would fight to the death to prevent them taking a single sugarcane of her wealth from his son. With such advice Saladin was sure to hold his own, even against his great mentor, Nur al-Din. In the end the two great leaders were spared the misery of seeing friends pitted against each other in battle when Nur al-Din suddenly died, on May 15, 1174.

The removal of Nur al-Din from the political scene was followed only a few months later by the death of the powerful King Amalric of Jerusalem, which produced a power vacuum in both Syrias, Christian and Muslim. Had Amalric been succeeded by a strong figure instead of the pitiful leper, Baldwin IV, matters might have taken a very different turn. However, Saladin found himself facing opportunities of advancement in the Syrian lands of his previous master, as well as in the lands of his Christian enemies.

The knowledge that the new king could not live long or ever father a child meant that there would eventually be a disputed succession in the kingdom of Jerusalem. As a result, two distinct parties grew up in Jerusalem and contended for power, dangerously splitting the strength of the kingdom precisely at the time that Saladin was striving to achieve a united Islam to pursue the holy war against the Christians. One of the two Christian parties was headed by Raymond III of Tripoli, regent in 1174 until the young Baldwin IV came of age. Raymond was supported by the native barons, who were second- or third-generation settlers, whose grandfathers had been among those who had conquered Jerusalem on July 15, 1099, the culmination of the First Crusade. Among these were numbered the brothers Baldwin of Ramla and Balian of Ibelin, as well as the Knights of the Hospital. These native barons were "Easterners" rather than "Westerners" in outlook and looked to establish good relations with their Muslim neighbors. They were often involved in Muslim political disputes, allied to one side or another, and preferred peaceful coexistence to territorial expansion. The other party consisted mainly of recent arrivals in the kingdom, knights who came with the Second Crusade in 1147–9 and brought with them the attitudes of Western Europe, and who were hostile to the Muslims and looked for Christian expansion south into Egypt. At first they were led by Joscelin of Courtenay, whose father had held and lost Edessa, but on his release from a Muslim prison in 1176 Reginald of Chatillon married Stephanie of Milly and became undisputed leader of the opposition to Raymond of Tripoli. As Lord of Kerak, Reginald became a thorn in Saladin's side and the man above all others who, for the Muslims, came to personify all that was bad in the Christian kingdom. With him was numbered another man, of furious temper and dangerous tendencies: the Master of the Templars, Gerard of Ridefort.

4

————————— +◆I◆I◆I+ —————————

A United Islam 1174–1184

THE DEATH OF NUR AL-DIN marked a watershed in Saladin's personal
life as well as in the history of the crusades, coming as it did at the same
time as the death of his father, Ayyub. Clearly the atabeg had been an ob-
stacle to his ambitions, yet in other ways Nur al-Din had exercised a profound influence on the younger man's political education. Like Nur
al-Din Saladin had adopted the jihad as his lifetime's aim, using religious
propaganda as a weapon every bit as potent as armed force. His father's
death brought Saladin leadership of the Ayyubid family as well as responsibility to forward the careers of his brothers and cousins. Now that
he was no longer indebted to Syria for men and money, he needed to
build a new Ayyubid dynasty in Egypt.

Events followed fast on the death of Nur al-Din. The chief officers of
his army promptly set about trying to win control of his eleven-year-old
son, al-Malik as-Salih. Meanwhile, Nur al-Din's nephews, Imad al-Din
Zangi and Saif al-Din Ghazi, the princes of Sinjar and Mosul respec-
tively, also cast predatory eyes on as-Salih in Syria. Saladin was prevented
from playing any part in Syrian affairs by a naval attack from the King of
Sicily on Alexandria, which kept him fully occupied simply holding
what he had won in Egypt. As a mark of respect to Nur al-Din, Saladin
acknowledged as-Salih as his suzerain. It would have been unwise to
have appeared to covet Syria so soon after the atabeg's death. However,
not everyone showed such scruples. Saif al-Din Ghazi invaded and an-
nexed all of as-Salih's territories beyond the Euphrates in al-Jazira, while

in August 1174 the eunuch Gumushtekin gained control of as-Salih and set himself up at Aleppo by imprisoning Nur al-Din's officers. The unity of Islam was now severely damaged and only the recent death of Amalric I, from dysentery, prevented the Franks from exploiting the situation. None of the atabeg's family possessed the necessary qualities to succeed him, and although Saladin had such qualities, he could not hope to win the support of Nur al-Din's family. As an outsider and a Kurd, he would inevitably face opposition from legitimists who already felt that he had committed treason against Nur al-Din by his actions in Egypt. To them he was truly "the dog barking at his master." He had been the creation of Nur al-Din, who repaid his master by stealing his lands and property.

Saladin was in a difficult position. As the de facto ruler of Egypt he clearly possessed greater resources and stronger armed forces than any of the Zangid rulers, yet as the vassal of Nur al-Din and now of his son he would find it difficult to justify intervening in Syria unless he was either invited to do so by those representing the young ruler or forced to do so by anarchy within the late Nur al-Din's lands. Logic surely demanded that he should succeed Nur al-Din as the leader of the jihad, and absorb the Zangid state into a greater Ayyubid empire. However, another possibility was for him to create a new political structure built on moral foundations and committed to the holy war, which he could persuade the Zangid princes to join either by peaceful means or by force. If he chose the latter, he would be upheld both by his inner conviction that he was doing God's work and by the public recognition granted to him by the Caliph of Baghdad. It would take Saladin twelve long years of campaigning before this dilemma was resolved.

In October 1174 Saladin crossed his own Rubicon by riding out of Cairo with just 700 riders and heading for Damascus. Everything that had happened in the past few months must have convinced him as a devout Muslim that God had preordained that he should take up the reins of the holy war surrendered by Nur al-Din. Controversy surrounds this episode: was Saladin riding to the aid of his new suzerain, as-Salih, prisoner of Gumushtekin, or was he, as most believed, taking the first step in the conquest of Syria? In one respect matters were simplified when the emirs of Damascus, failing to secure help from Saif al-Din Ghazi, called on Saladin to help them against Gumushtekin. This added legitimacy to his task and enabled him to gather reinforcements as he advanced into Syria, with Turks, Kurds, and Bedouin, all of whom had been loyal to

Nur al-Din, joining him in his expedition to rescue the late atabeg's son. As he approached Damascus he found that the Damascene army had drawn up to bar his way. However, their commanders were not prepared to fight Saladin and decided to join him when they heard his purpose from his own lips. In fact, words did not conquer Syria so much as the wealth of Egypt. Saladin learned the value of money not only in funding military campaigns but sometimes in making them unnecessary. The occupation of Damascus was a bloodless victory for Saladin, giving him control of the city he himself loved best, "the Garden of the World," as Arab poets called it. Possession of the city also gave him a strategic stronghold for future action against the Latin Christians. However, for the moment he could not give his mind to the holy war.

Saladin's presence in Damascus was justified primarily by the belief that he had come to restore the legitimate rule of Nur al-Din's son, as-Salih. As a result, Saladin must move on to liberate the boy from Gumushtekin's grasp at Aleppo. While he waited to hear from Gumushtekin, Saladin received a vitriolic message from the Zangid princes of Aleppo, Mosul and Sinjar, questioning his professed motives for being in Syria. As they said, "You want the kingdom for yourself; go back where you come from." Saladin's pretense, for pretense it surely was (however laudable its motive), of acting as the "protector" of as-Salih's legitimacy, could not convince the princes of Mosul or Sinjar that he was anything other than an upstart opportunist, motivated like them by greed and ambition. Their message cannot have surprised Saladin, but at least he knew now that the other states of Zangid Syria would not collapse like Damascus. He would have to wage war on his neighbors to achieve his long-term aim of uniting Islam under his rule so that al-Quds, or Jerusalem, could be restored to the faithful. This campaign of unification would earn him as much enmity from his coreligionists as thanks. For the next twelve years Saladin spilled Muslim blood, sometimes even using the Christians as his allies, in a long-term strategy that had as its ultimate objective victory in the holy war. Saladin was wise enough not to get drawn into purely dynastic squabbles, yet he cannot have been blind to the fact that unification of the Muslims would take place under his authority and that this would be interpreted as his fundamental aim, rather than his professed one of holy war. This troubled him and doubtless undermined the pleasure of his victories in 1187.

Saladin set out for Aleppo with an army of 7,000 men, having left

Damascus under the control of his brother Tughtekin. On his arrival at Homs in December 1174 he received the biggest boost so far to his campaign in Syria when he was joined by Nur al-Din's army commander, Fakhr al-Din ibn al-Za'farani. He moved on and reached Aleppo in the last days of the year, calling on Gumushtekin to hand over as-Salih to his self-appointed guardianship. But if Damascus had fallen into his hand like a ripe plum, Aleppo was not ready for plucking. The city was protected by some of the world's strongest fortifications and, without heavy siege weapons, there was no way that Saladin could seize the city, notably the citadel where Gumushtekin held as-Salih. Moreover, while the emirs of Damascus had welcomed Saladin, those of Aleppo absolutely rejected his authority. The Zangid princes challenged his motives and the boy as-Salih even appealed to the Shi'ites whose privileges had been revoked by his dead father. Gumushtekin would clearly stop at nothing to protect himself and as-Salih against Saladin. The eunuch even signed an agreement with Raymond of Tripoli, regent for the leper king Baldwin IV, to stage an attack on Homs, to draw Saladin away from Aleppo. The final insult to Saladin's legitimacy was the attempt on his life when the Aleppans paid Rashid al-Din Sinan, the "Old Man of the Mountain," to send his assassins to kill him. Thirteen of Sinan's men infiltrated Saladin's camp outside Aleppo. His life was saved as the assassins were discovered and cut down, one decapitated by an emir actually inside Saladin's tent and preparing to strike. The holy war must have seemed far from Saladin's thoughts when he saw the hostility he aroused among his fellow Muslims.

Saladin now found himself facing foes in all directions. While Raymond of Tripoli presented a threat from the West, the army of Mosul under 'Izz al-Din Mas'ud, younger brother of Saif al-Din Ghazi, marched to the relief of Aleppo from the East. Fortunately for Saladin the Zangids could not stir themselves to act in unison and Imad al-Din Zangi did not come to the help of his brothers at a moment when Saladin's position looked extremely vulnerable. Saladin strung out negotiations with his enemies until Egyptian reinforcements had reached him, whereupon he sought battle with the Mosulis at the Horns of Hama on April 13, 1175. Some 20,000 Muslim horsemen, Zangid and Ayyubid, met in battle for the first time and Saladin soon proved that he was more than a match for the foolish but courageous 'Izz al-Din Mas'ud. Saladin's troops from Egypt included those who had ridden from Damascus to Cairo with his uncle and himself, and these battle-hardened veterans were far too formidable for the green Mosuli troops. In fact, Saladin was content to rout his enemy rather than exterminate him, recognizing that blood spilled now would have to be avenged later. He wanted no legacy of blood, and he knew that the men who fled from him now would one day be needed to make up his own armies in the holy war.

Saladin returned to Aleppo and found Gumushtekin in more of a mood to negotiate. Consequently, while as-Salih nominally retained control of Aleppo, Saladin kept the territory he had conquered in northern Syria and the Aleppan troops were to be available to him for use in a future holy war against the Latin Christians of Jerusalem. The Caliph of Baghdad acknowledged Saladin's rights in Egypt, Syria, and Yemen, but warned him not to covet as-Salih's territories, particularly Aleppo. The caliph may have imposed conditions on Saladin, but he had obviously not convinced the Zangids that peace should be maintained in the lands of Islam. With Saladin back in Damascus, the Zangids decided to join forces against the new champion of Islam. In the spring of 1176 Saif al-Din Ghazi reached an agreement with Gumushtekin and as-Salih and the combined forces of Aleppo and Mosul met Saladin's army at Tall as-Sultan. In the ensuing battle Saladin again sought to spare his enemy while at the same time demonstrating his own superiority. As the defeated Zangids fled from the battlefield Saladin ordered his commanders to rein in their pursuing troops and, where they took captives, to treat them as brothers. After the battle Saladin released all prisoners, recruiting many into his own army and, with appropriate mockery, he returned the treasures looted from Saif al-Din Ghazi's tents, including the fine wines, musical instruments, caged doves, nightingales and parrots, and his singers and dancing girls. As Oliver Cromwell might have done in a later age, Saladin displayed such worldly vanities to his troops and sternly warned them against a life devoted to fripperies of this kind.

Saladin may have been able to vanquish the armies of Aleppo, Mosul, and Sinjar, but he had less success in combating the activities of the followers of the "Old Man of the Mountain." As he returned to Aleppo, hoping to negotiate a settlement with Gumushtekin that would hold, he suffered his second attack by assassins. During his siege of the fortress of A'zaz, four assassins infiltrated his camp and one managed to attack him in his tent, stabbing him in the head and neck before being cut down. Only the fact that Saladin was wearing a mail headdress under his turban saved his life, and his nerve was obviously broken as he staggered out of his tent, with his face bleeding and his garments ripped in the struggle. He had come closer to death than ever before. Chronicles record that he became excessively disturbed, suspecting every stranger of carrying a knife. He even sprinkled chalk and cinders around his tent to detect any suspicious footprints. His personal safety prompted him to break off his siege of A'zaz and instead attack the assassins' stronghold, but this led to a curious episode that indicated the psychological skills of Sinan's followers. One night Saladin awoke to glimpse a dark figure stealing out of his tent. On a nearby table there was a tray of hot scones, a familiar trademark of the assassins and designed to show how easily they came and went and how, if they chose not to kill, it was not because of a lack of opportunity. With the scones was a message that read, "We acquaint you that *we hold you*, and that we reserve you till your reckoning be paid." The message served its purpose. Saladin immediately broke off the siege and traveled to Aleppo, where he reached a peace agreement with his Zangid enemies. Saladin then returned to Damascus, where he married Nur al-Din's widow, Ismat al-Din Khatunthus, further legitimizing his claim to be Nur al-Din's natural successor.

Saladin's new preeminence in Syria may have brought him peace with his Zangid rivals, at least temporarily, but it pushed him up against the frontier with the Latin kingdom of Jerusalem far earlier than he was ready to begin the holy war. Consequently, like Nur al-Din, Saladin relied on the strategic "truce" to ensure peaceful coexistence as an alternative to continual war. The usual arrangement was that if a crusader of substance arrived from Western Europe, a powerful nobleman with his own troops, the King of Jerusalem would indulge the newcomer's yearning for battle against the Muslims by arranging a campaign, almost in the same way as at other times one might have arranged a ceremonial hunt. Once the Westerner had fulfilled whatever commitments he had made to the Church, he would leave for home, and the truce, temporarily suspended, would be restored between Christian and Muslim sections of Syria. Saladin may have found this cozy arrangement artificial, but it was convenient. Without it life for the common folk of Syria would have been impossible, as it was to become during the Third Crusade, with rival armies fighting a religious civil war in their fields and pastures, ruining their harvests and killing their animals.

However, in 1177 Saladin was to experience his first minicrusade when Philip, Count of Flanders, arrived in Palestine with a strong naval and military contingent. Philip had his own agenda that he did not reveal to the native lords, who hoped he would join them in a new attack on Egypt. When this proved impossible, Philip joined Bohemond III of Antioch and Raymond III of Tripoli in an assault on the northern cities of Hama and Harim. Saladin now made a serious miscalculation that almost ended his career and Islamic hopes in the holy war at a stroke. Thinking that the forces of the Christian kingdom would be depleted by their assaults in the north, he attacked Gaza and Ascalon in southern Palestine, near the Egyptian frontier. Both he and his mainly Egyptian troops were overconfident and undisciplined. Suddenly, to his astonishment, he was attacked by Baldwin IV and his army at Montgisard and routed on November 25, 1177. During the fighting Saladin narrowly escaped death: surrounded by three Frankish knights, he was rescued in the nick of time by a charge of his guards. Saladin had experienced the worst defeat of his career, more personally desperate even than Arsuf fourteen years later. However, he learned one important lesson, which was that the Franks could never be underestimated. The charge of their heavy cavalry was something to be feared. Furthermore, though in numbers they could never equal the troops that Islam could bring against them, each of their knights was like a fortress in himself, around which the infantry could gather and hold off a much larger force of Muslim soldiers. To defeat the knights of the kingdom would take the combined strength of Egypt, Syria, and Mesopotamia, and as yet he could still rely on perhaps only half of the princes and emirs that he would eventually need.

Emboldened by his success at Montgisard, Baldwin IV, with Templar support, adopted a more forward policy toward his neighbors. The king had come of age and had replaced the prudent regent Raymond of Tripoli with such advisers as the Master of the Templars, Odo of St. Arnaud, and the recently released Reginald of Chatillon, now Lord of Oultrejourdain. Consequently, Baldwin ordered the erection of a strong castle at Bait al-Ahzan, controlling the approaches to Damascus and no more than a day's journey from Saladin's capital. The area it overlooked was vital to Muslim Syria and was known as the "granary" of Damascus, consisting of rice and cotton fields, as well as groves of lemon trees. In peaceful times the area was shared by Christian and Muslim settlers and the border was marked by a single oak tree. Flocks grazed side by side and the common folk indulged in none of the frontier quarrels that occupied their lords. Nevertheless, Saladin could not view Baldwin's decision to build the castle as anything other than an act of extreme provocation, to which he must reply.

At first Saladin tried to pay Baldwin to stop the construction of the castle. He offered him 60,000 dinars and later 100,000 dinars, but when this compensation was refused he was left with no alternative but to destroy the fortress. The outcome was a brief border war along the Golan Heights during which Saladin inflicted two defeats on the Christians. The first of these involved the death of Humphrey of Toron, riddled with Muslim arrows while protecting the king from a similar fate. In the second battle, fought at Marj 'Uyun, Baldwin IV badly misjudged Saladin's strength and his army was trapped on a hillside; 270 knights were forced to surrender. Lost on this day were two famous warriors whose absence was a serious blow to the future of the kingdom. The first was Baldwin of Ramla, captured single-handed by the Kurdish chieftain Jamal al-Din Khushtarin. With the advantage of hindsight, this event can be seen as a crucial turning point in the whole future history of the kingdom and of the crusades. Baldwin was expected shortly to marry Princess Sibylla, sister of the leper king, and in due course to succeed the young king when his terrible disease eventually killed him. However, while Baldwin of Ramla was in a Muslim prison, Sibylla fell in love instead with the young Guy of Lusignan, who had only recently arrived in the kingdom. When Guy married Sibylla, it opened the way for him to succeed to the throne of the kingdom instead of Baldwin of Ramla. The second significant prisoner captured at Marj 'Uyun was the Master of the Templars, Odo of St. Armand. When Saladin suggested that Odo should arrange his ransom Odo refused, saying that Templars never gave ransom. As a result, the haughty Templar died in a Muslim prison and was succeeded by a man even more rash and arrogant than he was, Gerard of Ridefort, who was to bring disaster on the kingdom at Hattin. Saladin might have had reflections on the mysterious workings of the divine entity had he appreciated the significance of the capture of these two famous knights.

Saladin's army now closed in on the castle at Bait al-Ahzan, which had been the cause of the two disastrous battles for the Christians, and took it after a brief siege. The garrison of 1,500 was a large one and defended the castle by lighting fires behind the breaches to prevent the Muslim assault troops breaking through where the sappers had undermined the walls. Seven hundred of the garrison survived the siege and surrendered, whereupon Saladin, angered and tired by the constant campaigning, ordered any renegade Muslims inside the castle to be executed, along with all the Christian crossbowmen who were taken. The dead bodies were tipped into the castle well, which was filled in with earth and lime. But in the heat of a Syrian summer the decomposing bodies spread disease so quickly that the garrison scored a victory in death that had been denied them in life. Hundreds of Saladin's soldiers died of disease, including ten of his leading emirs. His nephew and one of his best commanders, Taqi al-Din, were also seriously ill in the epidemic.

The destruction of the castle of Bait al-Ahzan was achieved, but at a very high cost to both sides. Saladin was now convinced that he could not hope to overthrow the Christian kingdom without the full support of the military strength of Mosul and Aleppo. The Christian land was peppered with powerful castles; if each one took a toll similar to that of Bait al-Ahzan, Saladin knew that he would need both time and almost limitless resources. Yet time he could never guarantee if the Christian commander was able to traverse the kingdom and bring to the rescue of any imperiled castle a field army packed with Frankish knights.

On June 29, 1180, Saladin's implacable enemy, Saif al-Din Ghazi, died at Mosul and was replaced by his brother 'Izz al-Din, who wasted no time in demanding that Saladin accept his suzerainty over the Mesopotamian towns that the caliph had granted to Saladin. Saladin furiously refused, opening up the next round of civil strife. 'Izz al-Din's position was strengthened suddenly by the death of as-Salih on December 4, 1181, from colic or poison, depending on which chronicle one believes. On his deathbed the nineteen-year-old as-Salih ordered his emirs to swear allegiance to 'Izz al-Din as the only remaining Zangid prince who could possibly resist Saladin. For Saladin himself there could be no forgiveness for the treachery he had shown to the dynasty that had raised him so far.

For once events worked against Saladin. He was in Egypt when he heard of as-Salih's death and was not able to react promptly. Instead he sent messengers to his brother Farrukh-Shah at Damascus and to his nephew Taqi al-Din at Hama to prevent the Mosulis crossing the Euphrates and marching on Aleppo. However, he was to be thwarted for the first of many times by the man whom the Muslims came to regard as virtually the devil incarnate, "Brins Arnat," or as he was known to the

Christians, Reginald of Chatillon, Lord of Kerak. Reginald was in the process of invading Arabia from his desert strongholds of Kerak and Shawbak, and Farrukh-Shah had his hands full trying to contain this affront to Islam. As a result, he was not able to prevent 'Izz al-Din from reaching Aleppo, pillaging its treasury and arsenal, and leaving the city in the hands of Imad al-Din. Saladin impotently wrote to the caliph complaining that 'Izz al-Din had seized lands not his own and by so doing was weakening the holy war. Even as he wrote he must have wondered how weak these words would seem in Baghdad, particularly as the legitimate king, as-Salih, on his deathbed, had nominated 'Izz al-Din to succeed him. Saladin reminded the caliph that his brother, Farruck-Shah, had been defending the gateway to Arabia at the very moment that the Mosulis were stealing Aleppo from him. But in his heart he must have known that his only claim to Aleppo was in his own view of himself as champion of Islam. 'Izz al-Din was, in fact, legitimately entitled to rule in Aleppo, however damaging this might be to Saladin's perception of the holy war.

Deeds, not words, were needed if he were to oust the Zangids from Aleppo and so, in May 1182, Saladin marched northward with 5,000 troops, leaving Egypt, as it turned out, for the last time. He cannot have been optimistic of capturing Aleppo's massive citadel, but he knew that he must respond to this challenge to his authority. Before he reached Aleppo matters took a more hopeful turn. As he approached the city of Harran its governor, previously a Zangid supporter, Muzaffar al-Din Keukburi, came out to meet him, advising him to cross the Euphrates and march on Mosul, rather than continue north against Aleppo. Saladin agreed and his sudden change of direction took the Zangids by surprise, and a mutiny in 'Izz al-Din's army prevented him from coming out to oppose him. Eventually, the caliph arranged a truce between the two sides. But Saladin was welcomed in the trans-Euphratean region that had been allocated to him as little less than a liberator from unpopular Zangid rule, and he knew that he could not compromise with the Mosulis without losing the support of all those who looked on him as their hope for victory in the holy war. He therefore broke off negotiations with the Mosulis and attacked Sinjar, capturing it after a brief siege, and then moving on to take Dara. 'Izz al-Din responded by calling for help from all his allies, but when Saladin called up his nephew Taqi al-Din, the Zangid prince collapsed. Saladin now marched on from triumph to triumph, constantly informing the caliph that each step he took was but another on the road to the holy war.

In May 1183 Saladin camped before the forbidding walls of Aleppo, knowing that if he had to take the city by force there would be a blood-bath. He knew that the citadel was held by the elite troops of Nur al-Din's old guard, men he had known in his youth and whose services he would need in the struggle ahead. As a man in late middle age he felt a heavy heart at the thought that he had brought all this suffering on his people. His camp was full of young zealots and fanatics, who had no time for the old days or the camaraderie of the saddle that Saladin felt for those who held Aleppo against him. He had chosen the path of holy war and had equipped himself with the weapons of jihad, unquestioning obedience and fanatical hatred of all that opposed the faith. It was these weapons that he must unleash against the remaining men who had stayed loyal to Nur al-Din, a great Muslim like himself but now merely a memory. Saladin's hatred of spilling Muslim blood did not affect his zealots, who fought in the front line and sought martyrdom on the blades not of the infidel but of their own coreligionists. Saladin had to watch as one of his brothers, Taj al-Muluk Buri, was killed in the fight-ing, and it was this personal blow that caused him to call off the assault and withdraw some way from Aleppo. He had decided to allow his pa-tronage rather than the breasts of his soldiers to breach the city walls. He erected a fortress from which he welcomed all those who would join him to come to negotiate terms. He allocated Aleppan fiefs to his senior officers as though he had already taken the city and hoped that time would convince the city's governor, Imad al-Din, to give up the fight. Imad al-Din was not made of the stuff of heroes and was looking for a way out that might save face and would certainly save the rest of him as well. All he wanted was to leave Aleppo, where he was hated and reviled by the population, and return to his beloved Sinjar. Secretly he ap-proached Saladin with the idea that the cities could be exchanged, which Saladin was only too pleased to arrange. Imad al-Din was allowed to leave Aleppo with the treasure he had stored in the citadel and the Aleppans jeered him as he left, offering him a washtub instead of a crown to accompany his humiliating departure. Saladin was not con-cerned with what Imad al-Din took with him as long as he left him the "stones of Aleppo" and the soldiers that went with the city. On June 11, 1183, his huge yellow banner was unfurled on the battlements of Aleppo and his supporters flooded into the city amid general rejoicing. Those who had stood against him realized that he was the man of the hour and that further resistance was pointless. Nur al-Din's household troops, the Nuriyah, joined him to a man and he welcomed them with open arms.

Saladin had been in Syria for a year. During his absence from Egypt an incident occurred that showed him at his worst, impotently posturing and slipping into judicial cruelty of the kind that was typical of the age but not, fortunately, typical of him. Reginald of Chatillon had perpetrated an affront to Islam without parallel in the crusading period. He had launched a pirate raid in the Red Sea, landing near Mecca and planning to seize the body of the Prophet and hold it for ransom at his castle of Kerak. For a while the Islamic world seemed paralyzed with shock and to begin with Reginald's men had things their own way. When he heard what was happening Saladin could only tug his beard and hurl curses at the infidel. Fortunately, his brother al-Adil responded more effectively.

Reginald of Chatillon was the *enfant terrible* of the crusading period, a man of undaunted courage coupled with fiendish cruelty and respect for no authority. He was Outremer's answer to Conrad of Montferrat and was a thorn in everybody's side. Saladin felt personally insulted by Reginald and vowed to kill him with his own hand. This tells us much about Saladin, who rarely lost his temper and never allowed hatred of his enemy to blind him to responses short of death. Saladin felt that Reginald had challenged his perception of himself as the champion of Islam, as a man of greatness and generosity of heart; the concomitant sense of impotence drove Saladin to acts of violent revenge. Reginald brought out the worst in Saladin, and Saladin hated him for it and vowed to make him pay.

Reginald of Chatillon had come to Outremer in 1147, with Louis VII's crusade. He had none of the burning religious zeal of the knights who had traveled to the Holy Land with the First Crusade but was a young opportunist seeking an opening in a new land that offered opportunities unavailable at home in France. He was the younger son of Geoffrey, Count of Gien, Lord of Chatillon-sur-Loing. What Reginald lacked in money and prospects he made up for in his determination to succeed. He served Baldwin III of Jerusalem, and it was during the king's visit to Antioch in 1151 that Reginald's opportunity for advancement arose, an opportunity he seized with both hands. The recently widowed Princess Constance of Antioch, the greatest heiress in the land, fell in love with the handsome young knight and they became lovers, whereupon the strong-willed Constance decided that she would take Reginald as her consort. She had already rejected some highborn suitors suggested by the Emperor Manuel Comnenus and now asked Baldwin III to grant his permission for her to marry Reginald. Baldwin agreed and the lovers married in the spring of 1153. Heiresses who married elderly noblemen frequently found themselves widowed at an age where they preferred as a second husband a more virile partner. Whether or not Constance was satisfied with her young lover, her people were outraged by the behavior of this lowborn intruder. Reginald seemed born to the part, rubbing shoulders with emperors and kings, and playing the part of the tyrant when it suited him. Shortage of funds prompted him to stage a piratical raid on the Byzantine island of Cyprus, during which his men behaved like wild beasts, raping nuns, killing children, and cutting the noses and ears of the priests. When the Patriarch of Antioch complained of his behavior Reginald had the old man whipped, smothered in honey, and chained naked to a barrel in the blazing midday heat at the mercy of every passing insect. Reginald's rise had been meteoric, but his fall was no less spectacular. In November 1160 he carried out some rustling of sheep and goats and was captured by the Governor of Aleppo, who threw him into prison, where he stayed for sixteen years, unransomed and apparently forgotten. In 1176 Gumushtekin, eager to thank the Christians for their assistance against Saladin, released Reginald into a world that had changed. His wife had died in the meantime and Antioch was now ruled by her son from her first marriage, Bohemond III. Thrown back upon his own resources, Reginald showed what an enterprising man he was. Within months he had won the hand of another heiress, Stephanie of Milly, which gained him control of Oultrejourdain, and the castles of Shawbak and Kerak, the strongest in the kingdom. From these lofty perches Reginald could look down on the caravan routes from Cairo to Damascus, deciding which merchants, herdsmen, and pilgrims he would allow to pass and which he would drag off into his dungeons. In the gloomy, red-black stone castle of Kerak Reginald was his own master, and to the minds of the Muslims Reginald ceased to be flesh and blood and became a dark lord, "Brins Arnat," linked to the powers of Satan himself.

At the center of power in Jerusalem Baldwin IV was ailing, and Reginald therefore seemed encouraged to disregard government policy if it suited him. The four-year truce that the Christians had negotiated with

Saladin in 1180 had existed for no more than a year before Reginald broke it in a most dramatic way. Feeling frustrated at having to allow Muslim caravans to pass unhindered by his castles, Reginald decided to lead his troops to Taima, on the desert road from Damascus to Mecca, and there attack a peaceful caravan close to the oasis. This was just the first part of a plan that involved his going as far as Medina. However, prompt action by Saladin's brother Farrukh-Shah, who invaded Oultre-jourdain and ravaged Reginald's lands, caused the Christians to abandon the rest of the expedition and return to defend their homes. Saladin felt humiliated by the way Reginald was able to call into question his ability to defend the Muslim holy places from danger. He complained to Baldwin IV that one of his subjects had broken the truce but cannot have been surprised when the king failed to discipline the Lord of Kerak or gain the release of the Muslim prisoners taken from the caravan. All Saladin could do was indulge in "an eye for a tooth" by imprisoning Christian pilgrims who were shipwrecked on the Egyptian coast.

With the truce broken Saladin decided to invade the Christian kingdom, carrying out a razzia from south to north unchallenged by the royal army that, on Reginald's advice, had been stationed at Petra. The Muslims ravaged the Christian settlements, seizing thousands of prisoners and vast herds of animals. However, Saladin made no permanent gains, and when he returned via Galilee he found the Christians had anticipated his move and brought him to action near Belvoir. The two main armies clashed on an unbearably hot day, and though the fighting was inconclusive, casualties from heatstroke were heavy on both sides. With over a thousand men lost, Saladin had suffered a serious check and he had to withdraw his army from the pestilential area where he was forced to camp, an area filled with frogs and poisonous snakes.

The Lord of Kerak is perhaps the most interesting figure in the history of the kingdom of Jerusalem. Certainly no other Christian soldier, until perhaps the arrival of Richard the Lionheart during the Third Crusade, inspired such terror in the ranks of the Muslims. Saladin's hatred of Reginald, understandable in view of his actions, may have contained a degree of fear that Saladin did not wish to acknowledge. While Reginald shared the brute courage of the crusaders, he had a strategic vision that is only now being appreciated by historians. He realized that the future of the Latin kingdom would be fatally compromised by Saladin's union of Egypt and Syria. Reginald's own position in Oultrejourdain enabled him to intercept movements of supplies and troops between Cairo and Damascus. To a modern strategic eye the castles of Shawbak and Kerak were the dominant features on the map of the holy war. While the Christians held these castles the Muslims could never be secure.

Reginald's sixteen years in a Muslim prison had mellowed the young firebrand without dampening his appetite for action. He emerged from captivity in 1176, a man well advanced in years, but one who now spoke fluent Arabic and Turkish and who could communicate with the desert Bedouin of Transjordan and the Hejaz. He was able to pay such nomads to spy for him against the urban Muslims who comprised much of Saladin's strength. Reginald's strategy was to push the frontiers of the Christian state deep into Sinai and Arabia to create a *cordon sanitaire* between Christian and Muslim territory. To police these areas Reginald planned to establish fortified posts in the desert, linked to one another, by employing Bedouin tribesmen to inform him of any major Muslim buildup of military strength. From 1177 Reginald carried out numerous reconnaissance raids, some even striking deep into Egypt and advancing up the east bank of the Nile. Reginald recognized that water was the major strategic imperative in the region, and he therefore set about controlling the oases on which Muslim caravans depended on their desert journeys. In 1182 he wrecked the town of al-'Arish, took over the oasis, and drove away the Muslim population by destroying the date palms. He made no secret of his policy, claiming the whole of Sinai for the kingdom of Jerusalem and setting out to reclaim the Red Sea port of Eilat, which Saladin had taken from the crusaders in 1171.

With this in mind it is easy to understand Saladin's hatred of Reginald, for the Lord of Kerak not only interfered with the prosecution of the holy war but threatened to reverse the process and challenge Saladin in his own heartland. As he was far away and unable to protect the Muslim holy places, he could not maintain his claims to be the champion of a united Islam. In 1182 Reginald exceeded all his previous plans by launching a naval expedition into the Red Sea which so embarrassed Saladin that there could be no peace between him and Reginald until one of them was dead.

Reginald had been planning the most presumptuous of all actions of the crusading period, nothing less than the kidnapping of the Prophet Muhammad's body and its removal to his castle at Kerak, where he would either demand a ransom or charge pilgrims to see it. For the previous two years boats had been under construction on the Mediterranean coast at Ascalon, which were then transported in sections on the backs of camels to the Red Sea coast at 'Aqaba. Reginald intended to man these ships with freebooters, pirates, and desperadoes, and launch them on a piratical foray into the Red Sea, Islam's most important trading artery and also the center of the pilgrim route from North Africa. He could not have chosen a more vital area for Islam. Reginald's part ended when he captured the port of Eilat and returned to Kerak, but some 200 latter-day Vikings set out in five boats, appropriately painted black by way of camouflage, sailing down the African coast, helped by local pilots. The nature of attack was as savage as it had been in Cyprus, though Reginald was not there personally to add his own brand of terror. Having raided and wrecked coastal towns on both the African and Arabian coasts, Reginald's men bought horses from the Bedouin and rode to within a short distance of Medina, capturing caravans on the way. For six weeks these Christian pirates ran amok in the heart of Islam until al-Adil was able to transfer warships from the Mediterranean to the Red Sea, after which it was only a matter of time before their luck ran out. Eventually the Egyptian admiral Lu'lu hunted them down—not, as might be imagined, on the high seas, but some way inland, where the doughty seaman had pursued them by using the ships of the desert, camels. Saladin followed the saga with the frustration of knowing that he could do nothing to help. However, he was furious when he learned that al-Adil had promised the Christian prisoners quarter. His righteous indignation, fueled by hurt pride, would not allow him to show mercy. In one of his least commendable displays Saladin ordered the 170 Christian prisoners to be executed in public displays in Alexandria, Cairo, Mecca, and Medina. The wretched prisoners, shamefully mounted backward on camels, were killed by Sufis or Muslim holy men. It was an exercise in propaganda, and it is doubtful if al-Adil ever quite forgave his brother. He had given his word to the prisoners that their lives were safe and his brother had broken it for him. Saladin explained that there was a greater issue at stake than the men's lives, namely the sanctity of the Muslim holy places. If any of the Christians had escaped they might have revealed the weakness of the Muslim defenses and brought back with them even larger raiding parties so that, as Saladin told his brother, "Tongues in the East and West would blame us."

Although Reginald's Red Sea campaign had ended in failure, it had had an impact on the world of Islam out of all proportion to its size. Reginald of Chatillon weighed more heavily in Saladin's mind than any other Christian, and this is shown by two masking operations undertaken by Saladin during 1183 and 1184. Experience had shown him that no Muslim caravan, however substantial and well escorted, could move safely past the castle of Kerak. Thus when Saladin altered the administration of his empire, moving his nephew Taqi al-Din from Egypt to Hama, he had to assemble significant forces to protect the caravan.

In October 1183 Saladin marched south from Damascus and arranged a rendezvous at Reginald's castle of Kerak with al-Adil marching from Egypt. As it happened Saladin played the part of the uninvited guest at a wedding. His attack coincided with the marriage of Reginald's stepson, Humphrey of Toron, to Isabella, stepsister to Baldwin IV and stepdaughter of Balian of Ibelin. The union of the young couple was an attempt by the dying king to unite the two parties that were tearing the kingdom apart. It was no mean achievement to persuade Reginald and Balian to occupy the same room together, nor their wives Stephanie of Milly and the Empress Maria Comnena. There was enough hostility among the wedding guests to make Saladin's arrival redundant. Nevertheless, Saladin and al-Adil made a determined effort to capture the great castle at last, driving Reginald and his troops from the edge of the town up the slopes and into the castle. The Muslims almost broke into the castle itself but were held at bay by a solitary knight named Iven who held the bridge over the fosse while his comrades cut it away from under him. Just before the bridge toppled, Iven, riddled with arrows, was pulled to safety. Within the castle Reginald's people looked down at the town, swarming with Saladin's soldiers, who were pillaging the houses and shops. As they watched they saw the Muslim engineers erecting eight mangonels, which began tossing heavy rocks against the castle walls.

The wedding reception taking place within Kerak must have been one of the most surreal on record. Balian's squire Ernoul described this memorable occasion in his chronicle. While the guests danced and the music played, rocks crashed against the outer walls, reverberating throughout the castle. While the guests laughed and joked, the sound mingled with the screams and cries of pain and anger from the besieged soldiers on the ramparts. At night sleep was impossible. One of the most splendid of the anecdotes associated with Saladin occurred during this siege of Kerak. The mother of the bridegroom, Stephanie of Milly, was supervising the wedding breakfast and she specially prepared some dishes for Saladin that, it is reported, she delivered to him with her own hand. Astonished at this remarkable generosity, Saladin responded by inquiring in which tower the young married couple were to sleep. When he was told, Saladin ordered his engineers not to bombard that part of the castle for fear of disturbing the newlyweds. No similar story of any other medieval figure could be told with any chance that it was true. In the case of Saladin, it is one of dozens of similar examples of his natural generosity and its essential truthfulness is virtually guaranteed.

While the bombardment continued, the Muslims began trying to fill in the fosse to enable them to close in on the castle walls, but time was against them. No sooner had the Muslims closed in on the city than the defenders had lit a signal beacon on the highest tower to call for help. A relay of similar beacons then carried the message all the way to Jerusalem, and within hours an answering beacon had been lit on the top of David's Tower in Jerusalem to tell Reginald that help was coming. Baldwin IV was by now little more than an animated corpse, rotting away and carried in a litter, yet determined to lead his army to the rescue of his vassals. Leaving the command to Raymond of Tripoli, Baldwin nevertheless accompanied the army all the way to Kerak and was carried in triumph into the castle, to the acclaim of the garrison and the wedding guests. Once Saladin heard the news that the crusader army was approaching he called off the siege, withdrew his troops, and burned his siege engines.

Saladin besieged Kerak again the following summer, in the company of his nephew Taqi al-Din. Convinced that the massive walls of the castle were immune to the mangonels, which had failed once before, Saladin hoped to fill in the fosse and move siege towers close to the walls. This time Reginald had abandoned the settlement below the castle and had drawn the inhabitants within the castle walls before the Muslims arrived. The filling of the fosse was a massive task, made all the more difficult by the missiles that were poured onto the engineers by the Christian defenders. Rocks, jars of naphtha, burning oil, burning faggots and "Greek fire" (a naphtha-based mixture fired from catapults) were all thrown down onto the men working to fill the fosse. The more the Muslims tried to bring up fascines the more the Christians ignited them from above. One chronicler describes the scene at night with the Greek fire crashing onto the attackers: "In coming it made a noise like heaven's thunder. It seemed like a dragon flying through the air. So great a light did it emit, because of the great abundance of fire that made the light, that one could see as clearly through the camp as if it had been day."

As in 1183, Reginald had lit the beacon and had been told that a relief army led by Raymond of Tripoli was again on its way. The Muslims responded as they had the previous year by calling off the siege, but this time Saladin was prepared to challenge the crusader army that was approaching. However, Raymond of Tripoli outmaneuvered Saladin during the night and entered Kerak in triumph. Saladin's frustration at failing to capture Kerak for a second time was tempered by the fact that with the crusader field army in the extreme south of the kingdom, Muslim raiders were able to cross the river Jordan and attack numerous ungarrisoned towns and cities like Nablus, Sebastiya, and Jenin. By attacking Reginald's lands Saladin was stretching the resources of the kingdom to breaking point. Eventually, the crusaders in Jerusalem would have to decide whether it was worth the risk to other major cities of the kingdom to be available constantly to save frontier castles like Kerak, however strategically vital they might be. And Saladin must have noticed how easy it was to draw the main Christian army away from the center of the kingdom into areas that he could dictate. During these two abortive sieges of Kerak the germ of an idea may have grown in Saladin's mind; this was to reach fruition three years later at Tiberias.

5

─────────|◆|◆|◆|─────────

Preparing the Holy War 1184–1187

SALADIN WAS NOW approaching the final stage of his unification of the lands of Nur al-Din, preparatory to the holy war against the Franks. However, 'Izz al-Din still refused to accept him as the successor to Nur al-Din and continued to seek allies, even from as far away as Persia and Azerbaijan. In May 1185 Saladin decided that the time had come when he must settle his dispute with 'Izz al-Din at Mosul. Raymond III of Tripoli, the Frankish leader with whom Saladin was most ready to negotiate, was once again regent of the kingdom for Baldwin IV's nephew and successor, the boy king Baldwin V. A severe drought had struck Syria, both Christian and Muslim, and nothing was to be gained by destructive frontier warfare. Consequently, Raymond and Saladin signed a four-year truce, allowing Saladin to concentrate his attention on the problem of Mosul rather than the Franks at his back. He marched on the city, surrounded it, and for seven months a desultory siege ensued, maintained without much conviction by either side. 'Izz al-Din apparently tried to soften the heart of what he assumed was a ruthless conqueror in Saladin by sending several Zangid princesses to beg him not to conquer Mosul. At first Saladin scorned such diplomacy and dismissed the ladies and their charms. But when he was taken seriously ill, he relented and wondered if God was punishing him for the hardness of his heart to his fellow Muslims. After his recovery he withdrew his troops and sent envoys to Mosul to negotiate with 'Izz al-Din. It was what the Zangid prince had been waiting for and, like his brother Imad, he hoped to be able to save face and his territories if he gave Saladin what he appeared to want, which was his promise of military support in a future holy war. Saladin agreed. He had never wanted land for its own sake but for the men it brought him; they were necessary in his struggle against the Christians. With this settlement Saladin had finally united Egypt with the lands of Nur al-Din and was ready to begin the holy war against the kingdom of Jerusalem. It had been a lengthy process, but throughout Saladin had been sustained by an inner conviction that he was doing what was ordained by God. And, as he presumed was God's will, he had achieved unity of Islam without spilling more Muslim blood than had been absolutely necessary. His had been the way of the noble heart. Generosity had won him friends where physical courage could only have won him victory. Saladin the Lionheart was ready for what he regarded as his life's task.

It was the schism within the Latin kingdom that finally provided Saladin with the opportunity he had been waiting for. The split between native princes and recent arrivals, between Westerners and Easterners, between advocates of an aggressive forward policy and those of peaceful coexistence, flourished in the declining years of Baldwin IV, who was powerless to unite the factions. The death of the leper king in 1185, followed by the demise of the sickly boy king Baldwin V a year later, played into the hands of the "court" party headed by Joscelin of Courtenay. He saw an opportunity to oust Raymond of Tripoli as regent and become the power behind the throne by crowning Princess Sibylla, who would then offer the crown to her husband Guy of Lusignan. Joscelin tricked the native barons by asking Raymond to assemble the barons at Tiberias; while they were all out of the capital, he could then stage a "palace revolution." Guy and Sibylla were persuaded to seize control of Jerusalem and prepare their own coronation, joined in the coup by their allies the Patriarch Eraclius, the new Master of the Templars Gerard of Ridefort and, of course, greatest of them all, Reginald of Chatillon, who rode swiftly to join them from Kerak. The plotters then summoned the barons who were assembling at Tiberias to return to Jerusalem to celebrate the coronation of Guy and Sibylla.

Meanwhile, Raymond of Tripoli called on his allies to join him at Nablus. Balian of Ibelin and William of Montferrat, grandfather of the late king and father of the redoubtable Conrad, joined Raymond and together they rejected Sibylla's summons. Civil war loomed and Joscelin sent two Cistercian monks to warn Raymond that the coup was a *fait ac-compli* and that further resistance was unnecessary. In fact Joscelin was right. Of those in Jerusalem, only the Master of the Hospitallers, Roger of Moulins, had rejected the coup. As he held one of the three keys needed to unlock the crowns and royal regalia for the coronation, he was put under unbearable pressure by the conspirators until, in frustration, he threw the key out of the window and washed his hands of the whole procedure. The key was retrieved and soon Eraclius was crowning Sibylla Queen of Jerusalem. Sibylla then crowned a kneeling Guy her consort and King of Jerusalem. Next Reginald of Chatillon spoke to the assembled barons, asserting in a powerful speech that as Sibylla was the sister of the late Baldwin IV and mother of Baldwin V, her elevation to the throne was an act of legitimacy. His arguments were irrefutable. All that worried the assembled barons was whether her choice of a husband six years ago should have saddled the kingdom with the weak Guy of Lusignan as king.

When Raymond and Balian heard that the gates of Jerusalem were barred by the Templars they sent a soldier into the city disguised as a monk. This spy returned to Nablus with news of the coronation and the leaders of the native barons realized they had been outmaneuvered. Baldwin of Ramla had good reason to hate the new king, who had already robbed him of the woman he loved and now had compounded the crime by taking the crown that should have been his. He told his brother and Raymond, "I'll wager he won't be king a year. Lords, do the best you can, for the land is lost, and I shall leave the country, for I do not wish to have reproach or blame for having any share in the loss of the land. For I know the present king to be such a fool and such a wicked man that he will do nothing by my advice or yours. Instead he will prefer to go astray on the advice of those who know nothing. For this reason I shall leave the country." Raymond of Tripoli was not prepared to give up so easily. He attempted a countercoup by setting up a rival monarchy consisting of Queen Sibylla's sister Isabella and her young husband Humphrey of Toron, whose marriage at Kerak had included Saladin as an uninvited guest. However, Humphrey was more a scholar than a knight and was afraid of what men like Reginald of Chatillon and Gerard of Ridefort would do to him if he opposed them. Under cover of night he fled from Nablus to Jerusalem and confessed Raymond's plans to Sibylla, thereby gaining himself a full pardon.

With the collapse of his plans Raymond joined Baldwin of Ramla in exile. The rest of the barons, including Balian of Ibelin, swallowed their pride and returned to Jerusalem to acknowledge Guy as their king. Raymond retired to his wife's city of Tiberias, refusing to take an oath of loyalty to the new royal couple. On the advice of Gerard of Ridefort Guy now prepared to use force against the legal regent of the kingdom. Saladin, meanwhile, had been following events in the Christian lands with astonishment. Raymond was the wisest of the Christians and yet he was driven out of power. Baldwin of Ramla was their greatest knight and yet he was forced into exile. How could the Christians be stronger by the loss of such men? If civil war should threaten to break out in the Christian lands he must be prepared to take advantage of the situation.

The fall of the kingdom of Jerusalem is a story of the tragic overthrow of a great man. If Reginald of Chatillon was Saladin's enemy, Raymond of Tripoli came as close as any Christian could to being his friend. Yet loyalty and friendship were incompatible concepts in Raymond's situation. He owed no allegiance to Guy, who was simply a usurper, but he did owe loyalty to the realm, of which he was still the legitimate ruler. Had the barons' acceptance of Guy as their king changed his own legal authority? And if it had not, dare he use his power to overthrow Guy at the cost of civil war? If he did, the Muslims, now united under a powerful prince, would exploit the divisions within the kingdom and possibly overthrow it. Balian of Ibelin, his lifelong friend and ally, had taken the pragmatic line, accepting what could not be undone except at too high a cost. Raymond adopted a different line. As a fourth-generation inhabitant of Outremer, he no longer saw matters in black and white between Christians and Muslims. As regent of the kingdom in 1176 he had allied with Gumushtekin against Saladin and had frequently negotiated truces with the Muslims, when times were hard for the peasants on both sides of the Syrian frontier. In view of the threat facing him now from Guy of Lusignan and the court party, he felt he had no alternative but to turn to Saladin for help. With hindsight, one can judge Raymond harshly: on the one hand, he could be accused of treachery in allowing the Muslims free passage into the kingdom; on the other, without the issue of religion, Saladin was merely a neighbor helping Raymond to regain his position that had been usurped by his enemies. Yet surely Raymond was being shortsighted. Saladin was more dangerous as an ally than Guy could possibly be as an enemy. As a firm and public adherent of the holy war,

Saladin would never be satisfied by merely restoring Raymond to power in the kingdom. The price Saladin would charge for his help would be more than any Christian was prepared to pay.

Raymond contacted Saladin at Damascus and revealed his dilemma. Magnanimous as Saladin had always shown himself to be, he can be excused if he felt that "whom the gods wished to destroy they first made mad." The infidels were so at odds with themselves that they sought salvation in their most committed foe. Surely God had prepared the way for victory in the holy war. Saladin responded quickly by sending troops to Tiberias and releasing all Raymond's knights held in Muslim prisons. He sent verbal guarantees that if Raymond was attacked he would come to his aid within hours. Yet was Raymond really looking to use Muslim troops against his fellow Christians, even his friends like Balian of Ibelin, or was he merely threatening King Guy to deter his impetuous advisers like Reginald and Gerard? The fact was that a truce still existed between the kingdom of Jerusalem and Saladin. There was no need for hostilities of any kind unless Guy attempted to coerce Raymond, in which case the Count of Tripoli as the legitimate authority in the realm was entitled to defend himself in any way he could. And Saladin, of course, was only too eager to help the Christian kingdom to disintegrate at so slight a cost to himself.

In Jerusalem Balian of Ibelin, skillful diplomat that he was, was attempting to forge a compromise with King Guy and prevent a precipitate assault on Tiberias. As he pointed out, only Saladin would benefit from Christian fighting Christian. If the king would agree to disband his army he, Balian, would try to persuade Raymond to accept the new regime. Guy agreed to let Balian try. But before the diplomacy could take effect, Reginald of Chatillon had once again stepped into the limelight by breaking the truce with Saladin.

There is no point in asking why Reginald broke the truce at the precise moment that the Christians were least able to combat the Muslims. Reginald was a law unto himself, and the accession of a weak and junior knight like Guy to the throne hardly filled Reginald with a sense of fealty. He was already in the process of building in Oultrejourdain a state within a state and would eventually have pressed for independence from the rule of Jerusalem, like Tripoli or Antioch. However, unlike Raymond of Tripoli and Bohemond of Antioch he did not see himself as an Easterner, living peacefully alongside Muslim states. Reginald was aggressively expansionist, and his existence was inimical to the united Ayyubid state that Saladin was creating. Fate had placed the most dynamic crusader at the weak hinge on which the Syro-Egyptian state depended, and Saladin knew that the overthrow of Reginald was as vital a step in the holy war as the fall of almost any of the crusader strongpoints.

Early in 1187 Reginald attacked a Muslim convoy near Kerak. Rumors that Saladin's sister was with the caravan proved inaccurate but may have been just the additional bait that pushed Reginald over the edge. When news of the atrocity reached Saladin, he responded as usual by calling on King Guy for restitution. It was the first real test of Guy's authority, and he passed with flying colors. He caved in and proved that he had no authority at all. Reginald told Guy that within his own lands the Lord of Kerak was as much the master as the king was in his lands. It was a declaration of independence that, had time allowed, would have caused the breakup of the crusader state. This was all that Saladin needed to prove to himself that the time had come to put an end to the Frankish hold on Jerusalem. He began his preparations for the invasion of the Latin kingdom.

With the dispute between King Guy and Count Raymond still dividing the Christians, Balian of Ibelin offered to head a delegation from the king to seek a settlement. Gerard of Ridefort and Roger of Moulins went with him *ex officio*, though whoever thought that the presence of the former would help was much mistaken. The peace delegation rode toward Tiberias where Raymond was staying with his wife, Eschiva of Tiberias, and his stepsons. Fate conspired to wreck the best intentions of both sides. Balian's squire Ernoul left the only account of the extraordinary events that followed. On the journey to Tiberias the peace delegation stopped over for the night at Balian's castle at Nablus and, rather than riding out the next morning with the others, Balian decided to spend the day with his wife and catch the others up later. This left Gerard and Roger alone for a day, and that promised mischief.

Raymond's agreement with Saladin left him in Saladin's debt, and when al-Afdal, Saladin's eldest son, asked his permission to carry out a reconnaissance mission across Raymond's lands the count found it difficult to refuse his ally's reasonable request. Yet, as a baron of the kingdom, he would be accused of treason if he allowed the Muslims to use his lands as an invasion route. On the other hand, if he refused the Muslim request, would King Guy protect him in turn from the wrath of Saladin? It was a baffling problem, and Raymond responded as well as he could. He agreed to allow al-Afdal to pass through his lands provided that he damaged no Christian settlements. Moreover, his troops must cross the river Jordan after sunrise and leave before sunset. In order to avoid any military incidents he spread the word that the Muslims were not to be challenged or attacked. At the last moment word reached him of the royal delegation approaching Tiberias and he hastily sent messengers to inform them of the situation.

In the early light of May 1, Raymond watched from the battlements of Tiberias as Keukburi and al-Afdal led a powerful force of Mameluke cavalry, several thousand strong, across his lands toward Cresson. He cannot have thought that this force was preparing the way for the end of the Christian kingdom of Jerusalem, reconnoitering the terrain where the decisive battle of Hattin would later be fought. Assuming, as he did, that his friend Balian was leading the royal delegation, he can be excused for assuming that the approaching Christian party would ignore the Muslims and continue their journey to Tiberias. He cannot have known that Balian was not with the party and that the delegation was now led by the hotheaded Gerard de Ridefort. When Raymond's messenger reached the approaching delegation with his news Gerard virtually exploded with indignation. He would allow no Muslims in Christian lands and would fight those he met. He immediately summoned all Templars in the vicinity to meet him at the castle of La Feve, including the Marshal of the Temple, James of Mailly, with ninety knights. Joining up with forty secular knights at Nazareth, Gerard led his tiny army, supplemented by three or four hundred infantry, toward the Springs of Cresson, where Keukburi's army was watering its horses. At the sight of so large a Muslim force Roger of Moulins and James of Mailly rightly suggested withdrawal as they were outnumbered by twenty or thirty to one. However, Gerard and James broke into a furious dispute. Gerard, insulting his marshal, jeered, "You love your blond head too well to lose it." It was the sort of insult that no knight could allow to stand. Stung into action by Gerard's gibe, James spurred his horse into the middle of the Muslim force and was immediately killed. Ernoul's chronicle reports that before he rode off, he said prophetically to Gerard that at least he would die in battle like a brave man but that Gerard would flee like a traitor. The crusaders charged after the dying James and were swallowed up by the

Muslim masses. It was a massacre rather than a battle, and all the Templars were killed except Gerard and two others who somehow escaped. The death of the moderate Roger of Moulins was a further blow to the Christians, leaving Gerard of Ridefort as the voice of the Military Orders.

The first Balian of Ibelin heard of the disaster was when he and Ernoul rode toward Nazareth, only to meet Gerard riding the other way with his two comrades. Raymond of Tripoli received news of the battle in a more dramatic fashion. As the sun set behind the Galilean hills he once again witnessed Keukburi's Mamelukes riding back to the river Jordan, but this time they carried grim and bloody trophies on their upheld lances, the heads of Templars, and, preeminent among them, the golden tresses of James of Mailly. Raymond sent at once to inquire after his friend Balian and was relieved to hear that he had not been in the battle. Yet his mind must have been in turmoil. The disaster at Cresson had been the result of Gerard's rashness, yet in a deeper way Raymond knew that the fault had been his. Achilles-like he had retired to his tent, having been outmaneuvered by Joscelin of Courtenay and the court faction. His sulking had brought this disaster on the kingdom. Unless he made his peace with King Guy, Saladin would succeed in overcoming a divided kingdom and the Holy Land would be lost to the infidels.

Raymond first dismissed Saladin's troops, who had been sent to protect Tiberias, and rode back with Balian to meet King Guy. At the Hospitaller castle of St. Job Raymond and Guy embraced and then returned together to Jerusalem, where Raymond paid homage to Guy and Sibylla as his legitimate monarchs. But how deep the reconciliation went is shown by the fact that neither Reginald of Chatillon nor Gerard of Ridefort ever forgave the Count of Tripoli. Their control of the king meant that Raymond's advice could not prevail, even at the most vital moments.

Saladin showed appropriate anger toward Raymond for breaking their pact, but it was for public consumption alone. He never expected the Count of Tripoli so to forget his pedigree that he would abandon his faith and fight his fellow Christians. Saladin was happy enough to have used the opportunity to reconnoiter the land to the west of Tiberias, notably the plain of Lubiya, and assess its suitability for the campaign that he was planning to wage in the months ahead. What was needed now was to assemble the armies of Islam for the holy war. On March 13,

1187, Saladin rode out of Damascus to establish his camp at Ra's al-Ma', which became the mustering point for the troops arriving from his northern and eastern lands. Now that he had taken the decision to begin the holy war he would not sheath his sword again until he had fought a decisive battle against the Franks.

With his son al-Afdal in charge of the camp at Ra's al-Ma', Saladin headed south to Busra, to be in a position to protect the caravans of pilgrims returning to Damascus from Mecca, which had to pass within range of the castle of Kerak. One of the caravans this time indeed carried Saladin's sister and her son; after Reginald's earlier attack, intended for Saladin's family, the sultan was taking no chances. While he was in the south he was able to gather together his Mameluke regiments and the Nubian troops from Egypt who were to travel north with him to face the Franks.

Meanwhile, troops from throughout the Middle East flooded into the camp at Ra's al-Ma'. From east of the Euphrates came the troops from al-Jazira, commanded by Keukburi. From his capital, to the north of the camp, came the Damascene forces under the Mameluke emir Sarim al-Din Qaimatz, while from farther north still came the contingent from Aleppo under Badr al-Din Dildirim. Saladin's most able commander, Taqi al-Din, was meanwhile negotiating a truce with Bohemond III of Antioch, enabling him to march southward with his own feudal levies and the troops from Mardin, meeting on the way the forces from Mosul led by Fakhr al-Din ibn al-Za'farani. With the arrival of smaller contingents from Sinjar, Nisbin, Amid, Irbil, and Diyar Bakr, the muster lacked only the largest contingent, which Saladin was bringing from Egypt. It was one of the largest armies and the finest ever assembled by a Muslim leader, yet it was not as united as shared religious belief might have suggested. Saladin's army was vastly complex, containing soldiers of different color, race, nationality, language, and military tradition. Men who had only recently been enemies now found themselves brought together under one leader for the sole purpose of retaking al-Quds and driving the Christian interlopers into the sea. All men looked to Saladin for leadership. Without him there could be no unity and therefore no victory.

With the Muslim and Christian armies assembling on either side of the river Jordan, it seemed likely that a decisive battle might take place in the territory of Eschiva of Tiberias, which included most of Galilee. This would have suited Saladin, who needed to fight a battle, for he could not be certain that he could assemble such a mighty force again. If the Christians held their traditional position at Saffuriya, amid the lush, well-watered gardens there, they could defy Saladin without risking an encounter in the parched lands of Galilee, between the coast and Lake Tiberias. This is where Saladin would hope to trap his enemy, but how could he get such experienced leaders as Raymond of Tripoli and Balian of Ibelin to march to disaster on the waterless plain of Lubiya? Achieving this would be the equivalent of achieving victory itself, and Saladin knew that only human folly could deliver his enemy into his power.

With war imminent, Count Raymond traveled from Jerusalem to Tiberias to arrange with his wife for the defense of the city that he assumed would be at the center of the fighting. Presumably he warned Eschiva of her danger and begged her to abandon her home and take refuge in Acre, but she refused, even allowing him to withdraw much of her garrison and to take her four sons with him to join the royal army at Saffuriya. Eschiva's confidence shows a great deal about Christian perceptions of Saladin as a noble and generous man, who would never harm a lady. Raymond, recently his ally, felt that he could rely on Saladin's sense of honor to protect his wife. Nevertheless, he told Eschiva that if she was attacked she should withdraw into the citadel or if even this offered no safety, to take to the lake by boat and await rescue.

Saladin, having completed his muster, now moved to the south of Lake Tiberias and occupied the high ground, basing himself at Kafr Sabt, halfway between Tiberias and the crusader camp at Saffuriya. From this position he could overlook the plain of Lubiya, where he planned to trap the Franks and destroy them. But first he had to persuade them to leave Saffuriya. In this he was helped by a sound knowledge of crusader behavior, built up over many years of close association in peace and war with their leaders. His spies had kept him well informed about the dissensions within the Latin kingdom, and Saladin knew what he could expect from men like Raymond of Tripoli and Reginald of Kerak. But King Guy was an enigma. Could these "men of iron" really have chosen a man as apparently feeble as Guy de Lusignan as their king and military commander? All he could learn about Guy suggested that he was as weak as he was portrayed and that his control over his powerful vassals was limited, so that those in the political ascendant at the moment, and that meant Reginald and probably Gerard of Ridefort, would weigh with the king far more than the wiser voices of the moderates like Raymond and Balian. The fact that crusader tactics, evolved over a century of warfare against the Muslims, would argue against an advance away from "water and walls" did not mean that King Guy could not be drawn into a fatal break with the past if the lure was strong enough and the advice bad enough. Saladin reasoned that in the shape of Eschiva, lady of Tiberias, he might have just the bait for a chivalrous Western knight like Guy of Lusignan, which the more sophisticated and cynical local knights would reject. His decision was made. He decided to lay siege to Tiberias in the hope that the Christians would advance to Eschiva's aid as they had so often come to the help of Reginald at Kerak.

Leaving Taqi al-Din and Keukburi with the mass of the army at Kafr Sabt, Saladin personally led a force to attack Tiberias. As soon as it appeared before the city walls, the local population tried to buy him off with gold, but Saladin was relentless. His siege was almost immediately effective, with his engineers bringing down one of the city towers. Soon a breach was made and his troops poured into the city, killing and enslaving the inhabitants. Eschiva and her small garrison fled into the citadel, which was protected by a moat and powerful walls. For a while she was safe, provided that assistance came from Saffuriya. At once she sent out messengers to King Guy whom, significantly, Saladin made no real attempt to stop. As these desperate men rode across the plain of Lubiya, Saladin hoped to see them return soon with the whole Christian army.

King Guy's spies had been following events at Tiberias, and his scouts soon reported that the city was in danger of falling. At dusk on July 2 Eschiva's messengers rode into Guy's camp with her appeal for help and the king immediately assembled his leading councillors. One of the fundamental laws of the kingdom stated that the king had an obligation to go to the aid of one of his vassals if he was threatened by Muslim attack. It was so fundamental a requirement that, in a sense, it was one of the cornerstones of the entire state. How could a Christian enclave survive in the Muslim world, surrounded by hostile neighbors, if those living in distant frontier settlements like Tiberias or Kerak did not have the absolute confidence that the whole realm was committed to the defense of the smallest part? Yet Guy now faced a clash between military expediency and feudal obligation. He knew that if he failed to aid a vassal in danger then he was no longer entitled to be regarded as that vassal's liege lord. In fact, to fail Eschiva now would mean that every vassal in the kingdom would question their allegiance to him. As a king he would be finished.

Count Raymond's voice was loudest at the meeting that followed. After all, Eschiva was his wife and Tiberias his city. No chronicler who has left accounts of this famous occasion has been able to communicate the tension of the occasion. Everyone present, from barons and nobles to knights, knew what was at stake: nothing less than the kingdom, their homes, families, even lives. For many, an even greater consideration was that they were the guardians of the holy places, of Jerusalem, Nazareth, Bethlehem, the Holy Sepulchre, the True Cross—and so it went on. Hundreds of men crowded into the king's tent, illuminated by torchlight, and the babble of voices in many languages must have added to the confusion.

Raymond called for quiet and spoke in a voice that rose in confidence as he found that not everyone present blamed him for the disaster at Cresson and the death of so many brave knights. As an experienced soldier and the greatest landowner in the kingdom, he spoke with an authority that few others possessed. He told those assembled that the Muslim attack on Tiberias was merely a bait to trap them. He, above all men present, knew the mind of Saladin and he knew that the sultan would never harm Eschiva. If they refused to be drawn out of Saffuriya, Saladin would eventually be forced to abandon Tiberias and withdraw from their territory as his eastern and northern troops returned to their homes in Mosul or Aleppo. If, on the contrary, the entire military strength of the kingdom marched onto the waterless plateau that separated Saffuriya from Tiberias, they would risk a disaster of such magnitude that they would be undoing a century of Christian colonization in the Holy Land and, moreover, betraying the martyrs of the First Crusade.

Silence followed Raymond's powerful speech. Nobody wanted to be the first to challenge him, yet Gerard of Ridefort was shaking with anger at what he regarded as a craven speech by a traitor. "He has a wolf's skin," muttered Gerard, but when asked to explain himself he desisted, seeing that he was in a clear minority. King Guy had been completely convinced by Raymond's arguments and announced that there would be no march to Tiberias. Instead, the royal army would remain on the defensive either at Saffuriya or, in an emergency, before the walls of Acre. Saladin would never dare besiege the foremost fortress of the kingdom without risking total disaster if he had to retreat across the waterless terrain to the Jordan.

There was nothing further to be said, and as the evening turned to night, the crusaders retired to their tents, leaving Guy seated alone at a table, taking late refreshments. The scene has an almost Shakespearean feel to it, so great is the tragedy that is about to fall upon the kingdom. Guy started, becoming aware that not everyone had left his tent. From the shadowy corner a figure moved out into the torchlight, revealing himself as the Master of the Templars, Gerard of Ridefort, bitter enemy of the Count of Tripoli. Gerard had remained behind for one purpose only, and that was to change the king's decision to remain at Saffuriya. As Saladin was to learn to his cost, Guy of Lusignan was neither a coward nor as weak as he had been portrayed. Yet he was susceptible to bullying and, faced by the two formidable bullies Reginald and Gerard, he was putty in their hands. After all, these two men were among those to whom he owed his crown, and he felt unable to oppose them even when he knew they were wrong. It was with this knowledge that Gerard felt confident that he could change the king's mind about Tiberias.

Since the disaster at the Springs of Cresson, which he had blamed on Raymond, Gerard had been an even more bitter enemy of the Count of Tripoli, trying in every way to diminish his standing in the realm and convince everyone that he was a traitor, in league with Saladin. Gerard may even have believed his own lies and interpreted Raymond's speech as a way of leaving Saladin to ravage the kingdom unopposed. Whatever the truth, Gerard found a willing convert in King Guy, half of whose mind still did not entirely trust Raymond and was prepared to believe that the count might be prepared to side with the Muslims to regain his predominant position in the kingdom. Why, Gerard asked Guy, was Raymond so confident in leaving his wife at the mercy of Saladin unless he had already made an agreement with the Muslim leader? By encouraging Guy to stand on the defensive Raymond must be aiming to humiliate the new king in the eyes of his people. How would it look, Gerard insisted, if the new king remained with his full army while one of the cities of the kingdom was destroyed just ten miles away, and all its inhabitants were killed or enslaved? Gerard's arguments were quite overwhelming to Guy's weak mind and he might have stopped there, but Ernoul's chronicle records that the Master of the Templars used one more point that struck fear into Guy's heart. He revealed to Guy that he knew the minds of the Templars and that if the king remained at Saffuriya without offering to fight the Muslims, they would as a body remove their support from him as king. In view of the fact that Gerard had played a significant role in making Guy king the previous year while his Templar knights had barred the gates of Jerusalem to Raymond and Balian's supporters who were coming to challenge Guy's rights to the throne, Guy knew that without Gerard's support he was ruined. Regardless of the sense of Raymond's arguments, Guy now knew that he would have to do what Gerard wanted. The army must march to Tiberias at first light after all. Trumpeters were sent throughout the camp to issue the new orders.

Drowsy men, awakened by the call to arms, could not understand what had happened to change the king's mind. Only a few hours earlier the decision to remain on the defensive had been overwhelmingly agreed by almost all present at the royal council. Now everywhere there was noise and confusion as men came out of their tents shouting for news of why they were to march. Slowly the truth began to spread throughout the camp. To many it seemed impossible: the king had changed his mind or had it changed for him. The barons and knights grouped together and argued angrily. To advance across a waterless plateau in midsummer heat was madness. Everyone knew that it was a trap and that Saladin already held the high ground along the route of the march. And what hope was there of saving Tiberias anyway? It was already a smoking ruin. Those noblemen who met Guy now demanded to know why he had changed his mind, but they found the king almost ashamed of what he had done and he shouted at them, ordering them to obey him. In a feudal society it was enough for the king to give an order; it was for them to obey it without demur.

The Christian army assembled amid the sort of mutual recriminations that boded ill for the campaign ahead. Even the spiritual aid that the common soldiers sought came tainted. The Patriarch Eraclius brought the True Cross to Saffuriya but declined to ride with the army and instead passed it to the bishops of Lydda and Acre, who were to carry it in battle. For some the way Eraclius relinquished the priceless relic was symbolic. This remnant of Christ's crucifixion had been regained from the Persians by the Byzantine Emperor Heraclius in 627 as a result of a great Christian victory over the Fire-worshipers at Nineveh. Now it was being surrendered by another Eraclius who lacked the courage of his eminent namesake and was unprepared to risk his life for his faith.

Saladin's scouts kept a vigil on the hills overlooking Saffuriya throughout the night of July 2–3, 1187, and in the hours before first light they were rewarded by the sight they had been waiting for. The sleeping camp suddenly came to life and an immense activity replaced the previous quiet. It could only mean one thing, the spies reflected: the enemy was preparing to march. The fleetest mounts carried the message to Saladin at Tiberias: victory in the holy war could be won that day.

6

---◆◆◆◆---

The Battle of Hattin 1187

SALADIN WAS AT morning prayer outside the ruined walls of Tiberias
when the messengers arrived with the news he was waiting for: the
Franks were on the march. It was what he had hoped to hear without,
perhaps, ever daring to believe that King Guy would follow so desperate
a course. Elated, but with a due sense of the responsibility he bore, he
mounted his warhorse and galloped the six miles to Kafr Sabt, where he
had set up his headquarters. There he found that Taqi al-Din and Keukburi, good commanders as they were, had already sent out light forces to
harass the Franks, though not in such numbers that King Guy would be
seriously hindered from falling into the trap that had been prepared for
him. The plain of Lubiya, between Saffuriya and Tiberias, had been thoroughly reconnoitered by Saladin's spies and he knew that it provided
him with every natural advantage over the slower and heavier Frankish
cavalry.

From the high ground at Kafr Sabt Saladin was able to gaze down at
the Christian army, as yet no more than a lengthening dust cloud in the
far distance. He turned to his colleagues and with a grim smile reminded
them that the outcome of the holy war would be decided that day.
Among those with him was his son al-Afdal, now seventeen years old,
and Saladin's biographer Baha al-Din, both of whom recorded details of
Saladin's thoughts on this epoch-making day. Nevertheless, for a while
Saladin could do nothing but wait, so at this point it is necessary to follow the drama of the day amid the ranks of the Frankish army.

The Christian army, the biggest ever assembled in the history of the kingdom of Jerusalem, was so large that it traveled in three columns, rather than one. In an essentially feudal army command of the vanguard was accorded to the lord through whose lands the march took place, and so Count Raymond of Tripoli rode at the head of the army, with his personal contingent of knights. Behind him and in the center of the army rode King Guy himself, with the bishops of Acre and Lydda who carried the True Cross, while the rearguard, the position of greatest danger, was commanded by Balian of Ibelin, whose column also included the contingents of Templars and Hospitallers. Years of fighting in the desert lands had shown these descendants of Western feudalism that their Muslim opponents usually aimed to cut off the rearguard from the rest of the army so that it could be destroyed separately. As a result, the discipline of this section of the army was of paramount importance. As King Richard was later to demonstrate at Arsuf, four years later, the entire battle could turn on the composure of the rearguard and, in the commanders of the military orders at Hattin, King Guy was ill-served.

The formation of the Christian columns was designed to protect the vulnerability of the knights' warhorses. The knights themselves were regarded by the Muslims as almost indestructible in their heavy armor. As a result, the Muslim horse archers often chose to render the Frankish knights either helpless or, at least, ineffective, by unhorsing them. Once dismounted by the death of their mount, the knights could either be simply avoided or overwhelmed by sheer weight of numbers. To prevent this, Frankish tactics had developed close cooperation between foot and horse, in a way that was not practiced in Western Europe. For the crusaders, the armored knights were a prized weapon to be used only when the situation allowed, namely to break a concentration of Muslim cavalry that had strayed too close or who had hindered their own escape by leaving high ground, woods, or even water at their back. Yet knights who pursued a fleeing enemy too far, and certainly into desert land, were certain to be lost as the more mobile Muslim horsemen circled around them and cut them off from their fellows. On the march the main defense for the knights was provided by the infantry, who surrounded them and protected the horses with their own bodies, which were encased in leather or quilted tunics. In addition, of course, their own missiles, arrows, and crossbow bolts were used to keep the Muslim horse archers at a distance where their arrows could neither reach nor penetrate the defenses. Unfortunately, of course, the pace of the march was determined by that of the foot soldiers rather than that of the horsemen, so that the advantages gained by the infantry's human armor were sometimes lost by the slow advance of the column as a whole. The result was a compromise in military terms between weight and mobility, between speed and strength, and it meant that the outcome of each battle was determined by the extent to which a commander could successfully apply his chosen system of tactics. At Hattin, Guy lost so much momentum in the march that he succumbed to the better tactician in Saladin, while at Arsuf, Saladin himself lost control of his mounted troops and succumbed to a "counterpunch" by the better tactician in Richard of England.

The crusader army, which had begun its march in the cool of the morning just before dawn, was by now beginning to suffer from the oppressive heat of the sun. Although most of the local knights had learned to cover their armor with colored surcoats like their Muslim counterparts, some of the Western knights had not yet adapted to Eastern conditions and sweltered within their hauberks. All around them was evidence of the cosmopolitan nature of crusading armies. The air was filled with many of the languages and dialects of Europe and the Holy Land, with Western pilgrims marching shoulder to shoulder with Syrian and Greek Christians from the coastal ports and with the professional crossbowmen from Pisa and Genoa in their haquetons of quilted cloth or gambesons of leather.

Although Muslim skirmishers had kept the Christian army under constant attack from the early moments of the march, Saladin was keeping back the bulk of his army in readiness for the Franks' arrival at the waterless plain of Lubiya. Here he expected the heat of the sun to do half of his work for him. He could not know the desperate risk that King Guy had taken, marching without water carts and telling each man to depend on his own leather water bottle. Had he done so he would have known that God had delivered his Christian enemies into his hands, for there was no way that the Franks could force their way through his army to the water that they would desperately need within a matter of hours. Almost imperceptibly, Saladin fed more and more of his horsemen into the struggle so that as the Franks felt increasingly tired from the heat and from their efforts to repel the Turks, they noted how the enemy grew stronger all the time.

The sounds of fierce battle cries and the barbarous beat of Muslim drums seemed to echo through the hills. As more and more squadrons of cavalry swung down from the high ground and raced across the plain toward the Christian columns there was a veritable cacophony of sound. Even more than the ferocity of the fighting it was the noise that survivors of the battle remembered for the rest of their lives, particularly the incessant beating of the *naqqara*, or kettledrums. In the front of each *tulb*, or Muslim squadron, rode men clanging with all their might on timbrels, rattles, gongs, cymbals, and other instruments, while others simply blew trumpets to terrify the enemy and incite the passions of their own warriors.

From Saladin's own vantage point it must have seemed as if he had painted a great swath of saffron across the plain, which headed inexorably toward the Christian ranks. Below him, amid the eruption of Muslim horsemen that had burst out upon the plain at his order, were the yellow standards of his own Egyptian Mameluke regiments, each bearing the insignia of its commander. The regiment behind them was equally colorful, with red and jasmine standards and fluttering banners bearing roses, birds, and geometric patterns. Following the banners came the horse archers, resplendent in silk tunics over their cuirasses, who darted in and out and even away, in the manner of their Parthian forebears, constantly firing their arrows, which thudded into the shields of the Franks or ricocheted away from the gambesons of the infantry. It could be seen that many Christian warriors kept marching, even though as many as six arrows had struck them without piercing their skins. Undeterred by this clear demonstration of the Christian defensive superiority, the Muslims concentrated their efforts on the warhorses of the knights, without which these "iron men" were virtually helpless. Adding to the babelish sounds of battle were the piercing screams of these horses, bucking and tipping their riders, in their pain and terror, many struck in the faces by the Turks' cruelly barbed missiles.

The Christian infantry, when concentrated as for a march, was a terrible proposition for the Muslim light horsemen. The massed fire of crossbow bolts was more than the Turks could stand, penetrating their lamellar armor with ease. Only the slowness of reloading the crossbow prevented it from being a war-winning weapon at Hattin and elsewhere. On a small scale, King Richard's use of the weapon at the battle of Jaffa showed that in the hands of a good tactician a small body of crossbowmen could repulse and defeat an apparently overwhelming number of Turkish horse archers. At Hattin, however, the morale of the Christian infantry was affected by poor leadership and lack of water, which rendered them less effective than they might have been. Nevertheless, at this stage King Guy's army was more than holding its own and few casualties had been suffered, except among the horses. Saladin was undeterred, content to let the sun do his work for him, aware that exhaustion and thirst killed as ruthlessly as the arrows of his horsemen.

By midmorning the Frankish army had already been marching for five or six hours and most of the soldiers were suffering from both exhaustion and thirst, having used up the supplies in their water bottles. They had turned eastward into the Wadi Rummanah and were close to Mount Turan, where there was an important spring of water. Presumably everyone had expected to stop here and replenish their bottles. As a result they had not conserved their water as they might have done had they known they were expected to eke out their meager supplies until they reached Lake Tiberias. The decision not to stop at Turan to replenish the water is usually attributed to King Guy himself, though no satisfactory explanation has ever been offered for this extraordinary blunder. Certainly, the flank attacks by Muslim horse archers had been heavy, but surely no worse than had been expected. Even if morale was low it was hardly going to be improved by ordering thirsty men to march into a cauldron of desert heat without water. Nevertheless, that is what took place, and by midday, with the sun directly overhead and the heat intense, the vanguard led by Raymond of Tripoli had reached a point about eleven miles from Saffuriya.

Raymond was an experienced commander who had lived all his life in these conditions. He was as "oriental" as Saladin himself and he realized that the longer the army stayed out on this barren plain, without shade or water, the more certain it was to suffer disaster. With time now the real enemy, Raymond was in favor of pressing on as fast as possible, to complete the journey to Tiberias. Militarily this was probably the wisest decision, but it would have meant the knights spurring their horses forward and leaving the infantry behind. In terms of the survival of the kingdom it would have ensured the escape of the bulk of the mounted warriors, except perhaps those in the rearguard, who would probably have been cut off. The infantry would have to be written off, but in medieval terms such soldiers were easily replaced. Those who had been with the rearguard had been marching backward for several miles now, no mean feat over the sandy, rocky terrain and under constant attack, yet necessary if they were to present a strong "front" to their Muslim assailants. While Raymond at the head of the army had reached the conclusion that only a faster pace could ensure its survival, Balian of Ibelin and Gerard of Ridefort with the rearguard, probably several miles behind him, had reached an almost exactly opposite decision. With so many men falling from exhaustion or under the heat of the sun they sent a rider forward to tell King Guy that they would have to halt in order to allow the knights to charge the Turks and drive them away. This was exactly what Saladin had hoped would happen, for to halt in that dreadful place meant certain death for the Franks.

King Guy felt that he had no alternative but to comply with the rearguard's request, and so a general halt was ordered. When this news reached the vanguard, Raymond lost his composure. Was this king mad? The whole army of the kingdom was now virtually trapped in a desert, surrounded by Saladin's more numerous host of Turks. Matters were as desperate as they could be, and Raymond would have been less than human if his mind had not turned to his own survival and that of his knights if the army as a whole must perish. When he heard the king's news the vanguard was near the junction of the Meskenah and Lubiya roads. Only an immediate change of direction to find water could save the army, as Lake Tiberias was too far away and would, in any case, mean breaking through the entire Turkish army that barred the way. Instead, Raymond decided to head northward across the high ground to the springs at Kafr Hattin, where the army could find water and camp for the night, before resuming the march the next day. For Raymond the springs at Hattin were just three or four miles away. However, for the rearguard, at least a mile behind, they seemed an unattainable target for exhausted men constantly harassed by an active enemy.

The turn to the northeast was accomplished, but amid great confusion. Ordinarily the discipline of crusader columns was very tight, but by this stage discipline declined as the need to find water became more urgent. The knights, dependent as they had been on the infantry for protection, now spurred their horses forward and rode away from the cover of the infantry crossbows and gambesons, some of them preferring to risk death at the hands of the Turks to a lingering death from the agonies of thirst.

For Saladin the moment of crisis had come. So far he had been content to wear away the strength of his enemy in an attritional process, allowing heat and thirst to weaken the Franks. But now he would have to strike with his full force if the knights were to be prevented from reaching water at Hattin. Should he fail to stop them they might be able to establish themselves just a few miles from Tiberias and turn the entire campaign in their favor the next day. He immediately sent riders to Keukburi and to Taqi al-Din, ordering them to sweep around the Christian army and block the approach to the springs at Hattin. While he himself held the high ground at Kafr Sabt with his Egyptian forces, the two flanks of the Turkish army now poured onto the plain, attacking the crusaders in the rear and the flank. Regiments of Mamelukes, Syrian lancers, and Turkman horse archers moved at a gallop down the slopes in a relentless wave of colored banners and flashing steel. The Muslim numbers seemed limitless, and survivors later admitted that they had seriously underestimated Saladin's strength. While Keukburi's men engaged the column, Taqi al-Din's right wing rode into position, barring Raymond's approach to Hattin and safety.

Raymond may have been surprised by the number of his enemies, but he was not prepared to be blocked in his search for water. He knew that he must break through or die and if the army was lost here on the plain of Lubiya the kingdom was lost with it. He therefore prepared to charge Taqi al-Din head-on with his knights, risking anything to achieve his aim. However, before he could issue the order to charge a rider arrived from the center of the column, bearing the king's order to halt and make camp. The rearguard had again been forced to stop, and rather than marching on and abandoning it, as would probably have been wise at this stage, King Guy decided to halt the entire column and make camp, intending to continue the march at first light. Although the Turks continued their attacks until nightfall, King Guy set up his red tent near Meskenah. Chroniclers have tried to convey Count Raymond's reaction to Guy's foolish decision by quoting him as calling out, "Alas! alas! Lord God, the war is over. We are betrayed to death and the land is lost." These words may have been put into his mouth. In any case, Raymond had been predicting just such a disaster if the march to Tiberias took place, and he can hardly have been surprised at what eventually transpired. The only hope for the Christian army was to keep marching at whatever cost and to reach the water at Hattin regardless of losses. Saladin knew this and had prevailed upon Taqi al-Din to prevent it. Yet Guy, probably too exhausted to think clearly, had been unable to rise to the strategic thinking of Saladin and Count Raymond. His men would not be rested merely by camping on that barren plain, they would be a prey to their own desperate thoughts. The following day, far from feeling stronger for the fight, they would have passed over to the dull acceptance of fate. Saladin's stranglehold, which he had struggled all day to keep in place on King Guy's throat, had achieved its intention.

Saladin had realized the first part of his task, bringing the crusaders to a halt on the plain of Lubiya. As their camp spread out around Meskenah, he prepared to implement some psychological warfare to weaken their resistance for the next day. He first moved his own camp from Kafr Sabt to Kafr Lubiya, in effect surrounding the Christian camp completely. Chroniclers later wrote that so tight was his grip that not even a cat could have passed through Muslim lines to escape. As the light faded and darkness hid the two armies from each other, the crusaders found that they could clearly hear conversations from their enemy's camp, though their meaning was generally unintelligible. In the darkness the Muslims kept up a continuous rain of death from the skies, firing arrows high over the crusader camp to fall on the uncovered heads of the resting Christians. As a later crusading army was to discover on the march to Arsuf in 1191, darkness in that land brought out uncomfortable guests in the shape of scorpions or huge tarantulas that crawled into clothing and administered painful bites. Yet, however painful were the stings and bites of the insects, they could not distract the minds of the soldiers from the lack of water, which dominated thoughts and would not allow anyone to rest. The Muslims, aware of the Frankish predicament, appeared in the light of the campfires and were ordered by Saladin to be seen tipping water ostentatiously into the sand. And throughout the night the cries of the righteous, "Allah akbar" and "La ilaha illa Allah," echoed among the nearby hills.

The joy of victory to come was in the hearts of the Muslim warriors, who reveled in the misery they were able to inflict on their apparently beaten foes, but such thoughts, natural to the rank and file of any army, were far from Saladin's mind that night. He felt the burden of command even more heavily now that victory did indeed seem imminent. Saladin had campaigned for many years and knew how swiftly defeat could be snatched from the jaws of victory, particularly in battle against the

Franks. A single error on his part, or that of his generals, might present the "iron warriors" with a chance to charge against a concentration of his horsemen, perhaps trapped with rocky ground behind them. In such a case there would be no escape for the Turks, however mobile they might be on open ground. In fact, Taqi al-Din, with his covering force at Hattin, would face the greatest danger the next day. The knights of the vanguard would eventually be left with no choice but to charge, and if they succeeded in breaking through to the springs then Saladin's victory might be incomplete.

Saladin knew that appearances could be deceptive. Few Frankish knights had died so far, even though many now marched with the infantry, their horses having succumbed to the arrows of his horsemen. Such men could be remounted. Victory could be achieved only if these formidable enemies were slain or taken prisoner. Furthermore, their leaders must not be easily ransomed. Men of ability like Balian of Ibelin or Raymond of Tripoli must be prevented from re-forming the Frankish forces, while the devil of the Muslims, the much-hated Reginald of Kerak, must die if there was ever to be peace and security in the kingdom.

Throughout the night of July 3–4 Saladin personally organized matters that should rightly have been delegated to others. Perhaps it quietened his mind to keep busy, or perhaps he feared to be undone by the failings of an underling. In any case, it was at his command that the twin issues of water and arrows were referred to him personally. Throughout the hours of darkness a constant convoy of camels trudged to and from Lake Tiberias, bringing up thousands of goat skins filled with water, which were used to fill cisterns hastily cut in the ground. There must be no danger that his own warriors should suffer from the afflictions of the Franks. In addition, lines of dromedaries carried masses of arrows from Kafr Sabt and distributed them around the army, some circling around the Christian camp and taking reserves toward Taqi al-Din's right wing near Hattin. There must be no cessation in the arrow storm. Once the Frankish knights felt the fire lessening, they would emerge from the center of the column and rout the Turks with their charge and close combat superiority.

In the Christian camp there was no rest for anyone. Recriminations were doubtless exchanged by men now trapped and facing death or captivity the following day. It is equally certain, however, that these men were sustained by their simple yet profound faith. They would have sought consolation in the relic of the True Cross, which had been borne into battle with them as a reassurance that they did God's work and that He was with them in their suffering. Away from the tents of the lords and knights, the rank and file could not afford such reflection. Besides the inconveniences of desert warfare and the overwhelming feelings of thirst, many of them who had answered the *arrière-ban* must have wondered if they would ever see their homes in the coastal cities again. Most of these townsmen would never have been so far from the coast and would have found the conditions alien and unbearable. They would have blamed their leaders for bringing them to so miserable a fate and would have had little spirit for continuing the fight at first light. Only the professionalism of the Italian mercenaries and the spiritual convictions of the Western pilgrims would have maintained morale in the camp of this beaten army.

Light was not welcome as it gradually broke across the Christian camp. The sounds from within the Muslim camp told the Franks that their enemies were ready to renew the fight. King Guy ordered the army to form up as it had the day before, and once again Count Raymond led the vanguard. With him rode his four stepsons, the sons of his wife Eschiva of Tiberias, as well as Raymond of Antioch, with his northern knights. The rearguard again contained the knights of the Temple and of the Hospital, and this division was again commanded by Balian of Ibelin. King Guy, along with the redoubtable Reginald of Kerak and most of the nobles of the kingdom, rode in the center with the bishops and the relic of the True Cross. The army marched into the blinding light of the rising sun, and for a while Saladin did not molest them, again allowing the heat to build up and sap the strength of his enemies. However, grim episodes now followed each other at regular intervals. Men and horses fell by the wayside and were massacred by the pursuing Turks. Worse, several knights broke out of the column and rode toward the Turks, crying out that they wanted sanctuary and to adopt the Muslim faith. Of all the sights that were seen that day this was perhaps the most shocking for the Christians.

Saladin again concentrated his attacks on the Christian rearguard, hoping to break it off from the rest of the column and destroy it. Here rode the bitterest of his enemies, the white-robed Templars and the somber, black-mantled Hospitallers. With these men Saladin knew that the holy war must be fought and won. He would not ransom such ene-mies who would spit on his kindness and seek for any way to repay his softness with blows. In so bitter a fight there was sorrow for victor and victim alike. The chroniclers relate Saladin's sadness at the death of Man-gouras, one of his favorite Mamelukes, who fought his way single-handed into the Christian ranks against overwhelming odds, and died a martyr's death.

While the Frankish column struggled on toward Hattin they suffered an additional hardship. The Muslim irregulars had ignited a scrub and brushwood fire that, in the westerly wind blowing out of the Beth Netofah valley, blew hot smoke and ash into the faces of the parched crusaders. As well as intensifying their suffering, the smoke also provided cover for the Muslim horsemen as they rode up unseen toward the Franks. In the confusion produced by the smoke the Franks began to crowd together, losing the cohesion and discipline upon which their very survival depended. At last, the morale of the infantry began to crack: one by one and then in crowds they broke away from the column. With a unity of purpose that only shared suffering could give them, these exhausted men began to run and stumble in their thousands up the black, rocky slopes of the Horns of Hattin until the whole hillside was covered. Facing the collapse of the entire army, King Guy should prob-ably have abandoned his infantry and ridden on to save his knights. In-stead, he halted the column for the last time and pitched his tent to act as a rallying point. Riders struggled up the hillsides, calling out to the in-fantry to return to their duty, but nobody was listening. Even the bish-ops carrying the True Cross could not persuade the foot soldiers to return. They were calling to men who had abandoned themselves to death.

The Frankish column had now broken into three separate parts. Most of the nobles and knights of the kingdom were massed around King Guy's tent on the Horns of Hattin. At the van, however, Count Ray-mond could see that the day was lost and that nothing was to be gained by staying to die or be imprisoned with the bulk of the army. As a result, Raymond now did what he believed all the knights should have done the previous day. He ordered his own mounted men, with the knights of Sidon and Antioch, to form up into a concentrated and irresistible unit which would fling itself at Taqi al-Din's forces that barred their way. Taqi was an experienced commander who realized that he could not resist such a charge without suffering a disaster that might tilt the balance of the entire battle. As Raymond had the advantage of a downhill slope toward Kafr Hattin, his desperate charge would be unstoppable. Taqi's only option was to let the Christian knights pass unhindered, making the final defeat of King Guy even more certain. This, at least, was how he later explained his actions to Saladin. In the days after the battle many accused Taqi of cowardice for allowing Raymond to escape. Others, remembering the previous close relations between Saladin and Raymond, accused the latter of treachery in leaving the field before the battle was lost. In fact, neither Taqi nor Raymond had much option, and both did the only sensible thing possible in the circumstances. As Raymond's knights escaped to the north, Taqi al-Din's troops closed ranks again. There was to be no escape for the rest of the crusader army, even though isolated groups of knights tried to emulate Raymond's charge. Balian of Ibelin escaped from the rearguard at some stage, but there is no source that describes how he did so. Certainly, most of the Templars and Hospitallers who had been with him, including the Master of the Templars, Gerard of Ridefort, were taken prisoner as the battle ended.

It was only in the desperate final moments of the battle that the Christian knights showed their mettle and how, handled differently, they would probably have prevailed in hand-to-hand fighting. With escape impossible they sought victory by trying to kill Saladin himself. While their infantry huddled together on the hillsides under continuous fire from the Muslim bowmen, the knights made a series of tremendous charges, which carried the tide of the fighting virtually up to Saladin's tent, where al-Afdal recorded his father's reaction. Apparently Saladin's face turned ashen and he grasped his beard and tugged it violently in vexation. This was not at all what he was expecting. Surely the battle could not turn against him at this late stage? The first charge was turned back, but the knights re-formed around King Guy's tent and swept back toward Saladin. Now the fighting was desperate indeed and Saladin had to lay about him with his sword. Fearing that the Turks might give way, Saladin bellowed at all around him, "Give the devil the lie!" A few moments later the crisis had passed and the knights were in full retreat back to the red tent, which had become a symbol of their resistance.

Not far away a second struggle, equally symbolic, was taking place between Taqi al-Din and the knights surrounding the bishops of Lydda and

Acre who still guarded the True Cross. In the chaotic melee around the holy relic the bishop of Acre was killed, but his colleague, wielding a sword as readily as any knight, still fought for his faith. Taqi al-Din ordered his askaris to abandon their bows and join the fight with sword and mace. Soon numbers began to tell and the iron ring of warriors guarding the relic began to diminish. Suddenly, Taqi himself burst through the defenses and seized the relic from the bishop, riding exultantly out of the fight holding aloft the True Cross. This was the final blow to many of the Christians. Now it seemed that God himself had forsaken them. The relic had been borne into battle on all the famous occasions in the kingdom's history since 1099. It had represented the holiest of all Christian aspirations and had been a worthy source of martyrdom for countless thousands of crusaders, content to give their lives for its preservation. Its loss symbolized the fall of the kingdom as no other event could.

One can appreciate the excitement of the young al-Afdal, standing alongside his famous father during these final moments of a decisive battle that was changing the direction of history. The prince could hardly control his emotions as he saw the Franks, whom he had learned to hate as the enemies of the true faith, succumbing to the swords of the righteous. He exulted as the second Frankish charge was turned back and called out to his father that they had won. Saladin still had enough of the father about him to reprimand his son for his foolishness. Only when the red tent of the king fell could they be certain of victory, he snapped at him. At that moment, al-Afdal remembered, someone cut through the tent ropes and the tent did collapse. It was a symbolic moment. Saladin dismounted from his horse and prostrated himself, kissing the ground. Not far away, King Guy also sank to the ground, throwing his sword away and covering his head with his arms.

Saladin, his task as commander complete, now rode slowly back to his camp to prepare to receive his prisoners. All that remained on the battlefield was for his generals to enslave the Christian survivors. For King Guy and most of his nobles in the center there was to be no escape, even had they possessed the necessary strength and energy. So utterly overcome were most of them by the enormity of the disaster they had suffered that they scarcely noticed the Turks who came to make them prisoners. On the Horns of Hattin thousands of Christian foot soldiers were being chained and led away to captivity. It had been the greatest victory of Islam over the Christian conquerors of the Holy Land in a century. So many were the captives that there was a glut at the slave markets and prices plummeted to the point where one man was sold for the price of a pair of sandals. Of the noble prisoners the list included most of the great men of the kingdom. Along with King Guy, Saladin captured his brothers Geoffrey and Amalric of Lusignan, the constable, as well as the elderly Marquis William of Montferrat, Reginald of Kerak, Joscelin of Courtenay, Humphrey of Toron, Gerard of Ridefort, the Bishop of Lydda, the Marshal of the Hospitallers, and hundreds of men of lesser rank and distinction. The truth was that casualties had been light and few knights had suffered even wounds from the Muslim arrows. Although few had been mounted at the end of the fighting the Bishop of Acre had been the most prominent casualty in the hand-to-hand engagements. As usual, losses were heaviest among the military orders, who had borne the brunt of the fighting in the rearguard. During the second day's fighting, these doughty warriors had made charge after charge from the rear of the column to try to break the Turks' grip and to allow the column to advance to the waters at Hattin at a better pace.

With the excitement of the victory still in his mind Saladin had to try to administer justice to his prisoners. The most prominent captives were taken to his tent and treated with respect. The main problem facing him was how to deal with King Guy himself, who, it was noted, was closely accompanied by Reginald of Kerak. The stress of battle had made tempers short, and it says much for Saladin that he maintained his equanimity when dealing with these enemies of his faith. In the spirit of true chivalry he personally served King Guy with a goblet of iced water to quench his thirst, which, in Muslim tradition, was a sign that his life was safe. However, Saladin's brow furrowed when he saw that Guy passed the goblet to Reginald, against whom Saladin had a very personal grudge. Saladin quickly pointed out to Guy that it was he who had given the drink to Reginald, so that the inherent promise of safety did not apply. Saladin had taken a solemn oath to slay Reginald with his own hand if ever the chance arose. Reginald's crimes against Islam were so many that he can scarcely have expected any better treatment. Yet he made no attempt to placate his mighty foe, and when Saladin spoke to him he replied haughtily. He had never acknowledged any man his superior and, now in old age, he was not going to begin. When Saladin challenged him as an oath-breaker he replied, "I did only what princes have always done. I followed the well-trodden path." Saladin refused to allow his anger to master him and he left his tent for a while. When he returned he was more curt, offering Reginald conversion to Islam, something the old crusader would regard as an insult. When Reginald refused Saladin struck him upon the shoulder with his sword, cutting deeply into his neck. Reginald fell to his knees, whereupon a guard completed the execution by sweeping off Reginald's head with his sword. King Guy was not present at the execution, and all that he knew of what had happened was when Reginald's headless corpse was dragged past him by the heels. At this dreadful sight Guy's courage dissolved and he began to shake. Saladin hastily reassured him that his life was safe, and that kings did not kill each other. Reginald, he told Guy, was beyond forgiveness. In his heart Guy must have known that this was true.

Saladin's treatment of his prisoners has produced conflicting reactions among historians. The massacre of the Templars and Hospitallers and the execution of Reginald show a side of his character that lies uneasily with that of the magnanimous ruler, compassionate to the weak and helpless. On the other hand, in the context of the twelfth century and of the holy war in which he was engaged his actions make sense. These men were his enemies, and formidable ones at that. To release them merely meant that he would face them again in battle. Moreover, such fanatics would fear him the less for his clemency. Perhaps the circumstances in which Richard of England was to massacre the garrison at Acre were different, yet he appears to have had no conscience about the killing of Muslims. Apologists for Richard have cited Saladin's killing of the Templars and Hospitallers as justification for his actions four years later. Ironically, Gerard of Ridefort, most fanatical of the holy knights, was wined and dined by Saladin as if his noble birth somehow lifted him above the level of the common brethren of the order, who were rounded up for slaughter at Saladin's order. Those Muslim fighters who had captured the warrior monks and hoped to ransom them were paid 50 dinars each by Saladin so that he could execute them all in a single session. His biographer quotes him as explaining his action in these words: "I wish to purify the land of these two monstrous orders, whose practices are of no use, who will never renounce their hostility, and will render no service as slaves, but are all that is worst in this infidel race." Past experience had shown that these

men usually disdained ransom, so that he was faced with no strong reason to keep them alive. Going through the motions of offering each
man the chance of conversion to Islam, an offer that, not surprisingly,
was universally rejected, Saladin finally handed over 230 of these
knights to his Sufis, for execution.

7

—————|◆|◆|◆|—————

The Fall of Jerusalem 1187

At hattin saladin had reached the pinnacle of any Muslim ruler's power for centuries. His fame was tremendous both inside and outside the Muslim world. Yet his apparent victory in the holy war was an illusory one. He had shown the Muslims that a united Islam could, as a result of Christian disunity, overcome the Christian interlopers who had held Jerusalem and Palestine for a century. But the unity of Islam needed to be maintained if the victory at Hattin was to be a permanent one. And Saladin, probably exhausted by the emotionally draining experiences of the Hattin campaign, now made the error of judgment that allowed the Christians to renew their foothold in the Holy Land. Like a negligent householder confident in the security of his possessions, Saladin left a door unlocked through which one of the deadliest of his enemies made an entrance unchallenged. In killing Reginald, Saladin may have felt that he had rid himself of a foe of almost unparalleled danger. Yet in allowing Conrad of Montferrat to take the city of Tyre, Saladin condemned himself and his people to a dreadful war of attrition that ruined both them and him and sullied his reputation in the judgment of history. Without Conrad there would have been no Third Crusade, no Richard the Lionheart, no Acre, no Arsuf, and no restoration of Christianity in the land that Saladin had reconquered in the months after Hattin.

Saladin's victory at Hattin was a means, not an end in itself. The urge to see it as the final step in the conquest of the kingdom must have been very great, yet to do so was disastrous. King Guy had stripped the garrisons of all the castles and fortresses to equip his army, and now that the defenders were no longer in possession of these strongholds Saladin only needed to occupy them with his own men to make his conquest complete. And that is what he proceeded to do. But in the absence of any organized opposition he displayed a lack of urgency that gave the Christians a chance to cling on to some of what they had held, hoping that aid would come from the West. Saladin was undoubtedly misled as to the mood of the times. Everywhere his troops were greeted as liberators by the thousands of Muslim slaves who had been held within the kingdom. More surprising, the Syrian Christians, who had little love for their arrogant Latin coreligionists, also greeted Saladin with enthusiasm in view of his reputation for generosity and justice. Yet Saladin should have known how fickle public acclamation could be. Conquerors were usually received with shows of public adulation by the conquered, at least initially; only later would the acclaim turn to distrust and hatred.

In the days after Hattin Saladin found himself confronted with a difficult—if enviable—choice. Should he concentrate on capturing the coastal cities, where the Frankish Christians were mainly concentrated and through which any relief from Western Europe would have to come, or should he turn inland, mopping up the now ungarrisoned castles and capturing the symbolic target of Jerusalem for which, after all, the war had been staged in the first place? If his head must have told him that cities like Acre, Tyre, and Sidon were by far the most important strategic prizes, his heart would have whispered that the capture of Jerusalem was the gesture that all Muslims would understand. Unless he showed them that the holy city—the third holiest in Islam and the Prophet's original choice for his spiritual capital—counted most with him, the warriors who had followed him in the holy war might begin to doubt his sincerity. This Kurdish upstart, it was said by many who could not stomach his rapid rise to power, had used the holy war to advance his own power, not that of Islam. Until Hattin, his enemies said, his victories had all been at the expense of his fellow Muslims. In order to maintain the unity of his army, Saladin finally had no choice but to take Jerusalem.

After moving from the battlefield at Hattin, Saladin marched to Acre, the greatest city of the kingdom, where, to his astonishment, he found the walls manned by Christian soldiers and with war banners fluttering bravely in the breeze. It was an impressive show of strength, but, in truth, it was just one of many symbolic acts in an uncertain period. The inhabitants of Acre felt it necessary to demonstrate their willingness to resist Saladin if they were forced to the last extremity. They preferred to deal peaceably with him, to save their lives and their city from destruction. Saladin drew up his army for a symbolic assault, at which point the main gates opened and representatives emerged to discuss a surrender. Within a few hours Saladin was worshiping at the city's great mosque, liberated after ninety years of use as a Christian church. To public acclamation Saladin liberated 4,000 Muslim slaves and squandered the wealth of the city, which could have financed his later campaigns, on rewarding his captains and soldiers in an extravagant show of thanks. At Acre that day Saladin can never have dreamed that within a few years he would witness a Christian king massacring his garrison while he could not lift a finger to save them—for lack of money. Command of the city was given to Karakush, his favorite architect and engineer, who had organized the refortification of Cairo and who now brought the defenses of Acre up to a war footing, so that the city acted as the arsenal for Saladin's army within the new territories.

In order to facilitate the conquest of the entire kingdom Saladin decided to divide his army. There seemed no danger from any Christian field army, at least for the foreseeable future, and therefore he sent his captains to all points of the compass to restore Islamic rule to Palestine. Keukburi captured Nazareth, La Feve, Daburiya, Tabor, and Zarin and discovered masses of stores at the Frankish camp at Saffuriya. Husan al-Din Muhammad captured Sebastiya and Nablus, while Badr al-Din Dildirim took Haifa, Arsuf, and, after a fierce battle, Caesarea, one of the strongest fortifications in the entire country. Moving up from Egypt, Saladin's brother al-Adil took Majdal Yaba and, after a bloody assault, the city of Jaffa. However, it was in the north that Saladin made probably the greatest mistake of his career. He sent Taqi al-Din to capture Tyre and Tibnin. Taqi began by besieging the small and relatively insignificant fortress at Tibnin, only to find that its defenders, "heroes, fierce in their religion," made such a resistance that he was forced to ask Saladin for reinforcements. While this small siege was taking place, the survivors from Hattin, as well as the inhabitants from other captured cities and castles, were flooding into the seaport of Tyre, swelling its garrison. Even when Tibnin eventually fell, Saladin showed its garrison incredible leniency: he gave them five days to collect their possessions and allowed them to march to Tyre.

Why Saladin failed so signally in his strategic thinking is difficult to understand. His career had been built around almost continuous warfare, and yet he was an intelligent and just man who saw the consequences of this fighting on friend and foe alike. He would have preferred the ways of peace; he believed that his victory at Hattin would result in his first opportunity to rule a country at peace. If he erred in his strategic thinking it may be because he believed that peace had been achieved and that Hattin had been the last act in the war rather than the first in an even greater struggle.

Saladin has been accused, both by contemporaries and by later historians, of lacking urgency. Recognizing that the capture of Tyre would require a determined siege, he marched past it and instead headed northward to Sidon and then Beirut, which were much easier targets. Once he had captured these two cities he headed southward again but still ignored Tyre, traveling 170 miles in just ten days to secure the great fortress at Ascalon. Tyre clearly offered Saladin a challenge to which, for some reason, he felt unequal at that moment. Certainly his soldiers were tired and many disgruntled from the continuous campaigning. Perhaps he feared defeat at a time when everything seemed to be going his way. At the peak of his achievement, with the prize of Jerusalem within his grasp, he feared to be drawn into a terrible, prolonged siege against men made desperate by defeat and willing to sell their lives only at the highest price. And, if he was drawn into a siege of many months, as that of Acre was later to be, could that prevent him from ever seizing Jerusalem and earning final victory in the holy war? Furthermore, his closest advisers, men like his brother al-Adil in Egypt, were at pains to remind him of his common mortality. Dispatches from Egypt constantly stressed the need to make the capture of Jerusalem the immediate priority. Family obligation pressed al-Adil to remind Saladin that a simple case of colic could carry him off, or a stray arrow, and if he were to die the Muslims might lack the unity to complete his work. Such psychological pressure from within his own family was bound to be difficult to resist, and so Saladin turned away from the coast and made Jerusalem his target.

Before Saladin could leave the coast, however, he needed to settle the question of Ascalon and his most important prisoner, King Guy himself, who had been taken to Damascus straight from the battlefield of Hattin. Guy, along with the Master of the Templars, Gerard of Ridefort, was now brought to Saladin's camp outside Ascalon. Both were offered their freedom in return for persuading the garrison to surrender the great fortress. Guy agreed and sent a letter to the garrison telling them to surrender. However, these stout warriors assumed Guy's letter had been written under duress and refused to follow its instructions. Saladin, frustrated in his aim to trick the garrison into giving up, now found that he had a serious siege on his hands. During his initial assaults several of his leading emirs were killed, much to his anger, and he demanded that Guy bring his people under control. But defeat had destroyed any authority that Guy had over the garrison, who laughed at him and called down curses on him as a coward. It was a truly embarrassing experience, and one that undermined his chances of returning to power in Jerusalem if aid should come from the West. After a laudable defense, the garrison eventually surrendered and were treated with honor by Saladin. When he heard the news that his generals had taken Gaza and Darum and now held the entire coast except Tyre, Saladin turned inland and marched toward Jerusalem. After his failure to present Ascalon to Saladin, Guy was kept prisoner for a further year at Nablus and later at Lattakieh. Gerard of Ridefort bought his freedom at the price of the Templar castle of Latrun.

For a generation before the battle of Hattin, Saladin had known and respected many of the leading figures in the Christian kingdom, notably such men as Raymond of Tripoli, Baldwin of Ramla, and his brother, Balian of Ibelin, all of whom had been born in Outremer. He had understood these Eastern Christians far better than he had such newcomers as Guy of Lusignan or Reginald of Chatillon, who seemed merely rapacious and pillaging barbarians. Instead, Raymond and Balian were cultivated men who had adopted the ways of the East and even spoke Arabic. Both had escaped the debacle at Hattin and both, in their way, now faced a difficult future in a world dominated either by the successful conqueror Saladin or by the violent and alien crusaders from Western Europe, who had no time for the "effeminate" Eastern Christians who had lost the Holy Land to the Muslims.

After Balian had escaped from the rearguard of the army at Hattin he had made his way to Tyre, where most of the survivors of the battle had met. He knew that his own lands were lost and his mind turned to the safety of his wife, Queen Maria Comnena, and their children. In fact, the redoubtable Maria Comnena, who had been the wife of Amalric I of Jerusalem in her youth, had escaped from Nablus before the Muslims could close in on her and had made her way with the children to Jerusalem. Balian, aware that Maria could find no safety at Jerusalem in view of the certainty that Saladin would capture the holy city, decided to rescue her and take her back with him to Tyre. He knew—indeed had known for many years—Saladin's reputation as a man of honor, so he petitioned the sultan for permission to pass through Muslim lines and fetch his wife from Jerusalem before the city was besieged. Saladin lived up to his reputation. He gave Balian a safe conduct to fetch his wife but stipulated that he should stay in Jerusalem for just one night and should no longer bear arms against him. Balian swore to abide by these conditions and set off for the capital, accompanied by his squire Ernoul, whose chronicle of events has provided many of the most accurate details of events in the kingdom at this time.

In the minds of his critics, Saladin had just committed a further blunder through an act of kindness. The defenders of Jerusalem were being sent by their enemy a proven commander who might turn the war in favor of the Christians. Certainly Saladin showed more nobility than common sense in allowing Balian to visit Jerusalem. In the event, of course, not everyone could rise to the lofty heights of Saladin's own standards. When Balian arrived at Jerusalem he was not allowed to enter anonymously as he would have preferred. Instead, there was an outbreak of public hysteria that centered on his return and saw in him little less than a new Messiah. Logic counted for nothing. A single warrior, however famous or accomplished, was just a token and in no way represented the relieving army that the desperate inhabitants looked for every day. The Patriarch Eraclius and the leading officials of the Temple and the Hospital seized upon Balian, rejected his explanation of his oath to Saladin, and insisted that he take command of the garrison preparatory to the siege that they expected to close in on them any day. Balian was in an unbearable situation. He may have witnessed defeat in the holy war for himself in the rearguard at Hattin, but in Jerusalem the war was not over. Surely it was his Christian duty to fight for the holy city and for its helpless citizens against the enemies of his faith. An oath made to the enemy could not bind him and keep him from defending the holy places of Christianity. Eraclius insisted that an oath forced on him by an infidel should not be honored, and his words must have shredded the grizzled warrior's honor: "Know that it will be a greater sin if you keep your oath than if you break it; it will be a great shame upon you and your heirs if you desert the city in the hour of its peril and you will be unable to recover your honor no matter where you turn."

Balian was too experienced in the ways of the world to be entirely convinced by the patriarch's silvery tongue, and so, although he was given absolution by the church, he was not altogether prepared to break his oath to Saladin. He therefore explained his dilemma to the sultan, who again responded with a display of such magnanimity that it became legendary in his own lifetime. Saladin freed Balian from his oath and conducted Queen Maria with her children and young Thomas of Ibelin, Balian's nephew, under safe conduct to Tripoli. Before they left Saladin entertained the family in his own tent, giving the children costly garments and jewels and weeping at the downfall of such a great family. History records few, if any other, examples of nobility between religious foes.

Yet Saladin was a prisoner of history as well as a champion of the holy war. When Jerusalem had fallen to Godfrey of Bouillon and the Franks in the First Crusade, the Muslims and Jews who inhabited the city had been massacred in the worst and most brutal killings in the history of the crusades. Even the passage of a century had not erased Muslim memories of this holocaust. As a result, Saladin faced the responsibility not only of retaking the holy city but of closing a chapter in Muslim history. He must have been torn between his natural desire to achieve his aims in as bloodless a way as possible and the pressures from his generals and religious leaders who wished to wash the city clean with the blood of the Christians.

At first Saladin made it clear that he wanted no massacre, particularly as Jerusalem was packed with refugees who had fled there for safety from the castles and towns that had already fallen to his troops. He made this clear when he announced to the Christians, "I believe that Jerusalem is the House of God, as you also believe, and I will not willingly lay siege to the House of God or put it to the assault." He therefore summoned a delegation of Christians from the holy city and presented his conditions for a peaceful takeover. His leniency was such that it infuriated many zealots within his ranks. He offered to leave the inhabitants of Jerusalem free to fortify the city and to cultivate the land around to a distance of five leagues. He would even assist them with money and supplies. How-

ever, if no relief force came to their aid by the following Feast of Pente-
cost, then they would agree to surrender the city to him without a struggle and he would then convey the Christian inhabitants to safety in
Christian lands. Moreover, all Christian places of worship would be respected and pilgrims would be free to visit the holy places in safety. Such
surrender terms were unprecedented. Incredibly, the Christian delegation rejected Saladin's terms and responded with a defiance that would
have been laudable had it not been so illogical. They proclaimed, "Our
honor lies here and our salvation with the salvation of the city. . . . If we
abandon her we shall surely and justly be branded with shame and contempt, for here is the place of our Savior's crucifixion. . . . We shall die in
the defense of our Lord's sepulchre, for how could we do otherwise?"
Such words reminded Saladin of his own obligations to the holy war,
and, no doubt urged on by Muslim zealots as fanatical in their faith as the
Christians who had just defied him, he swore to take the city by assault
as had Godfrey of Bouillon a century before.

In the days ahead Balian of Ibelin found that greatness was thrust
upon him. He came to symbolize the aspirations of thousands of desperate Christians, and he can hardly be blamed if some of his usual common
sense was replaced by their faith. While they prayed for a miracle Balian
found himself in the uncomfortable position of having to fulfill their
wildly unrealistic hopes. As a seasoned warrior Balian must have known
that his garrison could not withstand a prolonged assault from the Turks,
but he knew that as a Christian knight he and those around him must
make the effort or die in the attempt. As a result he set about turning the
holy city into an impregnable fortress, before Saladin could cut off
Jerusalem from the outside world. Fifteen hundred knights had failed to
resist Saladin at Hattin; now Balian found himself with just two other
knights. He therefore knighted all noble boys over the age of fifteen and
did the same for forty burgesses. Yet it took more than a name to give a
man the qualities which only a lifetime of training could give. Boys and
fighting merchants were a scant substitute for all the men lost at Hattin.

An even greater problem faced Balian, and that was the loyalty or otherwise of the citizens of Jerusalem. Not all Christians within the city
would fight for him or even willingly resist Saladin in the name of Pope
Clement III in Rome. Thousands of Melkites, as the Greek Orthodox
Christians were known, as well as Syrian and Armenian Christians
would actually welcome Saladin as their liberator. The same thing had

happened throughout the kingdom as Saladin's generals moved from town to town and it was certain to recur in Jerusalem, where local Christians had never enjoyed the favors from the Latin Christians that they could expect under a tolerant Muslim leader like Saladin. In 1099, when the Franks captured the city, it had taken them only two years to expel the Eastern Christians from the Church of the Holy Sepulchre. The result was that the "holy fire" had not come to light the candles on the eve of Easter as had been traditional. The secret of this fire had, apparently, been known only to the local clergy and so the Latin conquerors had no alternative but to readmit their Eastern colleagues. Nevertheless, the Armenian, Greek, and Syrian churches had not prospered under Latin domination for the last century. As a result, their followers turned a deaf ear to Balian's appeals, even when he called them to protect their faith against the Muslims.

Whereas at Tyre Conrad of Montferrat had almost the entire remaining military strength of the kingdom, which had escaped there after Hattin, at Jerusalem Balian found that he had mostly civilian refugees and few soldiers. Those who had gone to Tyre sought safety in its massive walls; those who had gone to Jerusalem had gone there because of its sanctity. Balian's garrison contained a high proportion of priests who could offer little military help but served instead to maintain a kind of spiritual hysteria in which anything seemed possible, even military victory. Probably by the time Saladin's troops arrived to surround Jerusalem its population had been swollen to some 60,000, of whom perhaps 20,000 might have been of an age and sex to wield a sword and fewer than 6,000 of much use as soldiers. Yet 6,000 fanatics made up a formidable force when fighting from behind stone walls and with the belief that they were fighting alongside saints and angels. So inspired were many of these men that they tried to persuade Balian to sally forth as soon as Saladin appeared to fight to the death. Although Balian prevailed upon them not to seek martyrdom, some did open the city gates and charge out almost before Saladin's very eyes. After a brief skirmish the Christians found the martyrdom they sought, though not without impressing the Turks with their courage, however futile it proved.

While Balian faced such problems with the garrison, he also had to deal with the problem of arranging to feed a population that had swelled to three times its normal strength. In the last days before the Muslims closed the siege, Balian sent men to bring all the food and water from the surrounding villages. To pay the foot soldiers needed for manning the walls, Balian ordered all the gold and silver to be stripped from the roofs of the city churches; this was melted down by the Royal Mint and turned into coins. Day by day rumors reached the city of Saladin's progress along the coast, and when the city's delegates returned from meeting Saladin at Ascalon it was obvious that time had run out and Jerusalem's turn had come.

On September 20 Saladin made camp outside Jerusalem, having ridden up from Ascalon. He brought with him the bulk of his forces and prepared for battle, although he may still have hoped that the Jerusalem garrison would see sense and not force him to assault the city. One look at the battlements would have dispelled such a hope: they were crowded with soldiers and everywhere banners fluttered defiantly in the breeze. He had seen the same at Acre, but here in Jerusalem the defenders meant to lay down their lives for their faith. While his troops spread out along the western walls of the city, Saladin himself probed for weaknesses. Accompanied by his engineers and senior military advisers, he spent the first day in planning the assault. Yet for all the skills and experience at his disposal Saladin made the identical error made by the Franks a century before. Like them he assumed that Jerusalem's citadel had been situated where the walls were weakest and where it could strengthen them. As a result, Saladin ordered his assaults against the western walls where, for five days, his men struggled up difficult slopes and across tricky terrain. The result was that, in spite of his superiority in every respect, the Turks made no progress in their siege. From the towers of David and Tancred, which dominated the approaches taken by the Muslims, even defenders of limited ability were able to pour an effective fire on the best troops without risking themselves. Balian had placed mangonels in these high towers to fling stones at any siege weapons that the Muslims brought within range of the city walls. Saladin's engineers were quite unable to undermine the walls in the usual way as they risked the immediate destruction of their works and the collapse of their tunnels. Several of Saladin's best mangonels were damaged by counterfire from the Christian machines on their high towers, which enabled them to outrange the Muslim weapons.

Although Balian, probably alone of all the garrison, realized that all that had been achieved so far was some delay to Saladin's plans and some metaphorical blood lost, most others began to believe that victory was possible after all. The much-vaunted Muslim army had made no impression on the city's defenses after five days' fighting. Saladin, however, was frustrated rather than anxious. He had made a public announcement that his war was not with all the Christians but with the Latin Franks alone, who sought to rule the kingdom as conquerors. Eastern Christians were as welcome as they had always been in his realm and their religious freedom in Jerusalem was guaranteed. As a result, with little to fear from Saladin, these Easterners could not be relied upon to fight for their faith. Balian thus had no option but to try to buy the services of these men, many of whom had previously made up the infantry regiments of Frankish armies, fighting for pay.

Balian could take some satisfaction from the first five days' fighting. One mounted foray from the city had taken a Muslim column by surprise and had put it to flight. Otherwise, the fighting was generally at long range, with the Muslims unable to approach the walls without suffering a withering fire from the high towers and battlements. Even nature seemed against Saladin at this time. Balian exploited the blinding sun that afflicted the Muslims in their western position by attacking them each morning. By the afternoon, of course, the situations were reversed and Balian took up a defensive pose. Saladin was not prepared to concede the initiative to the Christians, and he ordered his engineers to exploit the wind that blew from the west. The Muslims filled their siege catapults with sand and dust and created a veritable sandstorm to blind the city's defenders by hurling it into the air, where it was caught by the wind and blown toward Jerusalem.

It must be observed that it took Saladin a long time to realize that he was assaulting the city walls from the wrong position. An experienced siege expert, as Richard of England undoubtedly was, would have rectified his mistakes within hours. Perhaps Saladin felt no sense of urgency. After all, he knew that it was only a matter of time before the city succumbed and there was no danger of a Christian relief army coming to the aid of Jerusalem's defenders. If this is what Saladin was indeed thinking, then he was badly misled. Every day he wasted outside Jerusalem gave Conrad of Montferrat time to make the city of Tyre invulnerable to Muslim assaults. Moreover, the patience of Saladin's own soldiers was not infinite. Every setback, however minuscule it might seem to Saladin, who was fighting to regain Jerusalem after a hundred years of captivity, seemed far more significant to his emirs and warriors, for whom each extra day at Jerusalem was an extra day away from their homes and families. When the appalling weather in December forced him to call off the siege of Tyre Saladin must have regretted the wasted week at Jerusalem.

On September 25, Saladin reached the decision to order the whole army to break camp and move northward. For a few blissful hours the Christian defenders believed that the sultan was raising the siege and marching away. Balian, however, can hardly have been fooled. He must have realized that the Muslims had suffered far too few casualties to make withdrawal likely. Instead, he must have known that Saladin was merely correcting his earlier mistake, which had allowed the Christian defenders to keep the Muslims at long range. Attacking from the northern side, Balian appreciated as nobody else, the Muslims would soon be able to fight the defenders hand to hand, and with their superior numbers it would only be a matter of time before the city fell.

Saladin established his new camp between the Postern of St. Lazarus, near the leper colony, and the Postern of St. Magdalene. Following the example of the crusaders of 1099, he had at last concluded that the breach would most likely be made between the Postern of St. Magdalene and the Barbican, exactly where Godfrey of Bouillon had entered the city in 1099. To commemorate this epic event the Christians had erected at this point a great cross. Ironically, this cross was to act as a sign to the Muslims as the point from which they could regain the city. Saladin now intensified the siege. Soon as many as forty mangonels were tossing rocks and "Greek fire" against the city walls with such an intensity that the defenders were, for the first time, almost helpless to resist. Hundreds of engineers from Aleppo and Khorasan now began to fill in the fosse on the west side, which had hindered the attackers in the first week. Sheltering behind men who advanced before them with covering shields, they reached the city walls and began their task of destruction. Dragging out stones and loosening the mortar with picks and levers, they began to dig shafts under the main walls, propping up the foundations with wooden beams. They eventually built a tunnel one hundred feet in length under the Barbican and, when it was completed, they burned away the struts that had been supporting the wall above. It was the traditional method of undermining medieval fortifications, and it worked. With a great crash the whole section of wall subsided, bringing down the great cross in as obvious a symbol of the triumph of Islam as anyone could have devised.

In case the garrison staged a sortie in desperation, Saladin had assembled a mounted force of some 10,000 men to cut them off. It was an example of "overkill," but it served its purpose. Jerusalem was now open to the Muslims. Saladin need only issue the order and the city would be assaulted and pillaged. In such a case a massacre was inevitable.

For the garrison the time for resistance was past. The Jerusalem militia, who had fought with such courage from behind the city walls, now faced the professional soldiers of Islam in open fight. Their courage now left them and nobody could be found to guard the breach, even though the city fathers offered bribes of undreamed-of riches to any man who would fight in the breach, or at least guard it. The priests now found their time had come. Processions of clergy around the battlements, constantly interrupted by showers of Muslim arrows, tried to maintain the morale of the beaten garrison as well as to invoke the help of armies of saints and angels. Fanatics pressed Balian to lead them out to attack the Turks rather than wait within the city to be massacred. After a hurried search a fragment of the True Cross was found in the possession of the Syrian Christians and they were prevailed upon to allow this sacred relic to lead the processions of monks, who intoned psalms and prayers and promised everyone who died in the fighting that they were absolved of their sins and certain of salvation.

Amid the chaos within Jerusalem and in an atmosphere of religious hysteria, Balian desperately struggled to keep a clear mind. He knew that all that was left for his garrison was death by martyrdom, but he was responsible for the welfare of thousands of noncombatants who would perish in an assault or suffer rape and slavery in the aftermath. Their hopes rested in his ability to negotiate with Saladin and, perhaps, to outmaneuver his noble adversary. With the help of the Patriarch Eraclius, Balian succeeded in subduing the military fanatics and prevailing on the people to risk a negotiation with the Turks.

There was no cessation in the fighting to allow Balian and Eraclius to prepare their arguments. Even as Balian fought his way clear of the city walls and made his way toward Saladin's camp in the valley of the Brook Kedron, the Muslims forced through the breach in the northern walls only to be physically thrown back by the defenders. Saladin believed he was on the brink of taking the holy city, and when his servants reported that Balian of Ibelin was outside demanding to see him Saladin refused twice, on the grounds that he had taken the city by force and there was nothing left to discuss. Saladin was uncharacteristically beside himself with rage at the ferocity of the resistance being put up by the garrison. The siege of Jerusalem, which he had expected to be little more than a formality, was becoming one of the hardest and bloodiest he had endured, and his losses were such that they called for Christian blood in compensation. At the third attempt Saladin did agree to talk with Balian, but even as they spoke a cry went up in his camp that Muslim flags were on the battlements. He turned to the Christian commander and asked him why he came to surrender the city when it was already in Muslim hands. Surrender was too late, he added, the city was falling by assault and his troops could not be denied the traditions of rape and pillage. Before Balian could respond the smile faded on Saladin's face as a sudden charge by the Christian defenders drove the Muslims out of the breach once more and threw down the Muslim banners. Saladin turned back to Balian, acknowledging that the ways of Allah were difficult to understand. Perhaps the city should not fall to the sword. He asked the Christian commander to return the next day to discuss the takeover of the city: Balian had at least gained a day's respite, and the feeling that the burden had now passed from his shoulders to those of Saladin.

Saladin was renowned as a man of his word, as his slaying of Reginald had proved only too well. When the delegates from Jerusalem had haughtily rejected his reasonable terms at his camp at Ascalon he had allowed his anger to rule him when he swore to take the city with the sword. Yet, for once, Saladin may have been looking for a way out of his dilemma. Oaths were a vital part of Muslim life, and all men of good faith made their observation an article of faith, yet was the cause of Islam served by a bloody massacre that would sully his name in the eyes of both friends and foes? When he looked for advice he found that his emirs were opposed to a massacre. Warfare was an expensive business, and many of them hoped to benefit from the ransoms of living prisoners, not the blood of dead ones. Moreover, Saladin's treasury was empty now that he had squandered the riches of Acre on rewarding his men. These same fighters would expect to be allowed to loot the treasure of Jerusalem if they had to fight to capture it, whereas if Jerusalem was handed over peacefully Saladin's officials could regulate the paying of ransoms so that the state treasury benefited as much as the common soldiery. Having heard such opinions from the more sensible of his advisers, he was finally forced back on what he felt himself. His word of honor as a warrior and as a Muslim could not be valued in money, but neither was it dependent on the blood he spilled. War—especially holy war—was not merely for the entertainment of kings and sultans like himself. The suffering that had been imposed on noncombatants by this "just" war to regain al-Quds had been great and, now that its end was in sight, it was incumbent upon honorable men to bring it to a swift and humane end.

Within Jerusalem, however, the Christian population knew that their fate was no longer in their own hands. Their lives and those of their children depended upon the decision of their enemy, the Muslim sultan, a man renowned for justice but nevertheless at war with their religion and all those who held to it. For a century Christians had ruled Jerusalem and had shown little love or consideration for their Muslim slaves or for the holy places of Islam like the Dome of the Rock and the al-Aqsa mosque. Now that the tables were turned could they expect pity from those whom they had treated so badly and whose mosques they had defiled?

All that night the air was filled with the sounds of prayers and lamentations in the streets of the holy city, while outside the ululating voices of Muslim women and the calls of the muezzins could be heard in the besieger's camps. At the Church of the Holy Sepulchre in Jerusalem women brought their daughters to bathe them naked in the water and cut off their hair in acts of penance and to render them less attractive to the Muslim soldiery if the city was taken by storm. Other girls were dressed as boys in the forlorn hope that they might escape rape. A wave of religious hysteria drove the people to acts of contrition. Barefoot and with their hair cut back to their scalps, thousands of women followed the monks and priests who carried the Corpus Domini and the Syrian True Cross in holy procession around the battlements of the city. As they did so their wailing increased at the sight of a sea of twinkling stars stretching out across the northern and eastern approaches where the Muslim campfires burned. Fanatics among them saw visions, and everywhere voices invoked the help of God and his angels.

Balian of Ibelin's state of mind that night can only be imagined. He had come to Jerusalem for just one night, to rescue his wife and children. Instead, God had found him a new purpose, a new responsibility beyond anything he had ever previously imagined. He had organized the defenses of the city as well as anyone could, but now all that he had with which to face the awesome power of Saladin was his native wit. He might even go down in history as the lord whose failure condemned the Christian inhabitants of Jerusalem to massacre.

The next morning the battlements of the city were crowded with a mixture of soldiers and citizens all jostling for a view of the lonely figure of Balian as he rode out to his meeting with Saladin. Balian had more trouble breaking through the crowded streets of the city than he did passing through the lines of the Muslim armies, drawn up for battle but otherwise silent. On his arrival at the Muslim camp he was taken into Saladin's tent, where the sultan greeted him with a grim propriety. Balian could see at once that Saladin was deeply troubled. The sultan began by berating the Christian commander with the attitude of the delegates who had come to meet him at Ascalon. He had offered them conditions of unprecedented moderation and they had haughtily flung them back in his face. Well, where were these delegates now? Saladin went on to say that he had shown them such kindness that he had earned nothing but harsh words from his own people. Consequently he had sworn an oath to take Jerusalem by storm. Now that he was about to achieve it, why should he listen to Balian's excuses? Balian could see that Saladin had worked himself into a fury with the Christians and that nothing other than the strongest response on his part could save the situation. He reasoned that all he had left was his life and the lives of the garrison, and so, as a warrior, he must be prepared to throw these into the balance. He therefore took the offensive and warned Saladin that unless fair terms of surrender were offered to his people they would have nothing left to hope for and they would fight to the death and would destroy much of the city before the Muslims could occupy it. Many chroniclers wrote impressions of the great speech that Balian made that day, but none recorded his actual words. The tenor of what he said, however, is probably accurately conveyed by the Muslim account of ibn al-Athir, who reports that Balian addressed Saladin and his emirs thus:

> O Sultan, know that we soldiers in this city are in the midst of God knows how many people, who are slackening the fight in the hope of thy grace, believing that thou wilt grant it them as thou hast granted it to the other cities—for they abhor death and desire life. But for ourselves, when we see that death must needs be, by God we will slaughter our sons and our women, we will burn our wealth and our possessions, and leave you neither

sequin nor stiver to loot, nor a man or a woman to enslave; and when we have finished that, we will demolish the Rock and the Mosque al-Aqsa, and the other holy places, we will slay the Muslim slaves who are in our hands—there are 5,000 such—and slaughter every beast and mount we have; and then we will sally out in a body to you, and we will fight you for our lives: not a man of us will fall before he has slain his like; thus shall we die gloriously or conquer like gentlemen.

Everything Saladin had seen so far of Christian fanaticism convinced him that Balian's threat was not an idle one. He was well aware that even if his troops did break into the city he would not have control of it for several hours, during which there was time for the Christians to carry out their threats, notably to desecrate the Muslim holy places and to massacre the Muslim prisoners. What Balian had painted was the picture of another holocaust like the one that had taken place a century before, when the crusaders had captured Jerusalem in the first place.

Saladin knew enough of the crusader mentality to take Balian's words seriously. Moreover, as the leader of the armies of Islam he owed it to his followers to do more than to destroy what he could not capture. His emirs had sacrificed much to follow him and they would hardly view it as victory in the holy war if they became masters of a ruined holy city, with their holy places laid low. He had driven the garrison to the point where they were willing to surrender, but if he offered them nothing to hope for but death they would seize the inevitable way of martyrs and do as much damage to their enemies as possible before they died. He had acted otherwise with the other cities of the kingdom and their garrisons had accepted his generous terms and surrendered willingly. Had he acted differently, much Muslim blood would have been spilled and the land that he was taking over would have been ruined. Saladin had found generosity a powerful weapon possessed by few, either of his predecessors or of his contemporaries. Most strong leaders ruled through fear, yet he had found that mercy and humanity sometimes opened doors; to break them down might cost him many casualties. If he were to grant clemency to the inhabitants of Jerusalem the message would go out that he had conquered men's hearts as well as their castles and that nobody, neither Christian nor Muslim, need fear to put their lives in the hands of such a man. And, after all, dead men paid no ransom. If the Christians were allowed to buy their freedom all would benefit and he would hold al-Quds just the same.

Saladin, who liked and respected Balian and was probably pleased to be spared responsibility for a massacre, agreed to accept the surrender of the city and now held lengthy discussions with the Christian leader to set the level of the ransoms to be imposed. Eventually it was agreed that each man should pay 10 dinars, each woman 5, and each child just 1 dinar. The many poor, estimated to number at least 7,000, were to be ransomed for a total of 30,000 bezants, paid for from the gold that Henry II of England had raised and that the Templars made available to Balian. Saladin granted everyone forty days in which to collect their ransoms, after which if they failed to pay they would be enslaved. Although the Christians were free to take their movable possessions with them, most sold what they could to the Muslim conquerors in order to fund their ransoms or those of their relatives and friends.

The occupation of Jerusalem by the Muslims in 1187 was in marked contrast to the horrors that accompanied the seizure of the city by the crusaders in 1099. There was no looting of buildings and no rape of the women. Saladin had posted his own guards on the streets as much to keep his soldiers under control as to ensure that the Christians behaved themselves. At this time of crisis it might be thought that the Latin Church would succor its people and be the rock upon which the Christians of Jerusalem could rely. Unfortunately, the leadership of the Patriarch Eraclius and his priests seemed based on indifference and parsimony. Rather than use church funds to ransom the poor, Eraclius paid just the 10 dinars for himself and left the poor to fend for themselves. Even Saladin was shocked at what he called "this unholy man."

When the forty days that had been set aside for the collection of the ransoms had passed, Saladin found that there were still many poor Christians who had not been able to raise the money. Previous conquerors, of whatever faith, would have wasted no more time and would have swept the remnants into slavery, but he continued to find ways to stretch his own rules and help the poor, particularly the widows and orphans of those who had fallen at Hattin. His compassion stood in stark contrast to that of the rich Jerusalemites, who seemed inspired less by the teachings of their Savior than by the selfishness of their own patriarch. Eraclius collected all the wealth of the church in Jerusalem and took it out of the city on a caravan of carts. Gold and silver ornaments, fine tapestries and carpets were loaded onto the carts in full view of the poor, who, lacking the means to pay their ransoms, were facing slavery in Muslim lands. Even Saladin's emirs were infuriated by the sight of this Christian cleric leaving the city as if in triumph. They urged Saladin to seize the wealth of this greedy and selfish man who, in the last days of the kingdom, was seen to be failing those who had regarded him as their spiritual link with God. But Saladin refused to break his oath to Balian to let those go who could pay their ransoms. As a result, although there had been enough money in the hands of wealthy Christians, some 15,000 poor Jerusalemites were taken in columns to the slave markets of Damascus.

The problem that faced Balian was to find refuge for those who had managed to ransom themselves. Three columns left the city, one led by Balian himself, and the other two organized by the Templars and Hospitallers. Each column was escorted by Muslim soldiers to protect them from the desert Bedouin tribesmen, who would have shown them no mercy now that their power was gone. Ironically, it was not their Muslim enemies who posed the greatest threat to the refugees. The Christian chroniclers relate with shame that it was the Christians themselves who fell upon their coreligionists and despoiled them.

After the capture of Jerusalem Saladin found that his enemies, rather than diminish, seemed to grow like Hydra heads. The holy city was merely a symbol of Christianity in the spiritual world; the heart of the Christian body was now at Tyre. If he wanted to end the holy war he had to capture this last remaining Christian enclave and disperse the garrison, now swollen to dangerous size. However, by leaving the greatest and most dangerous enemy until last, he had risked the possibility that his fighting men would lose their edge, dulled by easy victory and bloated with his largesse. Even while he was still arranging the ransoms at Jerusalem, the more astute strategists among his commanders were warning him to attack Tyre, which was, in their words, "the only arrow left in the quiver of the infidels." Yet even as they thought this they were already too late. Saladin's nemesis had already arrived at Tyre on July 14, in the person of Conrad of Montferrat, the formidable brother of William Longsword, first husband of Queen Sibylla. Longsword would have been the King of Jerusalem, but his death in 1176 from malaria resulted in opening the way for an interloper and a minor nobleman like Guy of Lusignan to take the throne. Now Conrad was determined to gain the prize that his brother had missed, and Guy's defeat at Hattin seemed to offer him just the opportunity. However, first he would have to win the kingdom the hard way, by retaking it from the hands of Saladin himself.

There are elements of historical license on the part of the chroniclers about the arrival of Conrad of Montferrat at Tyre. It is possible that the defense of Tyre owed much to the solid work of a survivor from the battlefield of Hattin, Reginald of Sidon. Just as Balian of Ibelin organized the defenders at Jerusalem, so did Reginald of Sidon at Tyre. However, Reginald's later involvement with Saladin has made him an equivocal figure, not to be praised too highly by later Western chroniclers. Therefore, in examining the role of Conrad in the defense of Tyre, it is necessary to allow for the fact that he was a relative of the rulers of France and Germany and, as such, benefited from the propaganda on which such rulers could always rely.

Conrad was the third son of the Marquess William of Montferrat, who had ruled a small principality in Italy, lying between Genoa and Milan, before coming to spend his last years in the Holy Land. The young Conrad served the Byzantine emperor Isaac Angelus so effectively that he earned himself the dignity of "Caesar" and the hand of the emperor's daughter in marriage. But Conrad was too fierce and independent a spirit to be satisfied with the luxuries of Byzantine court life, and he was sailing to find adventure in Outremer when, unaware of the disaster that had taken place at Hattin, he sailed into Acre, intending to land there. By July 14 Acre was in Muslim hands, and as Conrad's galley entered the harbor he was met by a Muslim customs boat, to whom he explained that he was merely a trader and from whom he learned that the kingdom had been conquered. Sailing away before he could be intercepted, he headed northward until he reached Tyre. Here, Reginald of Sidon was on the point of surrendering the city and Saladin's banners were even fluttering on the battlements when Conrad stormed ashore and was welcomed by the people of Tyre as if he brought salvation with him, instead of some boxes of treasure and a small force of soldiers. Conrad personally climbed the battlements, seized Saladin's banners, and threw them into the moat far below. It was the first step in the reconquest of the kingdom. Unanimously, the barons and knights of Tyre chose Conrad as their leader, until the kings of the West could organize a new crusade. Without realizing it, Saladin had come within a few moments of total victory in the holy war, only to have the cup dashed from his lips by this resourceful and charismatic Italian knight.

Saladin had been preparing to occupy Tyre and was rendered speechless by the effrontery of the newcomer. When he learned the identity of the arrogant knight who had thrown down his banners, he resorted to the sort of ruse that Richard the Lionheart might have employed himself, though more ruthlessly. Conrad's father, the elderly William of Montferrat, had been taken prisoner at Hattin. Now Saladin had the old man brought out into the open, and he warned Conrad that until he surrendered the city his father would be kept in the front line of the fighting. Saladin can hardly have believed that a Christian knight would submit to such blackmail, let alone a man of such severity as Conrad. The new ruler of Tyre disdainfully replied that his father had lived long enough already and that if necessary he would shoot the old man himself to remove the threat. Saladin had now felt the weight of Conrad's scorn. Shortly afterward William was taken to a place of safety and released.

While Saladin turned his attention inland to the capture of Jerusalem, Conrad used the respite to good purpose, strengthening the city's defenses by digging a deep ditch across the causeway from the shore that Alexander the Great's Macedonians had constructed 1,500 years before. By doing this Conrad had cut off Tyre from the land and the city was now an island, described as being "like a hand spread upon the sea, attached only by the wrist." In spite of his overwhelming numbers, Saladin would now find it difficult to concentrate his strength against even a few determined defenders. Meanwhile, if Conrad was able to rely on the naval strength of the Italian maritime cities, like Genoa and Pisa, Tyre might stand a prolonged siege.

Saladin did not return to Tyre until November 8, and by now it was far too late. Whatever his own thoughts, many of his commanders felt that their chance of taking the city had gone. Even though the kingdom had been conquered fairly easily, the strain on the rank and file had been great and the siege weapons, employed in numerous minor operations, were in need of repair or replacement. With winter approaching it seemed the worst possible time to be facing the greatest challenge of an entire year of constant fighting. And it was not only the common soldiers who were full of grouses. Keukburi, Saladin's left-wing commander at Hattin, was eager to undertake a pilgrimage to Mecca, while others, including Taqi al-din, felt they had been away from their homes and estates for too long. When Saladin arrived at Tyre in person he was very depressed at the condition of the siege train. Many of the mangonels were either too small or were simply worn out, and the morale of the troops was poor. After he had thrown himself into the job of revitalizing the operation he managed to cobble together seventeen fully functioning mangonels, and soon these were firing day and night. But Tyre was probably the strongest fortress in the entire kingdom, beyond even Acre, and had walls nearly twenty feet thick, far too strong for the stone-throwers available to the Turks. Nothing short of explosives could have breached such medieval walls.

A temporary improvement in morale was felt after the arrival of fresh troops from Aleppo, commanded by al-Zahir. Saladin was even emboldened to try an assault along the causeway. However, his men found themselves under attack from both land and sea. Frankish *barbotes*, warships fitted with shields to provide cover from behind which archers and crossbowmen enfiladed the Turks on the causeway, moved up and down the mole on either side, always out of range of the Turks on the shore. Saladin could see that with such seapower Conrad could easily control the causeway, and so he ordered warships to be brought up from Jubail and Beirut, to drive the Frankish ships into harbor and to keep them there. For a while Saladin's ten warships controlled the seas around Tyre and Conrad was forced to risk his limited number of knights in hand-to-hand fighting on the causeway. Prominent during this phase of the siege was a Spanish knight in green armor whose task was to lead out a special troop of knights to stem any breakthroughs. This knight, who carried a green shield and wore a green surcoat, bore a helmet fitted with stag's horns and made a great impression on friend and foe by his heroism. Even Saladin himself was forced to acknowledge the great part that the green knight played in the successful resistance.

During December there was little relief for either the garrison or the besieging forces. Saladin benefited from having the company of both his brother al-Adil from Egypt and his son al-Afdal, who came up from Acre, but the weather was already as grim a foe as Conrad and his garrison. Heavy and continuous rain flooded the tents and turned the ground into a muddy quagmire; snow was in the air and fell lightly on the hills. Worst of all, sickness was spreading through the Muslim camp and virtually extinguishing the morale of many men.

conquerors, and so the English fell victim to the native prejudices of the original inhabitants of the island. Tancred was as much to blame as anyone, seeking to strengthen his own position by appealing to the nationalism of the Sicilians, both "Griffon" and "Lombard" (Italian-speaking) against any intruders, among whom Richard's crusaders would be numbered. Both Griffons and Lombards tried to incite the English particularly, constantly referring to them as having tails and refusing to sell them food in the markets. There were even signs that the inhabitants of Messina were fortifying their city, expecting to be besieged by the crusaders. They had already weighed up the personalities of the two kings who were staying in their city, referring to Richard as the "Lion" and Philip as the "Lamb."

How early Richard knew that he would have to fight Tancred to gain what he was due cannot be ascertained. Suffice it to say that the Sicilians made no pretense of dealing humbly with the King of England or attempting to placate him. From the first they seemed willing to allow their visitors to be insulted and attacked so that some sort of retribution was inevitable. When Richard struck it was decisively. He seized a coastal fortress near La Bagnara, killed the garrison, and placed Joanna in an abbey there with a strong garrison, for protection. He next seized the Monastery of the Savior at Messina, evicted the monks, and used it as a barracks for his soldiers. A few days later a dispute over the price of bread led to some fighting between the crusaders and the locals that was only with some difficulty prevented from spreading. Richard now held a meeting with Tancred's ministers, hoping to find a peaceful solution to their dispute. Even as these notables, supported by Philip of France and Hugh, Duke of Burgundy, were discussing the situation with Richard, messengers came to report that fighting was raging all through the city and that the English were being killed. This was true, as Richard found out when he encountered one of his trusted liegemen, Hugh the Brown of Lusignan, whose party had been attacked by the Sicilians. As Richard soon saw, the locals had armed themselves and had ambushed the English crusaders. He had no alternative now but to send for his armor and to "assault the city by land and by sea." Once he had armed himself he set off with just twenty men; joining Hugh the Brown's party, they immediately set upon the armed townspeople. It was less a battle than a massacre and soon the Sicilians were fleeing before the armed crusaders like "sheep from a wolf." The English army, on the beaches outside

Messina, soon joined the action, though when the English galleys attempted to move up to support their king they were intercepted by Philip Augustus and prevailed upon to stay out of the fighting. A large force of Griffons and Lombards occupied a hill outside the city, but Richard led a small party of knights up a secret path and then burst upon the enemy, driving them down in headlong flight. Having dispersed the bulk of Tancred's troops, Richard now fought his way back into Messina, supported by the bulk of his army. Within minutes the city was his and the local population was in full retreat.

Richard allowed his victorious troops to plunder Messina, as was traditional when a city fell to assault, but after a few hours he reimposed his control as he took pity on the local inhabitants. Incredibly, while all the fighting raged around him, Philip Augustus and his French crusaders stayed within their lodgings, offering no help to their fellow crusaders and at ease with their Sicilian hosts. However, when he heard that Richard had raised his banners on the walls of Messina, Philip realized that he would have to react strongly or else Richard would have been able to usurp the authority of his feudal overlord. The French now demanded that the English banners be replaced by French ones, a demand that Richard simply ignored. Eventually, however, some of the nobles and prelates on both sides worked out a compromise. After all, the crusade ahead would be ill omened if the two kings could not cooperate on the voyage to the Holy Land. A simple solution was reached whereby the flags of both monarchs flew alongside each other, while the custody of the fortifications was left in the hands of the international authority of the Templars and Hospitallers. Philip, however, could not let matters end so lightly. As a result of the agreement he had reached with Richard at Vézelay, he insisted that the spoils of Messina should be divided equally between the two of them. So angry was Philip that it almost put an end to the crusade there and then. Richard went even so far as to order his ships to be loaded so that he could set off alone on the crusade rather than travel with so disagreeable a companion. Philip must have realized that he had gone too far, for the moment, and tempers were allowed to cool before the two restored their alliance.

Richard now renewed his demands to Tancred for his sister's dowry and these were transmitted to Catania, where the Sicilian king was staying, by some of the most distinguished of the crusaders, including the Duke of Burgundy. Later chroniclers, aware of the bad relations that were

to recur throughout the Third Crusade, report that the French representatives to Tancred carried a secret message from their king encouraging
him to resist Richard; whether or not this is true remains uncertain. The
French delegates did, however, return from Catania loaded with gifts,
while the English brought back an unsatisfactory reply. Tancred asserted
that he had given Joanna quite enough already and that he would be
guided in how to respond by "the custom of this realm." Richard per-
ceived this to be just a further step in defying him, particularly as two of
Tancred's ministers had secretly fled from Messina with all their movable
wealth. Master of siege warfare as he was, Richard had used the time
while the delegation was in Catania to build a huge tower overlooking
Messina, thus discouraging any further resistance to him. The wooden
fortress was known as Mategriffon, or "Kill-Greeks," and represented
Richard's determination to get what he came for. The Sicilians, however,
were not content to be dominated by this invader and began the sort of
harassing tactics that had caused Richard to take Messina in the first place.
When Tancred returned a defiant reply to Richard's demand for his sister's dowry, the people took courage from their king's tone and began refusing food to the English and attacking isolated parties. Again, the French
did nothing to help and it soon became apparent that Philip Augustus was
in touch with Tancred and was encouraging him to resist Richard's bullying tactics.

The inner politics of the Sicilian court were not immediately clear
to the kings of England and France. Tancred, however, was not so foolish as to challenge a warrior of the renown of the Lionheart. He had
regarded the arrival of two such puissant rulers as a heaven-sent opportunity to make alliances that might prove useful if, as he expected,
Constance should return to claim her right to the crown of Sicily. First
Tancred had sought to ally with France, but he soon discovered that
Philip Augustus was one step ahead and was already aware that Sicily
might eventually pass to the Emperor of Germany, and he wanted to
maintain good relations with him. As a result, Tancred decided it might
be better to come to an agreement with Richard over his sister's dowry
and settle the unpaid contribution to the crusade. He therefore proposed to pay Richard 40,000 ounces of gold, half being the dowry and
the rest the money for the crusade. Richard decided that he must accept this offer, and not unwillingly. Although it was not all that he was
due, it was so much more than he had expected that it would enable

him to get on with his crusade without further delay and, moreover, help to fund the entire operation.

Richard now drew up a treaty with Tancred, agreeing to keep the peace while in Sicily, where he was being forced to spend more time than expected due to the inclement weather and the difficulty of sailing at that time of the year. Moreover, and here Tancred scored an important point, should Sicily be invaded while the English were still on the island, Richard promised to fight the invader on Tancred's behalf. Part of the agreement also saw Richard's nephew, Arthur of Brittany, affianced to one of Tancred's daughters. Richard was satisfied with this settlement and turned his attention to his relationship with the King of France. Although none of the money he had been paid by Tancred could be construed as qualifying, under their agreement at Vézelay, for sharing with his co-monarch, he decided that some sort of "sweetener" should be paid to Philip in an attempt to restore relations that had become very strained. Also, Richard began restoring the loot that had been plundered when his men had seized Messina. The Archbishop of Rouen, who was traveling with the King of England, was called upon to excommunicate anyone who failed to restore stolen property to its rightful owner. Chroniclers were amazed by the extent to which Richard the bully became Richard the conciliator once he had got his way.

Details of Richard's stay in Sicily provide some of the best available evidence about his personality. The role of warrior-king, for which this member of the Plantagenet dynasty seemed fitted by both nurture and nature, is almost a contradiction in terms. Its essential incongruities can be illustrated by a minor incident during the journey to the Holy Land, in which Richard revealed the problems he faced not only as the leader of an army but as the preeminent symbol of Frankish chivalry. Significantly, Philip Augustus felt able to indulge his fellow monarch, thereby preserving Franco-Angevin relations in a matter of supreme indifference to the Machiavellian Frenchman.

Crusaders were traditionally expected to forget past grudges, at least while engaged in such great issues as those of the holy war. Unfortunately, Richard found this impossible in relation to one of Philip's bravest knights, William of Barres, whom Richard had imprisoned during a skirmish in July 1188 but who had escaped by breaking his parole. During the winter of 1190–91 old animosities rose to the surface. Richard was out riding with a group of English and French knights when they came upon a peasant with a cart full of canes or bulrushes. Immediately, Richard took a boyish glee in seizing the peasant's produce and organizing an impromptu tournament, arming the knights with nothing more fearful than the reeds. In the context of the event it would have been common sense for the knights to indulge the monarch's predilections and allow him to win. After all, neither life nor honor was at stake. However, as fate would have it, Richard found himself confronted by William of Barres, who appeared unwilling to enter into the spirit of the thing. The two soon fell to blows, using their horses to buffet each other and wrestling in an attempt to unhorse each other. It was obvious to the on-lookers that the mood had changed. When Richard's saddle slipped, tipping him to the ground, he demanded a remount so that the struggle could continue. The Earl of Leicester tried to separate the two men, but Richard bellowed at him, "Leave me to deal with him alone!" In real earnest, Richard now rode into battle against the French knight, knocking him from the saddle, but William clung to his horse's neck and refused to fall. Infuriated, Richard cursed William with the words, "Get thee hence, and take heed that I see thee no more, for henceforth I will be an enemy to thee and thine for ever."

What had started as sport ended in bitterness. Richard's petulance now drove him to demand of his fellow monarch that William of Barres be banished from Sicily and sent home to France. Even when some of the most prominent French nobles present went down on bended knee asking pardon on William's behalf, Richard was adamant that he must leave the crusade forthwith.

In the early days of spring 1191 a new quarrel sprang up between Philip and Richard. Everyone was growing bored with the delay in Sicily and many knights and lesser noblemen were complaining that they could not afford to stay much longer, especially as Richard had forced them to return the plunder they had taken from Messina. Richard showed understanding and was generous in his gifts to all members of his army, from high to low. His generosity, it must be noted, was based on the Sicilian treasure elicited from Tancred, but at least it was a heart-winning measure. On the other hand, one heart he could never win was that of Philip Augustus, who found Richard's procrastination very troubling and often tried to remind him that their duties were in the Holy Land, not in Sicily. Richard had not been able to concentrate fully on the crusade owing to reports that reached him throughout the winter about the troubles in England, where his brother John and the justiciars he had left to govern the country were in constant dispute. Several times he toyed with the idea of making a swift return home to put matters right, but eventually he decided to entrust that task to his companion Walter of Coutances, Archbishop of Rouen. Unknown to Philip, however, Richard's real reason for delaying in Sicily was that he was awaiting his fiancée, Berengaria, daughter of King Sancho the Strong of Navarre, who was being brought to Sicily for the marriage by his mother. When he heard that the wedding party had reached Naples, he sent some galleys to collect the two ladies and bring them to Sicily.

As King of England Richard has received even more criticism for his marital inadequacies than for his administrative failings. At every stage in English history it has been a fundamental requirement of each king that he marry and father an heir to the throne. Although Richard did marry, at the late age of thirty-three, he neither fathered any offspring nor even lived with his wife in order to make offspring a probability. This has prompted many historians to conclude that the case for Richard's homosexuality was proved. However, this may be too simplistic. There seems to be remarkably little evidence about Richard's sexual predilections, which is surprising in view of the attention that this subject normally receives in medieval chronicles. Richard may well have had a low libido and found Berengaria an unstimulating partner. Most rulers, Richard's father more than most, found alternative avenues if their conjugal path was either blocked or uncongenial. There is no mention of favorite mistresses or catamites in relation to Richard. His marriage to Berengaria seems to have been the political marriage par excellence. Feelings had absolutely no part to play. And in the twelfth century it was believed that no woman could conceive unless she had strong feelings for her partner. As a result, Berengaria must and did remain barren. But Richard could not divorce his wife without losing the vital alliance with her father, which helped him maintain his lands in Aquitaine during the years of the crusade and his captivity.

Although historians have tended to assume that Richard's mother was responsible for making the arrangements for the betrothal with Sancho of Navarre in 1190, it seems more likely that Richard had made secret arrangements himself the previous year. The reason for the secrecy, of course, was that as far as Philip Augustus was concerned Richard was still engaged to his sister Alice and was still prepared to honor the agreement made back in 1169. When the two kings had left Vézelay to begin the crusade in July, the marriage to Alice was still on the agenda, though Richard was looking for an opportunity to break his troth without so alienating Philip that the entire crusade collapse. The news that Eleanor of Aquitaine was approaching with Richard's bride-to-be blew all the secrecy away. When Philip heard the reason for Richard's delay in Sicily, he was furious. The King of England must either marry Alice or hand back Gisors and the Vexin. Richard was not prepared to do either. He now told the French king that his sister had been King Henry's mistress and had borne him a child. Richard assured Philip that there were many witnesses who could support these allegations.

Philip was now concerned with damage limitation. He had to save Alice's reputation, and that of his family as a whole, and he could no longer bring any pressure to bear on Richard for fear that the story would become public knowledge. He released Richard from his obligation to marry Alice in return for a token payment of 10,000 marks and settled the disputed territory of Gisors and the Vexin on Richard during his lifetime. If, however, Richard died childless then the territories would revert to France. These agreements formed part of the treaty drawn up at Messina in March 1191. There was no disguising the humiliation that Philip suffered at this turn of events and the hostility he felt toward the house of Anjou in general and Richard in particular. Hearing that Berengaria was due to arrive in Sicily on March 30, Philip sailed away from the island only hours before her arrival. Before his departure, however, he begged Richard to pardon his great knight, William of Barres, whose services would be essential in the crusade ahead. After some demur Richard agreed to keep peace with William, as all were involved in service to the cross, which should leave no room for grudges and petty quarrels.

Richard had accepted Tancred's friendship and hospitality at Catania, presenting his new ally with what he claimed was the sword Excalibur, recently dug up from a king's grave at Glastonbury. Astonished, some might say suspicious, at so high an award, Tancred replied with a generous gift that Richard much appreciated: four large ships, or "ussers," and fifteen galleys to accompany the crusade. Tancred also had a less pleasant surprise for Richard, nothing less than a letter from Philip Augustus, delivered by the Duke of Burgundy himself. The letter advised Tancred not to trust the King of England and promised that if he did decide to attack

the English he could rely on the French to help him. Tancred had originally seen the French as the more promising allies, but once he turned
to Richard he needed to impress him not only with his honesty but with
his power. The letter implicating Philip Augustus was a considerable
diplomatic weapon. If the letter was genuine it drove another metaphorical nail into the coffin of Franco-Angevin cooperation in the coming
crusade.

Richard's attention now turned to his wife-to-be, whom he placed
with his sister Joanna in his captured fortress of La Bagnara. Berengaria is
one of history's shadows. The very name evokes impressions of romantic
love, exoticism, perhaps even eroticism. Chroniclers refer to her as "a lady
of beauty and good sense" and "sensible rather than attractive." If, indeed,
Richard's libido was low, it is unlikely that a lady of this description
would do much to raise it for him. The fact is that for whatever reason
Richard did not spend much time with his wife and was severely criticized for this. In 1195 the chroniclers report that a hermit rebuked him
for his sins and afterward he spent more time with Berengaria, but she
remained childless. Because the marriage party had arrived in Sicily during Lent, the marriage could not take place immediately and Richard
decided to postpone it until his arrival at Acre. As it happened, news that
Archbishop Baldwin had died there led to a change of plan and the marriage took place in Cyprus instead. Eleanor stayed in Sicily with her son
for just four days before setting off for England again, her task having
been successfully fulfilled, although she may have been frustrated not to
be able to attend the wedding itself.

Meanwhile, the full strength of the English fleet had arrived at
Messina and was an awe-inspiring sight for the inhabitants of Sicily. Perhaps 200 vessels of all kinds bobbed proudly at anchor in the harbor, as
many as fifty of them being double-banked galleys that were the main
warships of their time, designed as a cross between the Viking longship
and the Roman galleys of antiquity. It was not long before the transports,
or "buses," began to be filled with all the paraphernalia of the crusade. At
last Richard was ready to sail away from Sicily.

The voyage across the eastern Mediterranean, from Sicily to Cyprus,
should have been a magnificent procession, so carefully had Richard organized the pattern of the fleet, but as mariners have found through
thousands of years, it is folly to think one can impose order on nature.
Sailing in the week of Easter, the English found that Maundy Thursday

gave them no wind at all, while Good Friday gave them nothing less than a storm. Richard seemed at his best, battling against the elements and helping those around him who lost faith. On April 17 his galley, leading as always, anchored off Crete, to await the arrival of the rest of the ships, which had been buffeted by the wind and blown off course. Soon his pleasant mood darkened as he came to realize that in spite of his organizational skills twenty-five ships were missing, including the one that carried Berengaria and Joanna and another that had much of his treasure. With no means of contacting the missing ships he had no alternative but to sail on to Rhodes, hoping to fall in with them or hear from passing ships of their progress. While on Rhodes he was taken ill and needed to recuperate for three days. During this time he sent spies to discover what they could about the ruler of the island of Cyprus, the "emperor" Isaac, whom he intended to visit before he reached Outremer.

Emperor Isaac Comnenus was a usurper like Tancred on Sicily, though he had less claim to the throne than had Richard's previous host. The Byzantine historian Niketas Choniates recorded this despot's dreadful behavior and personality, which must be judged in the context of the unpopularity that Isaac had earned among Cypriots in particular and Byzantines in general. According to this account, Isaac was unspeakably cruel and sexually perverted, debauching young girls at every opportunity. When excited he suffered fits during which his lower jaw trembled and spittle sprayed out along with strange bubbling noises. In view of his experiences with his father's "black bile" Richard must have felt a sense of familiarity with his atrocious host. In 1185 Isaac had been sent to become Byzantine governor of Cyprus and had, instead, thrown off the overlordship of Constantinople and made himself ruler. Lacking natural allies, Isaac had found a friend in Saladin. As a result, for six years he had cut off the traditional trade between the Cypriots and the Latin Christians of Jerusalem, who had always depended on food supplies from Cyprus. An Orthodox Christian, Isaac had no love for the Latin Christians of the Levant and did them as much harm as lay within his power. Unknown to him, Richard was now planning to put an end to this and to make a strategic base of Cyprus.

In fact, the storm that had dispersed the fleet had presented Richard with a good reason to intervene in Cypriot affairs. Some of the missing ships, including the one carrying the royal ladies, had landed in Cyprus and, while Richard was seeking them at Rhodes, they were attempting to enter the port of Amathus (modern-day Limassol). Even here they were not safe, for another storm now wrecked three of the smaller boats, smashing them on the rocks and shipwrecking their crews on the nearby beaches. It was almost as if Isaac had donned the guise of Prospero to work magic in drawing such guests to the island. Anchored offshore, and likely to fall within his power, were ships bearing the wife and sister of the King of England, along with his treasurer, Stephen of Turnham, in charge of the same king's treasure. However, at this point any similarity with Prospero ends, for Isaac seemed to display little magic and not much common sense. The mariners who were washed up on the beach were at first shown kindness by the local Cypriots but then promptly disarmed and imprisoned in a fortress, stripped of all their possessions, and treated like criminals. One William Dubois, armed with a bow he had secreted, shot down many of his assailants, while Roger of Harcourt found a horse and rode up and down the prison courtyard overthrowing his enemies as if he were at a tournament back home in France. Soon these stout-hearted warriors had overcome their gaolers, escaped from their prison, and fought a pursuing horde of Griffons until some knights were landed from the ships that had anchored off the coast and the rest of Isaac's men were put to flight. As hospitality to shipwrecked sailors went, Isaac had made a bad start.

Isaac, however, had greater matters on his mind. He wanted to take the royal ladies as hostages to ransom, a guarantee for Richard's good behavior once he arrived in Cyprus. On his arrival at Amathus, Isaac sent a courteous request and many gifts to Berengaria and Joanna, asking them to land. They were naturally suspicious, but they concluded that the longer they denied his request the more angry he would become and might even attempt to take them by force. Significantly, he was seen to be assembling troops on the shore opposite their anchorage. They concluded that if Richard did not arrive the next day they would go ashore. Fortunately, as the next day dawned his whole fleet was seen coming up from the direction of Rhodes. When Richard heard what had transpired he was furious, but he managed to calm his temper before remonstrating with Isaac for the way his people had treated the shipwrecked crusaders.

Thwarted by Richard's unexpected arrival, Isaac was in no mood to receive the two knights carrying messages of warning from the king, however subtly they might be expressed. The word "Pruht" in his chronicled response is difficult to interpret but probably meant something

along the lines of famous monosyllabic responses to demands for surrender, like the French "merde" at Waterloo or the American "nuts" in the
Ardennes in 1944. Isaac then went on to say, "Pruht, sires, who is this man
you call your king?" When the messengers reported this back, Richard
understood enough to reply in his own way: "To arms!"

In fact, Richard was facing a formidable task. He was going to have to
stage an opposed landing on an unknown shore, facing a well-fortified
infantry force drawn up behind barricades made of every available piece
of wood, from doors to old boats, casks, barrels, and so forth. In addition,
Isaac had also assembled some cavalry on the beach, against which the
English knights would have to fight on foot. Richard ordered his men to
crowd into the little cockleshells that were used for landing and to attack
the Cypriots without delay. Isaac drew up five Cypriot galleys, packed
with his best troops, in an attempt to prevent the English from landing,
but the English crossbowmen made short work of most of them, while
others managed to escape the deadly darts and swam to the shore.
Richard, ever eager to be at the head of his troops, refused to be rowed
ashore: as later at Jaffa, he waded to the beach, dressed in full armor, a
difficult and dangerous feat. Soon dozens of his knights were following
his example; having reached the shore, these tough fighters were routing
the Cypriots, who turned to flee, some into the town of Amathus and
some into the open fields. The chroniclers possibly overdramatize this action by relating that Richard found a horse, some kind of packhorse at
best, and challenged the "emperor" to joust. Isaac had no intention of
playing the hero and rode off on one of history's most famous steeds,
Fauvel, who has become part of the legend of Richard the Lionheart just
as Alexander's Bucephalus and Heraclius' Dorkon have entered the bes-
tiary of medieval heroes.

The English consolidated their bridgehead and Amathus surrendered
to Richard himself, so that he was able to bring Berengaria and Joanna
ashore and lodge them in comfort after their wearisome journey.
Richard now ordered that his horses should be landed and exercised, and
the next morning, with just fifty knights, he set off to look for the "emperor." It was not long before he met a squadron of Cypriot cavalry,
which he put to flight. However, the cries of these men alerted Isaac,
who had his entire army with him and was enjoying dinner nearby. He
had not expected to be followed by the English, as he did not believe
they had horses with them. Climbing to the top of a hill, Isaac watched

a curious engagement between his own troops and the English. The Cypriots vastly outnumbered Richard's little party, but, at least to his eyes some distance away, they seemed afraid to close in on them and simply fired a few arrows and shouted insults. After a while the English grew bored with this farcical and unknightly display and charged straight into the Greek masses, routing them in a matter of minutes. Again Isaac owed his escape to Fauvel, though his standard-bearer was killed and the standard taken by Richard's own hand. The English infantry had, meanwhile, reached the scene and they enjoyed the opportunity to loot the "emperor's" camp, which was lavishly decorated in an oriental style and was full of exotic luxuries. Richard had a proclamation issued, promising the people of Cyprus that he had not come to fight them and that his quarrel was only with the usurper.

During his voyage from Rhodes, Richard had spoken to people aboard a ship traveling to Europe from Acre who told him that Philip Augustus had arrived at Tyre, where he had struck up an alliance with Conrad of Montferrat. Ships traveling to the Holy Land from Rhodes and Crete carried word of Richard's progress, and it was this news that sparked off the controversy that was to create a schism in the crusader ranks throughout the crusade. On May 11 three galleys entered the harbor at Amathus, bearing important visitors. One of them was no less than Guy of Lusignan, accompanied by his brother Geoffrey, other members of their family, and leading adherents to his cause, including Bohemond III of Antioch and Raymond IV of Tripoli, son of the recently deceased Raymond III. As the King of France had allied himself with Guy's rival Conrad, Guy was desperate to secure the support of the King of England in his struggle to regain his kingdom of Jerusalem. In any case, Richard was his liege lord and he was doing no more than any wise vassal in the circumstances. Richard was overjoyed to meet him, particularly as he was just in time for the royal wedding, which took place the next day, May 12, 1191, amid a show of splendor and luxury aimed to impress the visitors from Outremer.

The ceremony was performed just after dawn, as was traditional, and was conducted by Richard's chaplain Nicholas in the Chapel of St. George in Amathus. It was a magnificent occasion, with everyone going out of their way to outdo each other in the brilliance of their apparel. Richard was never less than the true son of Aquitaine when it came to hosting a splendid celebration.

Following the wedding, Berengaria was obliged to undergo an even more arduous ceremony, her coronation as Queen of England. This took place in the small Orthodox cathedral at Amathus, where the Norman Bishop of Evreux officiated. (Traditionally such a coronation would have been carried out by the Archbishop of Canterbury, but, as described above, Archbishop Baldwin had recently died with the Angevin advance guard at Acre.)

At the completion of the ceremony Richard's seneschal appealed in a ringing voice to the assembled Angevin crusaders for their acceptance of the new queen. Thousands of voices replied in unison, "Vivat Regina." After the "political marriage" came the politics proper, with long discussions between Richard and Guy, during which the future status of Cyprus must have been one of the foremost considerations. Richard, on the advice of his allies the Templars, decided to pursue Isaac, overthrow his power, and place Cyprus under Latin Christian control. Taking refuge at his inland capital of Nicosia, Isaac called for a parley that duly took place in a garden surrounded by fig trees. The chronicles describe at some length what the Lionheart was wearing on this occasion. The magnificence of his attire was no mere affectation: he evidently intended to turn a fashion statement into a political weapon. It was a symbol of his wealth and of the kind of patronage he could grant. Furthermore, it was vital for him to outdo the King of France in all aspects of chivalry, from warfare, to fashion, to music, and even to generosity. Richard wore a tunic of rose-colored samite, a mantle "bedight with small half-moons of solid silver set in rows, interspersed with shining orbs like suns," a scarlet cap and an ornate silken belt. His sword had a golden hilt and its scabbard was finely chased and edged with silver. He wore golden spurs and rode a magnificent Spanish stallion, complete with a golden saddle encrusted with heraldic emblems in silver and gold. In the bright Cypriot sunshine the sight of the lofty Lionheart on his great horse must have dazzled the "emperor" Isaac, so that he fell at the feet of Richard's horse and swore fealty to him, promising to follow him on the crusade and equip 500 knights.

Isaac was not a man to be trusted. Having sworn fealty to Richard that evening he instantly mounted Fauvel, supposedly the fleetest animal in Cyprus, and rode north to Famagusta. When Richard heard the news he decided against hot pursuit, knowing already that Fauvel was faster than any other horse. Instead, Richard boarded his galley and sailed around to the north of the island, while Guy led his mounted knights along the coast road to prevent Isaac doubling back on himself. Richard's patience was growing thin at the time Isaac was costing him, a problem compounded when emissaries sent by Philip Augustus arrived in Constantia. Flying the flag of Jerusalem, a large galley pulled into the Bay of Salamis carrying Drogo of Merle and Philip, Bishop of Beauvais, from the crusader camp at Acre. They met Richard at an awkward time, just as he was discussing his final strategy for the capture of Isaac with his senior advisers. This, combined with the haughty demeanor of the emissaries, notably that of Philip, Bishop of Beauvais, a cousin of King Philip's and no friend of the Lionheart, produced an unfortunate scene. The emissaries began by berating Richard for spending his time killing fellow Christians in Cyprus while the enemies of his faith still held the Holy Land. They told him that the French would not besiege Acre alone while the Angevins wasted their time in Cyprus. Richard's Angevin temper, inherited from his father, now broke out in true earnest and a violent dispute broke out that ended with the French emissaries withdrawing amid curses on both sides. The King of France was justified in upbraiding Richard, if not quite so publicly, yet Richard had little alternative now but to complete the conquest of Cyprus. He dare not leave the island with Isaac still at large, a friend to Saladin and now a very personal enemy of Richard himself. Richard felt that the French complaints were justifiable, and this made him even more angry. He had declared hotly that he would not leave Cyprus for all the wealth in Russia, a curious comment in view of how little was known at that time in the West of the riches (or lack of them) in those almost-fabled lands. He had told the French emissaries to return to their lord and explain that he, Richard, was fighting the crusade here in Cyprus, explaining how the so-called emperor was an ally of Saladin and must be overthrown, so that food supplies could be sent to the Christians of Outremer as in the past. It is not recorded whether Philip Augustus believed Richard's description of Cyprus as the "storehouse of the crusade" or whether he, who knew the Lionheart's personality well, believed Richard was merely indulging his childish adventurism. Suffice it to say that Richard was going to accept no admonition from the French king's emissaries. That same night he set out for Nicosia, personally commanding the rearguard and expecting Isaac to stage an ambush. For all his character defects, Richard was a master of warfare, and he was able to "read" the plans of the feeble Isaac as if he were no more than a child. Like some wretched "Turkopole," as Richard described him, Isaac tried to harass Richard's column before unleashing the expected ambush on the English vanguard. Isaac, spotting Richard himself on his Spanish steed, even had the effrontery to fire two arrows at him, both of which were poisoned and both of which missed. Had Richard been with the vanguard he would undoubtedly have ended his chase after Isaac by personally cutting him down. He did make a token charge but, realizing that his horse was no match for Fauvel, he let Isaac escape once again, this time to the castle of Kantara.

While Richard showed unwonted patience, the Cypriot people were tired of Isaac's antics, which were bringing down the wrath of a powerful king upon their lands. The people of Nicosia duly offered up their city to Richard rather than force him to take it by storm. The King of England responded by declaring that the menfolk should shave their beards and so "Westernize" their appearance. As so often in his life, Richard now fell ill and took to his bed, appointing Guy of Lusignan to take command of his army and complete the campaign. Guy, acting with more ruthlessness than he ever showed as king in Jerusalem, besieged the castle of Kyrenia, where he took Isaac's daughter hostage. Although there seems to have been no intention of harming the girl, the mere fact that she was Richard's prisoner seemed to take all the fight out of her father. To his astonishment, Richard next heard that Isaac had promised to surrender "everything" to Richard so long as his daughter was safe and on the condition that he was not placed in iron chains. When Isaac came to meet Richard, he threw himself down and groveled at his feet. Embarrassed, Richard raised him up and asked him to take his place at the royal table for dinner. Isaac's daughter was brought in to meet her father and, in view of the fact that Richard had taken Fauvel for his own, the King of England decided that iron chains were no longer needed for the unreliable Isaac. The chronicles relate archly that Richard, in response to public knowledge that he had promised not to chain Isaac, had special manacles made from silver so that the "emperor" could retain his dignity.

The conquest of Cyprus had taken just fifteen days, and when the news reached Saladin he was astonished at the speed of the English victory. He was also uneasy at the reputation of this Westerner for whom, it seemed, all the Franks waited in the belief that he would bring them victory. However one views Richard's conquest of Cyprus—and he had many critics at the time as well as later historians who saw the campaign as little more than self-aggrandizement—it has to be conceded that strategically Cyprus was vital to a campaign in the Levant and was, moreover, of inestimable value in the maintenance of Christian supremacy at sea. Furthermore, Richard funded much of the Third Crusade from the money and treasure he pillaged from Isaac's castles and towns in Cyprus, as well as with the money he gained from his sojourn in Sicily. But now Richard knew that time was not in his favor. He must head for Acre and begin the great struggle for which he had left his possessions in the West.

10

———|◆|◆|◆|———

The Fall of Acre 1191

Fᴇᴀʀ ᴏꜰ ᴛʜᴇ ᴜɴᴋɴᴏᴡɴ was to be the undoing of the Muslim cause at Acre. Saladin had long dreaded the arrival of Frederick Barbarossa, but before the elation caused by the emperor's farcical end had died away, a much more real threat from the West burst upon the Muslims in the shape of Richard of England. For months the Franks at Acre had been uplifted by thoughts of the arrival of this famous warrior, boasting that they were conducting the siege of the city but faintly until the arrival of the Lionheart, after which they would assault Acre in full earnest. Saladin had good reason to believe them. His understanding of the psychology of these iron warriors had shown him the value they placed on the prowess of individual commanders. He had seen how a man like Reginald of Chatillon could bring out the best in his men or how the same troops would fight twice as fiercely when commanded by a Conrad of Montferrat rather than a Guy of Lusignan. As the common soldiery idolized the King of England, they would fight for him as for no other. The chroniclers all record that the coming of Richard "put fear into the hearts of the Muslims."

Richard had enhanced his reputation as a conqueror before he so much as set foot in the Holy Land. Saladin had been surprised and shocked at how swiftly and completely he had conquered Cyprus and now, on June 7, as Richard's fleet arrived off the coast of Palestine, Saladin had a further opportunity to appreciate the Lionheart's ruthlessness. A large Muslim cargo ship was trying to bring supplies and reinforcements into Acre and had the misfortune to be intercepted by the English fleet. The vessel was carrying French insignia and had, as further disguise, pigs loose on the deck in a way that would have been unthinkable in a Muslim ship. It was also carrying 700 troops to swell the besieged garrison. Once the ruse had been discovered, Richard ordered his galleys to capture the vessel and a brisk fight now followed. With so many soldiers aboard, the Muslim ship easily held off its attackers until the Lionheart threatened his men with the gallows if they did not take the prize. Men from the Christian galleys now swam under the enemy ship and lashed its rudder so that the Muslim vessel could only turn in wide circles. Under the king's orders his ships prepared to ram the enemy, whose captain, seeing his hopes gone, ordered his men to scuttle the ship to prevent the valuable stores from falling into Christian hands. Of the 800 soldiers and sailors aboard only thirty-five were taken alive, including some skilled military engineers from Aleppo and some emirs who were worth ransoming. The rest either drowned or were slaughtered as they tried to save themselves.

The next day, at dusk, Richard's galley reached Acre and the English king was able to gaze out at the city with its many towers; around it, in the words of the chronicles, "the world's people" were seated in expectation of its capture. Also, beyond Acre, Richard saw "the hill-peaks and the mountains and the valleys and the plains, covered with the tents of Saladin and Safadin and their troops, pressing hard on our Christian host."

The trumpets blared out throughout the crusader camp and bonfires burned along the beaches beside Acre in celebration of Richard's arrival. As Saladin's spies watched in awe, the newly arrived king's treasure trove was landed from his fleet along with thousands of new troops and tons of military supplies. Until that moment the crusaders, however numerous and well armed they might be, had lacked something that the Muslims possessed to their great benefit, and that was unity of command. Saladin imposed upon the many emirs and troops of different nationalities that comprised the army of Islam a unity that grew out of his iron conviction. Against this, Guy of Lusignan seemed a simpleton, Conrad of Montferrat an adventurer, and Philip of France a mere dilettante in the art of war. With the arrival of Richard of England the crusaders felt the presence of the same kind of iron will that the Muslims felt in their leader. Nobody questioned Richard's right to lead the crusade, for his military skills were renowned. His presence exuded confidence, inspiring his men to believe that while he led them defeat was impossible and failure in the crusade unthinkable. Not only did his own knights and common soldiers readily follow his every command, even liegemen of France chose to follow Richard rather than their own lord, Philip Augustus. Most prominent among the lords who joined Richard was Count Henry of Champagne, who had superseded Guy in command of the siege of Acre before the arrival of Richard and Philip. Henry was, in fact, a nephew of both kings, yet it would be unrealistic to suppose that all those who joined Richard's service did so as a result of conscious appreciation of his superiority over the King of France. Richard was not so idealistic that he believed his reputation alone would win him supporters among the freelance knights who were available at Acre. While Philip offered pay of three gold pieces a month, Richard's apparently bottomless purse enabled him to pay four pieces and secure the services of hundreds of extra troops.

No sooner had he arrived at Acre than Richard tried to arrange a meeting with Saladin. The sultan responded to Richard's approach by sending both the kings of England and France a gift of fruit and snow, mixed to produce a kind of sorbet that was much valued as a refreshing dessert in the desert; but he refused a personal interview on the grounds that "kings should not have speech with each other till terms of peace have been arranged." Saladin did, however, agree to send his brother, Safadin, as the Franks were to call al-Adil, but in the end Richard was taken ill and was unable to meet a man with whom he was later to establish the closest relationship. He did reply by sending Saladin a gift of a Negro slave. Richard's behavior at this early stage was unwise in that it might have suggested to his fellow crusaders, who had been besieging Acre for eighteen months, that Richard was not to be trusted. Diplomacy among princes was one thing, but diplomacy between Christians and infidels during a holy war was unacceptable in the eyes of the mass of the pilgrims who comprised the crusader armies.

The loss of the great supply vessel at the hands of the English fleet doubled Muslim woe. It was clear to the garrison that Acre's days were numbered. Yet, just as their prayers had, in their minds, extinguished the German threat from the north, so perhaps Allah was about to intervene for a second time. No sooner had the King of England set up his tent in the crusader camp than he was struck down by the prevalent camp fever,

"Arnaldia," which had already incapacitated Philip Augustus. But Muslim hopes were short-lived. At thirty-four Richard was not to be extinguished as easily as the seventy-year-old German emperor. Nevertheless, Richard's illness, during which it is said that all his hair and nails fell out, and the fact that some of the English transport vessels were held up at Tyre meant that for a while the Angevin onslaught on Acre was delayed.

Meanwhile Philip Augustus tried to maintain the siege himself, only to find that his military skills were inadequate. In the first place, many of his foot soldiers had been attracted to Richard's service by better pay, and as a result, the French king was often short of troops. Nevertheless, he planned an all-out assault on Acre and set about filling the ditches to allow him to maneuver his siege weapons close to the city walls. When he heard what was being planned, the invalid Lionheart refused to allow his own men to join the assault, particularly as he did not trust Philip as a commander. As a military decision this was probably correct, but in the context of a crusade that depended on shared faith and conviction, the decision was questionable. In the event the French assault was a disaster, being heavily repulsed and leading to a major Muslim counterattack that almost broke through into the Christian camp. One result of the French fiasco was that Philip's extensive artillery, with its portable shields and armored roofs, was burned by a sudden sally from the garrison of Acre. Philip was apparently reduced to tears. As usual, he blamed Richard for the catastrophe. The Lionheart had outbid him for the services of many of his own troops, who were supposed to be guarding his siege weapons from just such a threat.

Within days Richard was sufficiently recovered from his illness to be superintending siege operations, propped up in his bed with a crossbow, keeping up a steady and accurate fire against the defenders on the battlements. The siege now took on a final intensity. Huge mangonels, some of Richard's own design, were bombarding the walls or lobbing great stones into the city's open spaces. Some of the stones were especially brought by the Lionheart from the quarries of Cyprus, and one was reputed to be so big that it killed twelve men as it landed.

Once on his feet again Richard was in his element and ready to face the greatest challenge of his career. The walls of Acre, after all, had been built by the sort of military architects whom he knew well, the sort he and his father had employed to build their own fortresses in Europe, though admittedly none that matched Acre's enormous strength.

Whether Richard had been thinking of the task that lay ahead at Acre when he built Mategriffon at Messina is not known, but he had gone to great trouble to have the huge edifice dismantled and brought with him to the Holy Land. Now, with the deep ditches filled, it was possible to wheel up the siege towers so that Acre's high walls were actually over-looked. From the towers the Christian archers were able to control Acre's battlements, keeping up a relentless fire into the city that made every movement by garrison or populace a real danger.

Attrition was the most powerful weapon at the disposal of the cru-saders. While the Muslim garrison could no longer be reinforced, the ar-rival of first the French and then the large numbers of Angevin troops meant that the Christians were able to rotate their assault troops and keep fresh men in the fight. Richard's tactics combined infantry assaults with close investment by his engineers, who battered the walls in some areas and undermined them in others. He built armored roofs to protect his archers and crossbowmen quite close to the city walls and had indeed already operated from under such cover while recuperating from his fever. His main target was the Maledicta Tower and its adjacent walls, and it was kept under almost continual bombardment from the stone-throw-ers. A grim humor accompanied the fighting, with one of the French en-gines being christened "Malvoisin" or "Bad neighbor," while one of the Muslim ones, operating from within Acre, was known as "Malcousine." Several times the bad cousin defeated the bad neighbor, but fortunately the French were able to repair their machine each time. One of the most effective stone-throwers was the communal machine, financed by pious donations from individual crusaders and operated by pilgrims with no previous experience of war, known as "God's own catapult," which shat-tered part of Acre's strongest walls, reducing it to little more than the height of a man and requiring the Muslims to station most of their troops there to guard against a breakthrough. However, it was Richard's engineers who made the decisive breach on the night of July 5, when they brought the Maledicta Tower crashing down. Richard threw him-self into the battle, joining in the demolition work to accelerate the tower's collapse. So dangerous was the task of pulling the stones away from the breach that the king offered first two, then three, and finally four bezants for each stone pulled clear. However great the reward, his men knew that they were risking their lives under the walls, with Mus-lim archers hanging by their feet from the battlements to get better shots at them with their bows. Both sides were at the extreme of their effort, and only the supreme example of courage and leadership shown by the Lionheart at this time helped the Christians to prevail. Yet the very success of these major excavations proved the undoing of many of the infantry assaults. So much stone rubble was brought down by the miners and the bombardiers that the garrison still found much to act as barricades against the Christian attacks, each of which was prohibitively costly. On July 6 and 11 Richard launched full-scale assaults on the wrecked Maledicta Tower, but each was repulsed.

While Richard tightened his grip, Saladin did all he could to drag the King of England's fingers from the throat of Acre. As the crusaders prepared to attack, signalers from within the city contacted Saladin's camp with flashing lights or drumbeats to call on him to launch an attack on the Christian camp. This was almost a daily occurrence, but the fortifications there were now stronger than ever. After the collapse of the Maledicta Tower, Saladin launched a great attack with his field army to try to relieve pressure on Acre's garrison, but by now it was clear that he could not break the siege and relieve the city. This was the conclusion reached by the Muslim commanders inside Acre, and they knew that surrender was inevitable.

Saladin, on the other hand, alternated between hope and despair. He threw himself readily into every skirmish, and his efforts were so intense that his health suffered under the strain. On July 3 he ate nothing and drank only the medicine his doctors forced on him as he rode about the ranks of his troops, tearstained and virtually insane with passion. But in his despair Saladin was deceiving himself: Acre was lost from the moment he had allowed Guy of Lusignan to consolidate his camp, thereby providing the military strength of Western Europe with a landing place on the coast of Palestine. In a sense, the kings of England and France had arrived merely to administer the coup de grace to a fatally wounded enemy.

After July 11 the garrison simply could not continue the fight. Three emirs escaped by boat and made their way to Saladin's camp. He imprisoned them as cowards. The collapse of the Acre garrison had been cumulative. Each time they repulsed an assault they could not retire to rest like the crusaders; they had to endure continual bombardment from the siege weapons and constant missile fire from the siege towers. For them there was no rest. Richard sent emissaries to Saladin's camp to discuss peace. The men were no more than spies who, while they bought snow and fruit in the Muslim market, assessed the morale of the Muslim troops. It was clearly low. They reported back that unless Saladin could drive the crusaders away, Acre was doomed. This realization did not dawn on Saladin until a messenger brought him news at the end of the next day's fighting. The man, who had swum out from the doomed city, brought him an ultimatum from Acre's commanders, his old comrades al-Mashtub, a Kurd like himself, and Karakush, the architect from Cairo, who had ridden with Saladin when he had left Egypt to begin the holy war. Saladin knew the mettle of such men, and so when he read the despair in their words he knew that nothing now could save the city. They wrote that they must buy their lives from the Franks by surrendering Acre the following day unless, by a miracle or by the strong arm of the sultan himself, the Frankish siege lines could be broken. But Saladin's own troops had lost confidence in him and would not obey his orders. Only a group of Kurdish horsemen, kin to al-Mashtub, kept up the struggle to break the Christian siege lines, joined by such individual heroes as the Mameluke 'Izz-ad-Din Jurdik, who threw himself into the fray but could not effect a breakthrough. Saladin took the news so badly that for a while he seemed almost bereft of his senses. Certainly, he was never the same commander that he had been after Hattin.

On July 12 the Muslim commanders in Acre accepted Christian terms for the surrender of the city, with the garrison imprisoned by the Franks until their terms were met. Three were of particular importance. The True Cross lost at the battle of Hattin was to be restored, 1,600 Christian prisoners held by Saladin at Damascus were to be released and 200,000 bezants were to be paid to Richard and Philip Augustus, along with 40,000 to Conrad of Montferrat, who had negotiated the surrender. Throughout the crusader camp heralds proclaimed the news and warned that henceforth the Muslims were not to be injured or molested. The Acre garrison now emerged from the city and entered captivity while the Christian lords hastened inside, planting their banners on the walls and towers of the city. It was like a carnival, with Christians praising God, dancing, and jostling happily in the streets of the city that had denied them access for nearly two years. In the division of the spoils the best of the prisoners, the richest and most important at least, were divided between the two kings, along with the best lodgings within the city. As if to show that the relative positions of the two kings had changed somewhat since they left Europe, Richard gained possession of the royal palace while Philip Augustus had to make do with the Templars' house. It was an exact reversal of how it had been in Messina, and the King of France was not slow to notice how Richard's stock rose as his declined.

The problem facing the newly arrived crusaders was that they were the last reinforcements planned from Europe and therefore the entire strength of the crusading movement at that time was gathered at Acre. In spite of—some might say because of—the great success of the siege, they were now burdened with the unwelcome responsibility of 3,000 prisoners from the Muslim garrison. While some of them might be metaphorically worth their weight in gold, most were not only "useless mouths" who had to be fed at Christian cost but dangerous in that they had to be guarded by a large number of crusaders who were needed to fight Saladin's field army. Had the crusaders taken Acre by assault, many of these prisoners would have died in the fighting or been massacred in the aftermath, so the problem would not have arisen. Now, however, there were two alternatives facing the Christian leaders in dealing with 3,000 trained enemy soldiers: ransom them and release them to Saladin when the money was paid, or imprison them at Christian expense. The Byzantine emperor Basil II had found a third possibility when faced with a similar problem after the surrender of a Bulgarian army in 1014. He had blinded ninety-nine out of each hundred men and left a single-eyed soldier to lead each group of hundred men back to Bulgaria. Such ruthlessness had its intended effect when the Bulgarian state was crippled for years by the need to support so many blind men in a relatively primitive society. As God's representative on earth the Byzantine emperor had religious opinion on his side, and so whatever he did would have the backing of the only moral force that counted for anything in his day. Richard and Philip Augustus, however, had no such certainties. The fall of Acre was merely part of an ongoing war, and who was to say that the positions might not one day be reversed and Christian prisoners might fall into the hands of Saladin, as after the great defeat at Hattin four years before?

When Saladin heard that his commanders in Acre were contemplating surrender he was absolutely opposed to it. He wished them to fight to the last, and when his emirs sent to ask for his permission to accept the Christian terms Saladin refused. However, the sultan's wishes were overtaken by events and, even as he prepared to continue his attempts to aid the defenders, he saw Christian banners break out on the walls of Acre. The siege of Acre was over. All that was left for Saladin was to meet the ransom terms, just as Balian of Ibelin had when the Muslims took Jerusalem in 1187. At first all seemed to go well, with messengers traveling between Acre and Saladin's camp at Shefr' Am in complete safety. Saladin welcomed envoys sent by Richard to inspect the Christian prisoners at Damascus, who were due to be released. In doing so, at least in the eyes of the Christians, he was accepting the surrender terms made by his emirs at Acre, albeit without his authority. However, although the fall of Acre had imposed a period of peace between the warring sides during the negotiations, now that their task had been achieved the Christians had fallen to squabbling among themselves. The common soldiers who had borne the brunt of the fighting felt robbed that Acre should have been surrendered without their being able to pillage and loot so rich a city. Ransoming emirs was not their business. They demanded a share in the spoils or they would desert. The chronicles do not reveal which troops took this unspiritual if entirely reasonable view, but it is likely to have been Italian mercenaries rather than the troops of the feudal lords, particularly those English and French crusaders who had followed their kings in the hope of salvation rather than reward. Nevertheless, crusades were conducted as self-financing operations, and in the century since the First Crusade men had come to realize how expensive it was for them and for their leaders to support large-scale military operations thousands of miles from home. As a result, Richard bowed to the pressures from below and agreed to share some of the spoils with the rank and file, but only with those men who joined him in swearing their allegiance to the crusade for three years or until Saladin had surrendered the Holy Land to the Christians. Richard swore in public to honor this oath and many simple men joined him. Significantly, Philip Augustus did not swear, his mind already turning on the problem of how he could go home without too much loss of face, claiming that the capture of Acre released him from his crusading oaths taken back in France.

While the King of France wrestled with his conscience, the King of England was doing what he did best, apart from fighting, which was to make unnecessary enemies. A week after the city had surrendered, Richard took Berengaria and Joanna from the confines of their floating palace and allowed them to set foot on land. The royal party, after walking through the streets of Acre, now cleared of all vestiges of fighting or Muslim occupation, entered the royal palace where the ladies were to remain throughout the crusade. Reveling no doubt in the glory of the moment, Richard suddenly saw something that set off a temper. In the part of the city that was under his jurisdiction he saw an unknown banner flying from one of the towers. Not recognizing the heraldic device depicted on the flag, he asked his companions to whom the banner belonged and was told that it was Archduke Leopold of Austria's banner and it flew there because the duke and his men had besieged that tower. Richard could have left the German the little part of Acre that he had won and for which he had left his Austrian lands to travel with Barbarossa's crusade. It would have been the generous thing to do for a king whose conquests lay in his wake everywhere he traveled. But at moments like this the Angevins had no generosity. Their tempers drove out all reason. Just as Richard's father had called down the judgment of God on himself for his anger against Archbishop Thomas of Canterbury, so now a thoughtless moment would cost Richard his liberty and his English subjects their wealth. Once he heard that the banner was that of a petty nobleman, from Germany at that, he ordered his men to tear it down and trample it in the dust. He then sought out Leopold and angrily insulted him for his pretension. In the face of the undisputed leader of the crusade, for Philip Augustus had no interest in the military side of the crusade and appeared more interested in filling his treasure chests, Leopold of Austria could do no more than suffer in silence. But the insult was never to be forgotten or forgiven, and Richard's treatment of the proud Austrian showed little appreciation of how to command men. Burning with indignation, Leopold abandoned the crusade forthwith and returned home to plot his revenge.

Philip Augustus felt he also had reason enough to leave Outremer after the fall of Acre. Apart from the fact that proximity to Richard served only to remind him how much he disliked the English king, there was also a major financial incentive to return to France. In the first place, Philip of Flanders had died, yielding him an opportunity to benefit from the deceased's extensive lands on the borders of France. Furthermore, with Richard adding daily to his reputation as a crusader, he would not be available to defend his lands in Normandy and Aquitaine should Philip decide to settle any border disputes in his absence. Recognizing Richard's preeminence as a military commander, Philip requested leave of absence from him, sending four of his chief noblemen to explain to the Lionheart the fact that ill health made it essential that their king return to France.

Richard was scornful of such an excuse, saying, "If he leaves undone the work for which he came hither he will bring shame and everlasting contempt upon himself and upon France; so he will not go by my counsel. But if he must needs either go or die, let him do what pleases him and his folk." It is doubtful if Richard was much concerned whether the King of France went or stayed, as long as he left his troops behind to aid the crusade. Philip, however, though prepared to leave the fighting to those who enjoyed it, acknowledged nobody his master when political negotiation was concerned. If he was going to leave his troops, then Richard was going to have to pay them himself. Moreover, he would demand half of Cyprus, according to the agreement he had made with Richard at Vézelay to share all the spoils of the crusade. Richard refused to entertain this for a moment. The schism between the two became so wide that, but for the presence of numerous bishops and senior clerics to remind them of their spiritual purpose in the Holy Land, it is likely that they would have taken up arms against each other out of pure hatred.

While Richard and Philip maintained and even increased their hostility, a second dispute threatened the spirit of Christian unity. It concerned the question of who should be the king of the now apparently revived kingdom of Jerusalem. Guy was the man in possession, but many of his own people felt that he had lost the throne at Hattin and, with the death of his wife Sibylla, through whom he claimed the crown, it was time to turn to a more able candidate. That man was Conrad of Montferrat, whose tenacity in holding on to the city of Tyre had enabled reinforcements from Europe to come to the aid of the beleaguered Guy in the first place. This dispute mirrored that between Richard and Philip Augustus, with Guy seeking help from the King of England while Conrad chose the King of France as his protector. It was clear that until a decision was taken as to who occupied the throne of Jerusalem, no progress could be made toward reconquering the rest of the kingdom. At Richard's palace in Acre a meeting of the crusader leaders eventually decided on a compromise. Guy was to continue as king in his lifetime, but on his death he would be succeeded by Conrad and his new wife Isabel or by their heirs. It was a decision that solved nothing. A man like Conrad would not accept a mere parvenu like Guy as his liege lord, particularly when the throne should have been held by his family and would have been had not his brother, William Longsword, died so suddenly in 1177. Guy had merely picked up Conrad's lost property and, what is more, had squandered it by his abysmal leadership at the battle of Hattin. With his patron Philip Augustus now more determined than ever to leave for home and with Richard in the ascendancy, it became obvious to Conrad that he would be best served by returning to Tyre and waiting to see the outcome of what was clearly now an Angevin crusade.

Richard's efforts to persuade Philip Augustus to stay with the crusade were in truth halfhearted. Cynics might suspect that the King of England would have felt happier to have the King of France where he could keep an eye on him. Certainly he insisted that Philip take an oath before departing that he would not invade Angevin lands while Richard was on crusade, nor within forty days after Richard's return. On the other hand, the removal of his great rival left the Lionheart in undisputed command of the military campaign, which was how he and the rest of the crusader army preferred it. Hugh, Duke of Burgundy, who was to remain as commander of the French contingent, stood surety for his monarch's oath, but would henceforth be seen as Richard's lieutenant rather than fellow commander. The spoils that Philip had gained from the capture of Acre were handed over to Conrad of Montferrat. At the beginning of August the French king sailed with Conrad to Tyre and then embarked for Europe in some borrowed Genoese vessels. It was a thoroughly discreditable performance on Philip's part, particularly as his true reason for leaving the Holy Land had nothing to do with his health.

With Philip's departure there was no longer a focus of opposition to Richard's command. Although there were Germans and Italians present who much resented the Lionheart, the vast majority of the crusaders knew that their best hope of victory lay in following a commander of proven ability. Nevertheless, on one occasion only the intervention of the Templars prevented some dissidents from taking up arms and attacking Richard in person. Richard understood that soldiers needed to be kept busy if minor issues were not to assume too great a significance and lead to fighting. The Pisans and Genoese, forever at war with each other while at home in Italy, served together for their faith as long as Richard's strong authority prevailed. French and Angevin soldiers were also more accustomed to being on opposite sides than fighting shoulder to shoulder against the infidels. The problems of commanding an international army should never be underestimated, and Richard's achievement in getting the best out of men who, in Europe, had been brought up to hate and resent him was considerable.

In the weeks following the capture of Acre, Richard had time to assess the military situation and to devise a strategy for the campaign ahead. It had become very clear to him from what he had seen, and from what he had learned from the local knights and nobles and from the military orders, that a direct attack on Jerusalem, even if successful, would provide only temporary success. Once the Western crusaders returned home then Saladin, or his successor, would easily reconquer Jerusalem. The disaster at Hattin had resulted in the loss of many trained soldiers, so that the local Latin Christians no longer possessed the military strength to garrison the castles and fortresses, nor could they equip a major army to prevent the Muslims from constantly raiding the kingdom and undermining the everyday life of the people.

Meanwhile, Saladin faced the problem of having just thirty days to meet the conditions of a treaty he had neither signed nor agreed to. The sum demanded to ransom the garrison was simply too large for him to assemble at short notice. Nevertheless, the agreement had been signed, and August 20 was the day set aside for both sides to keep to its conditions. In the Christian camp Richard was facing a problem that had not been anticipated when Acre was originally surrendered. At that time Philip Augustus had been present and had taken half of the emirs and important prisoners for ransom. However, now a month later, he had left the Holy Land after handing the prisoners to Conrad of Montferrat, who had returned to Tyre, taking them with him. When Richard asked him to return them so that he could honor the agreement to ransom them to Saladin, Conrad simply refused. It was not until Richard sent Hugh of Burgundy to Tyre that Conrad complied. In his temper Richard had at first intended to go there himself and take the prisoners by force, but, fortunately for the future of the crusade as a whole, he was persuaded to let the French solve their own problems. Now that Richard was ready to meet his obligations under the Acre agreement, he expected the same of Saladin. However, Saladin was not ready and tried to delay, hoping to win more time to raise the sum required. In view of the tragic outcome it is as well to point out that there is no definitive account of what was finally decided. Richard and Saladin later accused each other of bad faith, but it may have been a result of the difficulties of working through interpreters.

The most pressing problem facing Richard, of course, was what to do with the Muslim garrison of Acre. He could not keep them imprisoned after the main army marched south from Acre without having to leave behind a large force of guards. The longer he allowed Saladin to delay ransoming these prisoners, the later the crusaders could begin their campaign. For all he knew, Saladin might have a military reason for his delaying tactics. For instance, he might be expecting reinforcements to reach him from Egypt. Richard felt that the Acre garrison was now keeping him prisoner in Acre when he should be marching south to begin the campaign to regain Jerusalem. On August 20, the day Richard believed he had agreed with Saladin that the first installment of the ransom should be paid, Richard moved the whole Christian army out of Acre and spent the morning awaiting news from the Muslim camp, but none was forthcoming. At midday, watchers on the hills saw Richard ride out of Acre with an array of his knights. These Muslim spies reported that the King of England's army was now occupying the whole plain outside Acre. What they next saw terrified them and caused them to send instant appeals to Saladin for help. The Muslim garrison of Acre, numbering perhaps 3,000 men, was marched out of the city, roped together, with their hands bound behind them. As soon as they passed within the lines of Christian soldiers there was an appalling massacre: the crusaders leaped upon them, stabbed them, and hacked off their heads. Everything happened so quickly that Saladin's watching troops could do nothing except charge madly against the assembled crusader ranks and add to the Muslim casualties. Vengeance was all that was left, and Saladin's troops kept up a futile assault until nightfall brought an end to the fighting. Three thousand Muslim prisoners, the whole garrison except the few emirs who could pay their own ransoms rather than rely on Saladin, lay dead on the plain outside Acre, victims of either an atrocity or a calculated military decision, depending on which chronicle one believes. Who was to blame? Again there is no easy answer. Richard felt justified in doing what he did, because in his eyes Saladin had broken their agreement and the fate of the prisoners was in his hands. Militarily, the 3,000 Muslims comprised a drain on the crusader army and a potential risk to Acre if they were allowed to remain there. If Saladin failed to ransom his soldiers then the fault was his, not their captor's.

Saladin's handling of the problem of the Acre garrison has left him open to as much criticism as was leveled at Richard himself. Modern historians have questioned whether Saladin ever intended to ransom men whom he could not afford to pay and feed and keep in the field with his army. Mere numbers were not a problem for the Muslim armies of this period. It was quality rather than quantity that was needed in action against the Frankish knights, and no commander could afford to support an army too large for the countryside to support. Moreover, a massacre of the kind perpetrated by the Christians might serve a propaganda purpose in the holy war, enraging Muslims everywhere and making them more determined to avenge their fallen comrades. It might also undermine Richard's reputation, even among his own people. However, if Saladin hoped to gain a propaganda victory with the lives of his slaughtered soldiers, he was to be disappointed. Richard's reputation may have declined in the eyes of his coreligionists, but as a demonstration of his ruthlessness it scored a propaganda triumph over Saladin's emirs and soldiers. After the fall of Acre no Muslim garrison could be relied on to resist Richard. The very existence of the Lionheart seemed to diminish the morale of Saladin's troops, even if the sultan himself was present.

Saladin's anger in the aftermath of the massacre was as great as at any time in his career. He even allowed his men to commit atrocities against Christian prisoners, aware that after the massacre of their families and friends they needed an avenue for revenge. It was not his way, yet twice before he had bowed to public pressure and allowed such acts of vengeance, after the capture of Reginald's pirates in the Red Sea and with the killing of the Templars and Hospitallers after the battle of Hattin. Nevertheless, Saladin soon reined back his feelings and once again was saving Christian prisoners from the natural wrath of his soldiers on the grounds that "blood never rests" and that the holy war was a just war that spilled no unnecessary blood.

11

—————|◆|◆|◆|—————

The Coast Road 1191–1192

THE FALL OF ACRE marked a watershed in the history of the Third Crusade. For Philip Augustus of France it was a symbolic achievement that enabled this unenthusiastic crusader to justify his return to France. For Richard of England it marked the end of an uneasy alliance with his main European adversary and an opportunity to enjoy outright control of not only the crusading army but also the strategy to be adopted by the crusade as a whole. As a warrior Richard far outshone Saladin. However, as a student of men Saladin had an advantage that Richard could hardly even suspect. Richard made enemies among his powerful allies, notably in Philip of France, Conrad of Montferrat, and Leopold of Austria, men who could do him harm; and the friends he made were among his enemies, like Safadin, who could do him no good in the long run.

Acre provided the crusaders with a foothold in the Holy Land and a base from which to begin the reconquest. As a result, Richard took his time about beginning to exploit his success. Under his personal supervision the fortress city was repaired and remilitarized, with the command of the garrison being given to two of his most trusted lieutenants, Bertram of Verdon and Stephen of Longchamp. Berengaria and Joanna took up residence in the palace, along with the captive "Damsel of Cyprus," daughter of the dethroned "emperor" Isaac Comnenus.

Although Acre had returned to being a Christian city, for the Westerners it remained exotic. After the horrors of the siege many easily succumbed to the luxuries of an Eastern way of life, where loose women were quite unlike the dirty drabs to be found in Western cities. Richard had extreme difficulty clearing the inns and brothels in order to get his men on the road to Ascalon. By August 23, however, the army was ready to begin the march south. This was to be the decisive event of the entire crusade. If by completing it Richard succeeded in his strategic aim of taking control of the entire coastline, he would be able to use his supremacy at sea to support a march inland from Jaffa to capture Jerusalem. Unlike Guy of Lusignan's army on its fatal march to Tiberias, Richard's army could gain continual reinforcement and replenishment from the fleet. However, until the coastal cities of Caesarea, Jaffa, and even Ascalon were in his hands, Richard knew that to march inland toward Jerusalem might involve risking a second and even more devastating "Hattin."

Almost a century of Christian occupation of the Holy Land had taught the crusaders how to combat their Turkish enemies; modern historians neglect this fact at their peril. The local knights of Outremer were far from being headstrong and, even if the disaster at Hattin and the foolhardiness of a man like Gerard of Ridefort seem to indicate the contrary, the knights of the military orders were the backbone of Richard's army and men on whom he knew he could rely for local information and tactics.

However, Richard was always prepared to hazard his own life in a way that he would never have asked of others. Frustrated by the delays around Acre, he made personal forays, accompanied by a few spirited knights, against raiding parties of Turks. One such, just before the army left Acre on its march south, might have cost the life or at least liberty of its commander. The incident also illustrates the multinational nature of the crusader army. There had been a Turkish raid on the crusader camp. As Richard was mounted at the time, he chased after the retreating Turks in the company of a Hungarian count and several of his Hungarian knights. As the chronicles relate, Richard "pursued the Turks further than was expedient," so that the Hungarian nobleman and the king's marshal, Hugh of Poitou, were taken prisoner. Virtually invincible in combat, Richard was untouched, yet he made several charges in an attempt to rescue his marshal, only to see him swept away into captivity by the superior speed of the enemy.

The journey from Acre to Jaffa was a distance of some eighty miles, along a broken road with eight rivers to be crossed. Moreover, it was conducted in the heat of a Levantine summer, all the time under harassment from an army two or three times as strong as the Christian force. The march, irrespective of the victory at Arsuf, must be counted one of the greatest in military history and sufficient alone to elevate Richard the Lionheart to the ranks of great commanders, as well as to give the lie to those who believe that the art of generalship was asleep between the time of the Romans and the Renaissance. History records the achievements of many "great" generals, where victory alone is enough to build reputations, without any consideration of the quality of both the opposing commander and his troops. Richard's victories at Acre, Arsuf, and Jaffa were achieved at the expense of an inspirational leader in Saladin, who led an army that had not known defeat under his command and who had enjoyed years of continuous success against the Franks. Seen in this context, Richard's military achievements are outstanding; the difficulties he had to overcome must not be underestimated. He had numerous insubordinate knights in his own ranks, as well as those in the Templars and Hospitallers, and had to enforce his command over men of many different nationalities, some of whom, notably the French, were actively hostile to him. Richard moved his army with a chesslike precision that, on a smaller scale, resembled the Duke of Marlborough's famous march to the Danube, before the battle of Blenheim in 1704.

A century of warfare in Outremer had provided Richard with clear lessons. In a sense, his march to Jaffa was a return to traditional Frankish tactics that had been forgotten or disregarded by Guy of Lusignan only four years before at Hattin. The strength of the crusader armies lay not so much in the hitting power of the Frankish knight alone, as the Turks so often assumed, but in the combination of such mounted strength with the defensive "armor" of the infantry, notably the crossbowmen, whose weapons were far more effective than those of the Turkish horse archers they faced. If the crusader leaders managed to curb the natural élan of their knights and hold them ready to administer the "shock" to the enemy, victory would be theirs; but if their knights charged prematurely and allowed themselves to be drawn in pursuit of the retreating Turks, they would fall an easy prey to their more mobile opponents. And, above all, the Franks should never forget that they were strangers in Outremer and were unsuited to the climate and the desert and mountain terrain. Were they to allow themselves to be drawn away from the coastline, where they were able to be supplied by their command of the sea, they would suc-

cumb to a more skillful and well-adapted enemy. It was with these fundamental facts in mind that Richard prepared his march from Acre.

In medieval times moving an army was a vast exercise in logistics.
Normally thousands of packhorses, mules, and ox-drawn wagons would
have been needed, but in the peculiar circumstances in which the crusaders found themselves—they were, in fact, no more than an invading
army with a toehold on the coast—men would have to serve as beasts of
burden. As a result, Richard divided his infantry into two parts, alternat-
ing them throughout the march: those not fighting could be "resting" by
marching along the beach, flanked on their right by the sea and the fleet
and on the left by the cavalry. The price they paid for being safe was that
they had to carry the baggage.

To the left of the infantry on the beach was the cavalry, which was organized into twelve squadrons that covered the entire length of the column, a distance of several miles. They were assembled by nationality, but
were also studded with "star" knights to give leadership and inspiration
and to help coordinate their efforts with the infantry who marched on
their left. Richard alternated the vanguards and rearguards between the
Templars and the Hospitallers, who had vital local knowledge and who
were also equipped with swarms of light horsemen, or Turcopoles, who
fought in the style of the Turks and who helped to scout for the army.
Behind the military orders came first the English and Norman contingent of knights who had traveled with Richard himself and then the
French knights commanded by Hugh, Duke of Burgundy. Finally, the
Syrian knights, the local chivalry who had survived Hattin, rode either
with Guy of Lusignan or under those who no longer recognized Guy
and favored Conrad of Montferrat.

To the left of the knights and acting as a form of human armor for
their horses marched the other half of the infantry. These men, who included most of the crossbowmen, marched so close together that it was
said that a casually thrown apple could hardly have struck the ground
without first striking one of the Frankish foot soldiers.

We are fortunate in having accurate and detailed accounts of
Richard's great march from Acre to Jaffa. Among the chronicles of the
Third Crusade is that of Richard of Howden, who marched with
Richard's army. There is also the detailed and balanced Muslim account
by Baha al-Din, a man much trusted by Saladin himself, who shared the
sultan's councils at this time.

Richard realized that in the tremendous heat of late August he would have to move his army with due caution, using only the morning for marching and resting on every alternate day. As a result it took him nearly nineteen days to march the eighty miles from Acre to Jaffa. On the other hand, he knew that he had with him virtually the entire military strength of the crusading cause and a second Hattin would lose the Christians their final foothold in the Holy Land. In addition, the Turks harassed his army continuously. While Saladin played a similar role to Richard's as general and strategist, he never tried to emulate the English king's personal performance as a warrior. In a very real sense Richard was the supreme warrior of his time.

Richard had the choice of two roads south from Acre: one an inland route, the best approach to Jerusalem; the other following the coast, a longer road to the Holy City but one that enabled the crusaders to keep in close touch with the fleet offshore, their lifeline to Cyprus and Western Europe. Richard chose the latter, an old Roman road now much reduced to little more than a track. From the high ground about two miles inland, Saladin was able to watch the crusaders' every move and harass them whenever he chose. However, as at Hattin, Saladin chose to let the march develop relatively unhindered so that he could attack the crusaders as they became tired and dropped their guard.

On the first day Richard led the vanguard himself, riding with the knights of the Temple as if throwing down the gauntlet to the watching Turks. Directly behind him were his English and Norman knights surrounding the royal banner that marked the rallying point for the crusaders in battle. Emulating the example of the Milanese forces at the battle of Legnano in 1176, Richard had affixed the royal standard to a very tall pole, possibly even the mast of a ship, which was covered in iron to protect it from being cut down or burned, and fixed to a wagon drawn by four horses. A select body of knights were set aside to guard the banner, and the mobility of this massive emblem enabled it to be used effectively to issue silent commands in the confusion of battle.

The first day of the march demonstrated the problems the crusaders would face very clearly. The old Roman road soon began to break up with the passage of so large an army, and the rearguard, traveling in the dust of those ahead of them and struggling across the broken ground, began to fall behind. The Turks, watching continually for any sign of weakness, swooped down on the confused rearguard, trying to separate it from the rest of the army and sweep it into the sea. However, Richard had made allowances for just such an eventuality and had positioned himself, and a group of select knights, on the extreme left of the march so that he could ride to the aid of any section that was in danger. When John Fitzluke rode forward to tell him of the danger to the rearguard, Richard at once galloped to the rescue, falling upon the Turks "like a thunderbolt," in the words of the chronicler, who continued, "and they fled before him like the Philistines from the face of the Maccabee." It was to be just one of many examples where Richard's personal involvement in the fighting turned the tide in the favor of the crusaders. Saladin, watching from the hills, must have been impressed. But this shrewd man must also have realized the importance of this one great warrior to the Christians and considered how each such personal intervention must have tired him.

At times it seemed as if nature itself was at war with the crusaders. As the column passed along the seashore the heat became unbearable, with many men fainting and others, already overburdened with the heavy baggage they were carrying, falling and dying in the burning sands. Richard had the dead buried where they fell and the sick transported to the ships off the coast so that the Muslims would not see how many men he had lost. Each night, as the army camped, the crusaders were tormented by an enemy unseen in daytime but every bit as numerous and as insistent as their Muslim foes. Albert of Aix had called them "serpents" when the men of the First Crusade had encountered them a century before; although their sting was as painful and dangerous as that of a snake they were, in fact, tarantulas. These huge spiders crept inside the clothing of the soldiers, inflicting painful stings. For those who could afford them there were ointments and antidotes to "assuage the tumors" that swelled up on the injured body, but many sufferers sought a solution in sympathetic medicine, hoping that the "touch" of their leaders or better still of the king himself would effect a cure. In the event, prevention was found more effective than any kind of cure, and the men resorted to a cacophony of noise in an attempt to keep the spiders at bay. According to the chronicler, this was done by clashing together "shields, helms, saddlegear, poles, jars, flagons, basins, pans, plates and anything else that was handy for making a noise."

The Franks moved on without further interruption and made camp at Cayphas, now the modern city of Haifa, little more than ten miles from their starting point at Acre. Here they rested for two days. Their journey so far had been less a battle with the Turks than one with the climate, the terrain, and their own transport. Carrying the heavy baggage typical of Western campaigning was impossible in the heat of a Levantine summer. As a result, the decision was taken to cut back on baggage as far as possible and the beach around Cayphas became a dumping ground for unwanted paraphernalia. On August 27 the march continued, wending inland around the point of Carmel to Carphanaum and then back toward the sea at Athlit, where they waited for a further two days until the fleet was able to put in to shore and supply much-needed provisions.

Saladin must have been impressed by the crusaders' discipline and he must also have reflected on how much more daunting an opponent the English king was compared with Guy of Lusignan at Hattin. So far, apart from the confusion in the rearguard at the start of the march, Richard had given the Turks no opportunity to break up his formation. The occasional raids by Turkish horse archers had been easily dispersed by the crossbowmen, without the knights having to emerge from their infantry "armor." Nevertheless, Saladin was no passive observer and he kept shifting his camp down the line of the crusader advance, seeking an opportunity to bring his enemy to battle. Near Carmel the hills were too steep for him to launch his cavalry. He knew that patience was his ally: just as Richard knew that he dare not risk a second Hattin, so Saladin was aware that he possessed the one unified Muslim army. Were he to be caught in the open by a charge of these "iron men," Jerusalem and the holy war might both be lost.

On the approach to Caesarea the crusaders crossed the "river of crocodiles," named after two swimming knights had been devoured by the reptiles. Once again the fleet brought in supplies to the port of Caesarea, including reinforcements in the shape of some of the "lazy folk" who had been rounded up at last in Acre and reminded of their duty. The first blood spilled by many of the crusaders on the march came from scratches on the faces of the foot soldiers from the thick bushes that covered their path. Moreover, their feet were constantly disturbing a host of small rodents known as jerboa, which kept leaping up in their hundreds, at first alarming and eventually amusing the Europeans, who had not seen their like before. Each evening, before everyone slept, the peace of the night was broken by the voice of one of the priests crying out loudly, "Sanctum Sepulchrum Adjuva," or "Help us, O Holy Sepulchre!" At once the entire host would take up the cry of the solitary voice, after which the priest would repeat his cry twice more and then peace returned, leaving each crusader alone with his fears and his thoughts, but secure in the knowledge that he was carrying out God's will.

Saladin was becoming restless. His waiting game, though essentially the right tactics, was having no effect of breaking the discipline of this remarkable army. After the crusaders marched out of Caesarea on September 1, he knew that he would have to increase the pressure by unleashing his light cavalry from the hills. Full-scale fighting broke out as the Turks attacked all along the line of march. But the Turks faced the eternal problem of harassing crusading armies on the march. If they stayed out of range of the Christian infantry crossbowmen, they could not inflict casualties on the knights' mounts with their own arrows, which were lighter and less penetrating than the quarrels or bolts fired by the crossbows. If, however, they closed in and attempted to make their shots count, they risked very heavy casualties from the Frankish infantry. And, if the crusading knights charged and caught them on open ground, they would suffer annihilation. It was a fine decision for both sides, and for the moment, neither was prepared to risk all in a general engagement. Baha al-Din describes the problems Saladin's warriors had in getting to grips with the Christian knights, who were guarded by the infantry cover on their left.

> The enemy moved in order of battle: their infantry marched between us and their cavalry, keeping as level and firm as a wall. Each foot-soldier had a thick cassock of felt and under it a mail-shirt so strong that our arrows made no impression on them. They, meanwhile, shot at us with crossbows which struck down horse and man among the Muslims. I noted among them men who had from one to ten shafts sticking in their backs, yet trudged on at their ordinary pace and did not fall out of their ranks.

During the following week Saladin became more and more desperate as he failed to break the discipline of Richard's army. Throughout this time the main bulk of the Muslim forces was little more than two miles away from the crusaders' line of march and there was a continual series of skirmishes as he threw increasing numbers of his men onto the infantry wall but without success. All the chroniclers, including Baha al-

Din, report the death of one of Saladin's favorite Mamelukes, Aiaz el-Tawil, a mighty man who carried a lance thicker in the shaft than any two of the Christian lances. He had been in the habit of challenging individual Christian champions to single combat until at last he was overmatched. The Christians cut off his head and refused to allow the Muslims to regain his body, whereupon his friends cut off their horses' tails in their misery. The crusaders reached a river, which they named the "Dead River," about three miles beyond Caesarea, and crossed it safely in spite of the fact that the Turks had tried to make it a trap by concealing it with reeds and rushes. Again thwarted by the careful progress of the Christians, the Turks withdrew to a position farther up the same river and for two days the armies camped peacefully. Richard, in one of the forays, was wounded in the side by a spear, but it was just a flesh wound and it served only to "excite him against his enemies."

Matters now took a distinct turn in favor of the Muslims. The coast road beyond Caesarea was so bad that it became almost impassable for the thousands of horsemen who traveled with the Christian army and Richard was forced to make a strategic decision to move up the left bank of the Dead River until he reached the inland road. Here the terrain was quite woody and the Turks were able to conceal their movements until the last moment, when they fell upon the crusaders. Even so, Saladin was not yet prepared to risk an all-out fight. He had made a choice of battleground, and as yet the Christians had not suffered enough attrition to weaken them so that his victory would be assured. As a result, Saladin merely increased the harassment of the Franks until they felt they were involved in a continuous walking battle against an enemy that never flagged.

Richard matched the efforts of the Turks with his own tireless patrols up and down the column. Many times each day he and his picked men swept the Muslim horsemen away from the Christian ranks, returning with even more Turkish heads bouncing from his saddle. But for every head Richard was tying to his saddle, the Turks were responding by killing a warhorse on which the knights depended for their military success. More and more of the Western knights found themselves walking of necessity with the infantry, carrying their lances in the hope that they would find new mounts. In the Christian camp horse meat was fetching a high price that was putting it out of the range of the common soldiers. Ever aware of the plight of the common soldiery, Richard intervened by offering a live horse to any knight who would give his dead one to the footsloggers.

On the morning of September 5 the crusaders left their camp at the Salt River and moved toward the forest of Arsuf. Here Saladin was waiting for them with the whole of his army. He had decided that if he was going to prevent Richard from reaching Jaffa it must be done here, where the wooded terrain helped him conceal his movements. Ironically, at this moment of greatest danger, the Christians had finally convinced themselves that the great Muslim leader was prepared to seek a peaceful solution to the war and would parley with them. At his camp on a hill in the forest of Arsuf, Saladin was surprised to receive a messenger from the Christian leaders asking for a meeting to discuss terms. In fact, many of the Western crusaders were eager to return home and were only too aware of how difficult it would be to move inland from the coast to capture Jerusalem. Saladin was waiting for reinforcements and was happy to allow a meeting to take place that day between Richard and Safadin, with Humphrey of Toron acting as interpreter. Clearly both sides were simply playing for time, because as soon as Safadin asked Richard what were his conditions for peace, the English king replied, "One condition only, that you restore the whole land to us, and go back to your own country." Not surprisingly, this put paid to the discussions and both sides continued their warlike maneuvers.

Richard had already heard a rumor that the Muslims intended to set fire to the forest as his men were marching through it, and he was keen to march in a southwesterly direction to regain the coast. For a few hours the fear of fire dogged the crusaders' footsteps, but in the event they emerged safely near a creek called Rochetaille, from which they could see the sea. But the crusaders also learned why Saladin had not fired the forest, for there facing them was Saladin's whole army, numbering some 30,000 warriors, outnumbering them by probably two to one.

Richard knew that he would have to fight a full-scale battle before reaching Arsuf, and before he broke camp on September 7 he paid particular attention to the formation his men would take up in that day's march. The administration of the army showed immense skill, reflecting Richard's appreciation of not only his own strengths but those of his Turkish foes. Moreover, he had to bear in mind the divisions within his army, between his own Angevin forces and the French, between the Syrian supporters of either Guy of Lusignan or Conrad of Montferrat, and last, but by no means least, the undisciplined nature of the military orders and their tendency to regard themselves as a law unto themselves.

By now the crusading army was divided into five large battalions. In the vanguard rode the Templars, with Richard's Angevins and Bretons behind and then the Poitevins commanded by Guy. In the center of the army, clustered around the standard, were Richard's English and Norman knights, while behind them came the mass of the French knights. In the rearguard rode the knights of the Hospital and the Syrian knights. Parallel to the divisions of knights were similar divisions of infantry, with an extra thickening of crossbowmen, particularly in the rearguard, which was expected to come under particular pressure. For once Richard abandoned his own personal battle with the Turks and moved from the flank of the army into the center, where he would be able to coordinate the action of individual divisions by trumpet calls. Instead, Hugh, Duke of Burgundy, with a body of picked knights, including such heroes as James of Avesnes and William of Barres, took over Richard's roaming role and rode up and down the column ensuring that indiscipline did not threaten the cohesion of the whole. In addition, Richard's nephew, Count Henry of Champagne, rode on the flank with special responsibility for coordinating the movements of infantry and cavalry. In view of the difficult conditions, in both climate and terrain, and in the face of a vastly superior enemy, Richard's organizational skills rose to a supreme level.

It must have been apparent to Saladin for some days that he was facing a far more formidable enemy than he had defeated at Hattin. A growing sense of admiration is apparent in what the Muslim chroniclers wrote of the English king from this time onward. Though they believed him a butcher for the terrible way he dispatched the prisoners at Acre, they detected a consistency and an honesty in this man, the Lionheart.

Richard's army set out just before dawn and the vanguard had reached the outskirts of Arsuf by nine o'clock. In the gardens of the city they began to pitch their tents, but the rest of the Christian army was not going to reach Arsuf without a far greater struggle. Saladin now committed his entire army to the attack, and soon thousands of Turkish archers were keeping up a heavy fire on the rest of the column. As usual, the greatest pressure fell on the rearguard, and here Saladin planned his greatest stroke, hoping to cut off the Hospitallers from the rest of the army and destroy them before Richard could come to their aid. So heavy was the attack on the infantry at the rear that they were forced to march backward to enable them to keep up a steady fire on their assailants. As they did so, they fell farther and farther behind the divisions ahead of them. More and more of the knights were toppled headlong in the sand as their horses were killed beneath them, and the Turks, emboldened by the fact that the Hospitallers had been ordered not to retaliate by leaving the center of the column, now closed in and fell to hand-to-hand fighting in which the sword and *latt* (bronze) mace replaced the arrow as the main killing weapons.

Never before had the Hospitallers shown such discipline. Many of them had lost their steeds without being able to strike a blow against the enemies of their faith, and their bitterness against the king's orders was almost tangible. Several times they sent riders forward to acquaint Richard with their plight, but every time the answer returned that they must resist the urge to charge the enemy. Even when the Grand Master, William Borrel, rode forward to speak to the king, begging him to allow them to relieve the pressure on the rearguard by charging the Turkish cavalry, Richard merely replied, "Be patient, good Master: one cannot be everywhere." In fact, Richard knew precisely what he was doing and was not prepared to make his plans public. He had already devised a prearranged signal by which two trumpets in the vanguard, two in the center, and two in the rear would sound simultaneously to order a charge. Unfortunately, he found his charge preempted by two of the rearguard, the Marshal of the Hospital and Baldwin Carew, a Norman knight. Forcing their way through the ranks of the infantry, they dashed into the midst of the Turks, roaring "Saint George!" The entire rearguard, virtually acting as a man, followed them in a charge that sent their own infantry spinning in all directions.

Great confusion followed. Had Saladin been able to exploit the situation as he frequently had at Hattin, the battle would have been won and the Christians would have been swept into the sea. Yet, once again, Richard proved the readier soldier and, showing remarkable self-control, he ordered his trumpeters to sound the charge, and, in perfect order, division after division followed the French knights as they swung through gaps in the infantry and delivered a devastating charge against the Turkish center and left wing. The Turkish right wing was already shattered and in full retreat from the impact of the Hospitallers' charge, and Richard himself, "quicker than quarrel from crossbow," was hammering home his advantage as Saladin's army was sent reeling back in headlong flight. Rarely had the advantage in battle turned so suddenly. The indiscipline of two men had been exploited by their commander, who had unleashed the pent-up fury of an army that had been taking punishment day after day without the chance of responding.

So sudden and apparently well coordinated was the change from passive defense to all-out attack that Baha al-Din, who was present on the battlefield, assumed that it was prearranged. The effect was immediate and devastating. As he wrote:

> On our side the rout was complete. I was myself in the center: that corps having fled in confusion, I thought to take refuge with the left wing, which was the nearest to me; but when I reached it, I found it also in full retreat and making off no less quickly than the center. Then I rode to the right wing, but this had been routed even more thoroughly than the left. I turned accordingly to the spot where the Sultan's bodyguard should have served as a rallying point for the rest. The banners were still upright and the drum beating, but only seventeen horsemen were around them.

The right wing of the Turkish army had been in close contact with the rearguard of the crusaders and had therefore borne the full weight of the charge of the Hospitallers and the French squadrons. The charge had been so rapid that both Muslim foot and horse had been crushed together and overrun, so that casualties were very high. Thousands of men died in the confusion, and even the mobility of the Muslim horsemen could not save them from the weight of the Frankish charge. The Muslim center and left wings had escaped more lightly; they had attempted to flee, but many had died in the pursuit. Although Richard himself had led a squadron into the attack and had reached the fighting, the bulk of his cavalry, in fact perhaps two-thirds of his knights and all of the vanguard, had not reached the fleeing enemy or crossed swords with them. The truth was that Richard's rearguard had inflicted a defeat on an army perhaps ten times their number.

Having won so complete a victory in a matter of minutes, Richard was shrewd enough to realize how often hotheaded pursuit by Western knights had snatched defeat from the jaws of victory. It was vital, therefore, that order should be restored and his pursuit of the retreating enemy should be reined back. Already the fleeing Muslims had turned back and were beginning to cut off some of the scattered knights. It was in this phase of the battle that the great French knight James of Avesnes was killed after an epic struggle against overwhelming odds. Moreover, some of the Turkish leaders were restoring order, notably Taqi al-Din, who rallied a strong force of 700 Mamelukes around his famous yellow banner. It was becoming apparent to Richard that the battle was not yet over. Re-forming his squadrons, he and his erstwhile enemy William of Barres now led a second and then a third charge against the Muslims, driving them in total rout into the forest of Arsuf. As it became clear that they had lost their appetite for the fight, he refused to pursue them farther. He led his knights back to the camp that the infantry had set up at Arsuf before pillaging the corpses on the battlefield.

This gruesome process was as old as organized warfare and was one way in which impoverished soldiers could supplement their minimal pay. Muslim warriors, notably the rich Mamelukes, concealed on their persons much of their portable wealth in the shape of gold coins. As a result, the aftermath of the battle of Arsuf was memorable for the crusaders less in terms of prisoners and ransoms than from what they could strip from the thirty-two emirs whose bodies were found on the battlefield. Estimates of Muslim casualties cannot be verified, but the figure of 7,000 dead, though enormous for the twelfth century, may well be no exaggeration. Certainly, the crusaders had plenty of time to count the bodies, as the Muslims were unprepared to renew the struggle at that time.

Saladin reassembled his army, moved south to the river of Arsuf, and began to harass the crusaders once again. It was all that he could do in the circumstances. Richard had clearly demonstrated the superiority of the Western knight in open battle, and Saladin now realized that he was facing an enemy whose military skills were superior to his own. His personal fear was that Richard might choose this moment to alter his route and take the opportunity to make a dash for Jerusalem. With Muslim morale at a low ebb the mere appearance of Richard and a few hundred knights would probably have won him the holy city, but Richard was not prepared to gamble with his hard-earned victory. He had decided that he needed Jaffa as a base for the reconquest of Jerusalem and he was not prepared to jeopardize that aim. As a result, Saladin was given time to recover, and this has tended to conceal the decisive nature of the crusaders' victory at Arsuf. Richard's victory had been a psychological one as much as a physical one. From this moment onward the Muslims lacked confidence in engaging the crusaders in battle, and even the rumor that Richard was with a squadron was enough to make the Muslims seek safety in flight. As Baha al-Din wrote, "God alone knows what intense grief fills his [Saladin's] heart. All our men were wounded, if not in their bodies, in their hearts."

On his return to camp Richard heard the news of James of Avesnes' death, and this took the edge off the celebrations. Although the Christians had lost few men in the battle, the Frenchman had been one of the foremost knights in Europe for many years and he was as well known to the rank and file as any of the great noblemen. He had led a squadron of French knights in the initial charge with the Hospitallers and had been cut off by a mass of Muslim horsemen after his own horse stumbled and threw him. Fighting with a couple of his kinsmen beside him, James was surrounded by the enemy and yet succeeded in killing, according to Turkish observers, fifteen of their men before he was cut down. This loss was hard for the crusaders to bear. Accusations were leveled against the Count of Dreux and his men for not rescuing him. Both Richard and Guy attended the burial, and the whole army stood in silence, shocked by the loss of so virtuous a crusader.

Meanwhile Saladin needed to restore morale to his beaten troops, particularly to inspire his emirs on whose loyalty he was entirely dependent. This was not easy. So great was the fear of Richard that one emir from Aleppo told Saladin:

> Never have we seen his like; or met with his peer. He is ever foremost of the enemy at each onset; he is first as befits the pick and flower of knighthood. It is he who maims our folk. No one can resist him or rescue a captive from his hands.

Such speeches from his emirs convinced Saladin that his only hope against Richard lay in persuading the crusaders that they might remain masters of the coast, but once they turned inland and tried to march on Jerusalem they risked disaster. In addition, Saladin now began to listen to those of his entourage who advised him to play on the divisions within the crusader camp, particularly on those between the adherents of Guy of Lusignan and Conrad of Montferrat, and to try to outlast the King of

England who, Saladin's spies told him, was already uneasy about the fate of his own lands in Europe.

On September 9 Richard resumed his march south from Arsuf and Saladin, much to his relief, was temporarily reassured to see that Jaffa rather than Jerusalem was his target. This gave the Turkish leader breathing space to bring up reinforcements, for it would take the Christians some time before they could refortify the cities of Arsuf and Jaffa, which the Turks had dismantled during the panic that followed news of Barbarossa's abortive crusade. As a result, Saladin continued to use his army to block the road through Ramla that led to Jerusalem in case Richard should change his mind, and merely sent harassing bands to skirmish with the crusader column as it continued its march to Jaffa.

Egypt was the heart of Saladin's dominions, and for too long he had taken it for granted, simply using its wealth and manpower to fight the holy war in Syria. It was probably not until the crusaders continued south from Arsuf rather than turning, as he had feared and expected, inland toward Jerusalem, that a doubt began to nag him. Supposing that Jaffa was only the initial target of the march, not as a base for an attack on Jerusalem but as a further step on the way to Ascalon, gateway to Egypt itself? In such a case Saladin might find himself so completely outmaneuvered by the crusaders that he would be forced to choose between the holy war and Jerusalem on the one hand, and his power base in Egypt on the other. Seizure of Egypt had propelled him to power, after all, why could it not prove his vulnerable point in the holy war? Certainly Richard thought seriously and hard about staying in touch with the fleet and marching to Egypt, having fortified the entire coastline to get there. It would have been a brilliant plan, limited only by probable shortages of manpower and divisions within the crusader leadership, where the French knights eventually prevailed on him to remember that they had traveled to the Holy Land to recapture Jerusalem, not to spread the Angevin empire into Africa.

Waiting only long enough to convince himself that Ascalon was Richard's eventual target, Saladin moved swiftly to preempt his opponent. He knew that he could not garrison the city to resist the crusaders; furthermore, his men would rather seek immediate terms to save their lives than risk a repetition of the brutal fate of the Acre garrison, so that Ascalon would pass into Christian hands in a virtually undamaged state. This could not be allowed to happen, for the next port along the coast from Ascalon was Alexandria itself. Leaving his brother Safadin with the bulk of the army guarding Jerusalem, Saladin rode out at the head of some select squadrons and traveled to Ascalon at a gallop. It was a heart-breaking decision he had been forced to take, for Ascalon was known to his people as "Syria's Bride" and was a vital piece in his defensive jigsaw. He told his companion Baha al-Din that he would rather lose all his sons than be forced to pull a single stone from the walls of the city. It was probably Saladin's lowest point during his war with the Christians. Nevertheless, there was no place for emotion in the holy war and he ordered his soldiers to force the townspeople from their homes before dismantling the city walls and razing the entire settlement to the ground. In ten days, with Saladin working like a laborer with his bare hands, they reduced the great city to a pile of rubble.

While Saladin was demolishing Ascalon, on September 10 Richard arrived at Jaffa, which he busily refortified. As usual, the English king supervised much of the work, occasionally joining in the heavy lifting to keep himself in trim, while his lazier companions indulged themselves in the orchards and vineyards that surrounded the city. It was a time for rest and consolidation while they waited for the fleet to arrive with their supplies. In fact, just as had occurred after the capture of Acre, there was such a release of tension that a holiday atmosphere prevailed, a strange contrast to the grim determination of the two leaders in the holy war, both laboring in the heat while their followers enjoyed a break in hostilities. To spin out some time the crusaders played their usual card, that of a round of diplomacy with the urbane Safadin. Although they can hardly have believed that this sophisticated man was deceived by their pedestrian ploys, Safadin obviously felt that his brother could also benefit from a truce.

It was only when the refugees from Ascalon began to arrive at Jaffa that the crusaders realized that it was Safadin rather than themselves who was spinning out the negotiations and that the Muslims had more to gain by delay than they did. For the refugees from Ascalon carried with them the astonishing news that Saladin was demolishing their city. Unable to believe this, Richard sent Geoffrey of Lusignan down the coast by galley to see if the rumors were true. Geoffrey duly returned with confirmation. Richard immediately began issuing orders for a forced march to seize Ascalon before it could be finally leveled. As he said, "The Turks are razing Ascalon; they dare not fight us. Let us go and recover it. All the world ought to hasten thither!" At this moment Hugh, Duke of Burgundy, and other French noblemen intervened and the chance was lost.

This definitive moment is another example of the marked contrast between the two leaders in the holy war, the intellectual Muslim and the Christian man of action. Essentially it was the difference between short-term opportunism on the part of Richard and the fundamental long-term strategy of Saladin. Richard was eager to exploit the temporary weakness of Saladin by striking at Egypt. However, the crusaders had not included in their calculations the possibility of capturing a country the size of Egypt, nor had they manpower to hold down a population that would prove hostile in the long term. Even if Richard were to win the initial battles and to capture Alexandria, how could a monarch hardly capable of keeping his lands together in France maintain an administration of a Muslim country in Africa? It was temporary madness. The notion of Saladin planning to conquer the Isle of Wight would have been an equally mad equivalent. Curiously enough, Saladin did once assert his intention of taking the holy war into the lands of his European enemies, but this was merely the language of the holy war and far from a feasible option. On the other hand, the idea of the Lionheart on the Nile was by no means impossible in the short term.

Richard was then reminded of his duty to the crusade: although he was virtually funding the entire enterprise himself, it was as a pilgrim that he had traveled to the Holy Land, not as a conqueror. Richard could not understand the defensive strategy Saladin adopted after his defeat at Arsuf. He referred to his great enemy as "a man bereft of all counsel and of all hope of succor." In this he was closer to the truth than anyone could have guessed. At the very moment that Saladin needed the strength of a unified Islam he was threatened by the collapse of everything he had built up.

Having completed the demolition of Ascalon, Saladin next moved to Ramla, whose walls he similarly pulled down, and then returned to Jerusalem, where he concentrated on strengthening the defenses. He had made his choice: Jerusalem would be held at the cost, if necessary, of his entire army and even his own life. While Richard was writing letters to his ministers in Europe, promising that the holy city would fall within weeks, Saladin was digging in his heels and preparing to outlast the crusaders in a war of attrition. Had the sultan known what was really going on in Richard's mind he would have been much relieved. The truth was that Richard was close to exhaustion, both physical and financial, and besides the letters promising victory there were others that begged for reinforcements of men, money, and supplies.

The crusaders' short idyll at Jaffa had worked to undermine the iron discipline that Richard had imposed on his army. News had reached Acre that Richard had taken Jaffa and had cleared the coast road south. This emboldened the tourists among the crusading pilgrims to leave the comparative safety of Acre to travel southward, some arriving by boat at Jaffa while others risked the journey by land. The result was that there arrived at Jaffa hundreds of "useless mouths," as the pilgrims were described. Even worse, some crusaders decided that by fighting their way to Jaffa they had completed their obligations to the crusade. As an immediate advance on Jerusalem was out of the question, they gave up the cross and went by sea to Acre, en route for their return to Europe. The resultant reduction of the army was not fully appreciated by the leaders until they called in the troops who had been resting outside Jaffa in the orchards and vineyards and saw the extent of the depletion. The job of Provost-Marshal fell to Guy of Lusignan, who was ordered by Richard to return to Acre and round up as many of the truant soldiers as possible. During this difficult time, Richard concentrated on his usual tactics of personally carrying the war to the Turks, riding out daily to collect Turkish heads, and then offering to negotiate with Safadin. Saladin's brother seemed to enjoy the diplomatic battle with the English king, although it held little more meaning for either side than a game of chess. However, while this shadow diplomacy was going on, a very real change took place when a message arrived from the only crusader whom Saladin feared more than Richard himself: Conrad of Montferrat. Conrad was offering an alliance to Saladin by which he would help the sultan regain Acre in return for the cession to him of Sidon and Beirut. This offer was clearly treacherous to the cause of Christianity, but it should be remembered that Conrad felt he owed no allegiance to Richard while the English king continued to support his rival Guy of Lusignan as King of Jerusalem.

Richard obviously took the news of Conrad's offer to Saladin very seriously, sailing from Jaffa to Acre to help support Guy's disciplinary efforts. Although he planned a meeting with Conrad, this did not take place. Within two weeks Richard was back in Jaffa with his wife and sister as well as a large number of the soldiers who had drifted away earlier.

On September 29 Richard went falconing with a group of companions, all unarmored and lightly armed. This outing almost caused him to end the crusade in a Muslim prison. The chronicles relate that after some sport he was resting, or even napping, when a squadron of Turks swept down on the group of knights, hoping to capture Richard. They failed to identify him—to their eyes the Franks all looked alike—and Richard apparently mounted Fauvel and charged into action, felling Turks left and right. His companions fared less well and several were killed, including the renowned knight Reynier of Marun, his nephew Walter, and the brothers Alan and Luke of Stabulo. In the confused fighting, the Turks were closing in on Richard when suddenly one of the Frankish knights, William of Préaux, called out in Arabic that he was "Melec Richard," whereupon the Turks abandoned Richard and swept William away into captivity, convinced that they had the famous Lionheart.

On his return to camp Richard was received with acclamation by the rank and file, who also expressed much sorrow for the loss of William of Préaux. Some of the Frankish nobles, however, notably those led by Hugh, Duke of Burgundy, were irritated by the way in which Richard toyed with them all, even at the risk of his own life. They upbraided him for his lack of a sense of duty to the cause, which was surely more important than his own pleasure, either in hawking or in collecting Turkish heads to hang from his saddle. In reply, Richard conceded that he had been irresponsible in the past but added, "Who can entirely turn his nature out of doors, even with a pitchfork?" The fact was that Richard had been incredibly lucky so far. He had not only survived wounds and chronic ill health but had avoided numerous missiles in battle, any one of which could have ended his life and the crusade at a single stroke. His critics were right, but Richard was not good at taking advice when it came to his own affairs. His continued risks won him the love of the common soldier but not the respect of the more serious crusaders.

The diplomatic maneuvering with Safadin had started as lighthearted bartering or time-wasting, but now it took on a more serious tone as Richard began to seek a nonmilitary solution to the war. Again he used the sultan's brother as a means of communication with Saladin himself, and the negotiations after his return from Acre became more intricate, possibly even tongue in cheek. Richard began by sending Safadin a magnificent horse, a present grand enough to suggest the seriousness of intent. Richard then spelled out the issues that were in dispute between the two sides, telling Safadin that Jerusalem was to the Christians a non-negotiable issue as it was the most "sacred seat of their Faith" and was the reason above all others that they had come in arms to the Holy Land. The True Cross taken at Hattin should be returned to the Christians for whom it was a sacred treasure, whereas to the Muslims it was simply a piece of wood. Finally, Richard claimed, the crusaders insisted that their land up to the west bank of the Jordan should be returned to them. Saladin rejected all three conditions. Richard can hardly have been surprised at this as Jerusalem was as non-negotiable to the Muslims as it was to the Christians. Nevertheless, Richard had intended his conditions merely as an opening gambit in this metaphorical game of chess, for he had a "sacrifice" to make that he hoped might sow confusion in the royal ranks of the enemy. The "sacrifice" in question was no less than his sister, the former Queen of Sicily, his beloved Joanna. Richard proposed to Saladin that Safadin should marry Joanna: the two would reign over the land of Jerusalem, with Joanna holding the city itself as her royal seat, while Richard himself would endow her with Acre, Jaffa, and Asacalon. Neither Saladin nor his brother was much in favor of this scheme, but by the time their messengers had returned to the Christian camp there had been further developments. Richard had apparently not told Joanna of his scheme, and the good lady, "furious with indignation and wrath," told him in no uncertain terms that she would not marry a Muslim. Richard, feebly, replied that he would try to win Safadin for Christianity and, on this weak note, the idea collapsed. And now that his military affairs had improved, Richard was ready to march out of Jaffa on his way to Jerusalem. To work up an appetite for the fray he led several armed reconnaissances, rescued some crusaders from certain death, killed some Turks, collected their heads, and began to supervise the rebuilding of the fortress of Casal Maen, which commanded the road from Jaffa.

According to the main Christian chronicles Richard received a message while at Casal Maen that nearby, perhaps two miles away, a group of Templars was under attack by an overwhelming force of Turks. First sending fifteen knights under Andrew of Chauvigny to the rescue, the king then mounted his horse and set off after them to lead the rescuers in person. However, once they came in sight of the skirmish they saw that the Templars were vastly outnumbered and were doomed. The earls Hugh of St. Pol and Robert of Leicester, who were with the king, called him away, warning him that to attempt a rescue meant certain death. As they said, "If mischief should befall you, there would be an end of Christendom!" Richard replied, "I sent those men here; if they die without me, may I never again be called king." Thereupon he spurred his horse forward and, of course, put the Turks to flight. During the struggle Richard slew one of the greatest of the Turkish warriors, a huge man known (incorrectly) to the Christian chroniclers as Ar-al-chais. Baha al-Din records the same incident as a minor Turkish success but does not record Richard's presence.

Richard duly complained to Safadin about the breach of their negotiations inherent in the attack on the Templars. It is doubtful if the Turks took this seriously in view of the fact that Richard was merely waiting for an opportune moment to swoop on Jerusalem. They placed far greater importance on their negotiations with Conrad of Montferrat, for whom Reginald of Sidon was acting as go-between. Safadin continued to entertain Richard, on one occasion in his tent with a beautiful singing girl and dancer, to which Richard responded by "knighting" Safadin's son. Meanwhile, Saladin still hoped that an alliance with Conrad might break up the Christian army so that in the event of his death the crusaders would have to return to their own lands. When the King of England became aware that he was not alone in negotiating with the Turks he began to lower his demands. As a result, when Saladin presented the two Christian propositions before a council of his emirs, the official one from Richard and Conrad's unofficial offer of alliance, they preferred to deal with that of the king. But Richard had stirred up a hornet's nest in the crusader camp and he was being heavily criticized for his willingness to marry a Christian lady to a Muslim. Even his own supporters, among whom the chroniclers should be included, were baffled at his lack of dipomatic skill and tried to present him as a simple Christian warrior duped by wily orientals.

Peace negotiations having failed, Richard now faced a winter campaign to capture the holy city. The crusaders soon discovered why the Muslims sent their soldiers home for November and December. For three months the rain fell incessantly and Richard's soldiers found scant shelter in the ruins of the towns that Saladin had demolished, including Ramla and Lydda. While Saladin kept a much-diminished force together in Jerusalem, the crusaders were still harassed by guerrilla bands that Saladin had sent into the hills for that purpose.

Christmas 1191 came and went, with the crusaders huddled in one filthy camp after another, with no dry clothes, limited food, and numbers decreased daily by disease, malnutrition, or Turkish arrows. On January 3, 1192, Richard ordered the army to advance on Jerusalem once again, as much for something to do to maintain morale as with any real hope of retaking the city. The army marched to Beit Nuba, and it is reported that the pilgrims who accompanied the army were borne up on the idea that they were within hours of visiting Christ's Holy Sepulchre. The inner warmth of faith sustained some of them through appalling weather conditions as rain turned to sleet and snow, with tempestuous winds. Many of the poorer crusaders died of exposure and the chroniclers report that "armor rusted, clothes rotted, biscuits and bacon turned putrid." It was in these terrible conditions that the knights of Outremer, notably the Templars and Hospitallers, decided that they had had enough and the march inland would have to stop. Among the reasons they gave Richard for turning back was that if they were cut off from the coast they would all starve in the hills; and that even if the city was captured, it would be lost to Saladin (or another Muslim leader) the next year when most of the crusaders expected to return home after worshiping at the Holy Sepulchre. Despite the strength of these arguments, Richard and Hugh, Duke of Burgundy, realized that the whole point of the crusade would be lost if they did turn back when within sight of victory, and they would carry the blame. Richard, in particular, agonized over the decision and did not give way easily. He demanded to see a map of Jerusalem and, after studying it for a while, concluded that it would be difficult to capture the city in view of the weakness of his forces. True, it was no Acre, but neither he nor his army was the powerful force of six months before. The Templars advised him to retreat from Jerusalem and refortify Ascalon, so that he could use it as a powerful base either for a renewed attempt on the holy city or, indeed, an invasion of Egypt. Richard acknowledged the weight of this argument and the army turned back on Ramla. Just as the collapse of Barbarossa's crusade had seemed to Saladin like a case of divine intervention, so Richard's turning back from Beit Nuba seemed similarly inspired by Muslim prayers. Saladin had almost lost hope, and his lack of confidence seemed to have affected Muslim morale. Few of his emirs had believed they could hold Jerusalem against the fearful Richard. They had insisted that if they were to endure a siege Saladin or one of his sons must endure it with them. News that there would now be no siege seemed like a miracle to them.

In the event it was not Muslim morale that was now the problem but the collapse of fighting spirit among the crusaders. The rank and file had believed that capture of the city would be easy, and felt that to turn away at the last moment was both foolish and treacherous. Unaware of the issues of higher strategy, they blamed Richard with unusual bitterness, losing hope and faith simultaneously. Richard, burdened by communal guilt, devoted much of his time to saving the common soldiers who were sick and helpless, arranging for carts to carry them in safety back to the coast. It was the least he could do. The Duke of Burgundy's French contingent voted with their feet by deserting the crusader army, either traveling to Acre to restore their strength in the brothels and alehouses there, or joining Conrad of Montferrat at Tyre and becoming part of the plots that were aimed against Richard.

Infuriated by the loss of his allies, for whom he had been paymaster for so long, Richard struggled with the remnants of his army through dreadful conditions. The roads on the approach to Ascalon were so broken by the passage of thousands of men and horses that they had become little more than swamps, in which men and mules fell and drowned. When the crusaders reached the city they found it in ruins, as Saladin had left it. The sea was so stormy that no ships dared come into the harbor. The Christians spent a week seeking shelter, like rats burrowing in the broken masonry, beneath ground or in caves dug out of the solid rock. Most of the stores that had traveled inland with the army had been lost on the return journey through the swamps, and once the fleet did try to bring in food supplies, the ships were caught in a storm and many dashed to pieces. With characteristic resolve, Richard refused to succumb to despair and ordered the wood of the wrecked vessels to be collected from the beach; this was used to construct new, simpler galleys, ideal for use on that coastline in better weather.

Meanwhile, messengers were sent by Richard calling the French soldiers back to duty. Some said that they would come, on condition that they be released at Easter, when they wished to return to Acre for transport back to France. Richard had no option but to agree to this, and once the crusader army was reinforced he set about rebuilding and refortifying Ascalon. To give some idea of how powerful the city had been before Saladin dismantled it, the chroniclers tell us that the original plan of the city had fifty-three separate towers. The city itself had been built over a long period when the crusaders had enjoyed peace and security in the face of a weak and disunited Islam. Now a few thousand exhausted soldiers had to attempt to restore the demolished city to its former power while also facing the greatest of Muslim warriors with an army three times their own strength. Money was too short to hire local masons and laborers, so Richard became the main architect himself and his knights put aside their weapons and took up the tools of the artisans they professed to despise.

Richard was now plagued by internal divisions. He was eager to mend relations with Conrad of Montferrat, calling on him to rejoin the crusade and honor his obligations to Guy, who was still, on paper at least, his liege lord as King of Jerusalem. Conrad was hardly likely to respond to this approach, particularly as he regarded Guy as a weakling. So while Richard continued to support Guy there was no chance of a reconciliation with Conrad. Furthermore, Richard now found his always troublesome French allies prepared to abandon him altogether. The problem was one of money. In August 1191 Philip Augustus had left Palestine, putting his army under the command of Hugh of Burgundy, but with not a sou with which to pay the soldiers. The impecunious duke had been forced to take a loan of 5,000 marks from Richard, but by February 1192 the money was exhausted. With a potential riot on his hands, Hugh approached Richard for a further loan, which the English king, already aware that Philip Augustus had broken his promise to respect his Angevin lands in France, refused. After a heated argument, Hugh withdrew his troops from Richard's command and took them back to Acre, where they allied themselves with Conrad's supporters and joined the marquis in fomenting trouble between the various Italian contingents who garrisoned the city. While the Pisans had taken the side of Guy and his overlord, Richard himself, their Genoese opponents took the side of Conrad and the French. It was not long before Acre was torn by communal fighting between Pisans and Genoese soldiers and sailors. Incredibly, a second siege of Acre took place as Conrad's ships from Tyre attacked the city from the sea, while the French and Genoese besieged it from the land, the Pisan garrison using mangonels and stone-throwing trebuchets as defense against Conrad. It was truly the nadir of the entire crusading period, showing the world of Islam that however serious their own disunity, the Christians were in equal disarray.

For three days the Pisans resisted Conrad, during which time messengers headed south to call Richard to their aid. As usual, Richard was a tireless overlord. He was, in fact, at Caesarea, on his way north to meet Conrad, and once apprised of the situation he drove his horse into the night, arriving in person just after news of his imminent appearance had sent Hugh and Conrad fleeing back to Tyre. Acre was safe—at least from the Christians. To ensure this Richard had meetings with both Conrad and Hugh, failing to achieve much with the former but settling the latter's debts when he handed over to Richard some of his most valuable Turkish prisoners. Richard now tried to renew his negotiations with Saladin, offering through Humphrey of Toron the Temple of the Rock in Jerusalem to the Muslims, so long as the rest of the city was returned to the Christians. Some of Saladin's emirs thought that Richard's offers were becoming almost acceptable, but with the weather improving Saladin began to look again for a military solution.

The military position in which Richard found himself on April 1 was worrying: Conrad and Hugh had refused to join him against Saladin; and the French soldiers who had stayed loyal to the crusade were now insisting that Richard honor his word and let them return to Europe; so it was with a much-reduced army that Richard viewed the prospect of campaigns in 1192. The chroniclers write that 700 French knights, some of the best in his army, left him at this time and set off for Acre, as a first step in their return to France. To lift morale Richard held an Easter Day feast in his camp, ensuring that all those loyal to him ate and drank well. Now that the ground was firm again the Christians rode out and captured two Muslim caravans, bringing them many prisoners and enormous wealth in the form of horses, asses, camels, and sheep. Richard even began hunting for heads again, leading raiding parties out as far as Darum, reconnoitering the city and probing for weaknesses. It seemed that the problems of the winter were passing and that the king was becoming himself again. And then a messenger arrived from England bringing news that shocked the entire camp.

The letters the messenger brought were from Richard's justiciars, who begged him to return to England at once—his brother John was attempting to seize the kingdom for himself. The message was clear: if Richard stayed with the crusade, he might lose his lands, both in England and in France. The actions of his brother and Philip Augustus were against all the teachings of the church and the traditions of chivalry. The

[195]

possessions of a crusader were supposedly sacrosanct, but there were always priests available to salve the conscience of a sinner and absolve him from such rewarding crimes.

Richard was not entirely ignorant of affairs in England during the earlier part of the crusade. However, until Philip Augustus returned to France he had felt that his justiciars and his mother were quite capable of controlling John. Now matters had gotten far more serious. Richard's Chief Justiciar, William Longchamp, had remained in control of the situation until the summer of 1191, in spite of minor tensions with Prince John. Even while he was at Messina Richard had heard something of this and had sent Walter of Coutances, Archbishop of Rouen, home from Sicily with letters authorizing him to take over from Longchamp if the situation demanded it. However, Walter of Coutances traveled back to England in the company of Queen Eleanor, making slow progress. In the meantime, Longchamp had come to an agreement with Prince John that, if Richard should die on crusade, he would support John's candidacy for the throne. However, in September 1191, Longchamp made a blunder that enabled John to oust him from power. Richard's half brother Geoffrey, the Archbishop of York, had sworn before Richard's departure for the Holy Land not to return to England for three years. Breaking his oath, he landed at Dover and Longchamp ordered his arrest; Geoffrey took refuge in a nearby priory, where he was besieged for four days and eventually dragged out from the altar and thrown into prison. This reminded everyone of the Becket murder, and Prince John was able to work up the clergy to such an extent that Longchamp was forced to flee, disguised as a woman. Longchamp was apparently captured by a "half-naked fisherman" on Dover beach and consigned to Dover gaol for a week before escaping to Flanders in disgrace.

Free of Longchamp, Prince John now found that he had to contend with the more formidable combination of Walter of Coutances and Queen Eleanor, who had arrived in England from Sicily. Philip Augustus had also returned from the Holy Land and was eager to take his revenge for the humiliations Richard had heaped upon him. He promised John all the Angevin lands in France if he would take the hand of his much-abused sister Alice. Before John could accept he was warned by his mother and Walter of Coutances that if he made any agreement with Philip Augustus he would lose all his lands in England. For a moment

John came to heel and when, in frustration, Philip Augustus tried to invade Richard's duchy of Normandy he found that none of his vassals would join him to attack the territory of an absent crusader.

Hearing of these events Richard acted swiftly, assembling his foremost supporters and telling them that he might have to leave at short notice; they must choose who would stay on crusade and who would return to England with him. Those who preferred to stay told him that they would do so on one condition: if he left, they must have the leadership of a man skilled in war. In other words, they would not suffer another Hattin; they wanted a better king than Guy. Richard therefore asked them whether they would prefer Conrad of Montferrat. With a single voice they replied that they would willingly follow Conrad but none would follow Guy. Richard recognized that however loyal he felt to Guy as his liegeman, Conrad was the better choice. He therefore sent his nephew Henry of Champagne to Tyre to tell Conrad of the decision and to ask him to accept the throne. He also hoped that the divisions within the Christian host would now be resolved and that the Duke of Burgundy would return with Conrad to restore the army to full strength. In the meantime, Richard remembered that he could sweeten the pill for Guy by offering him the recently conquered island of Cyprus. He had originally planned to sell the island to the Templars, but they had paid only part of the purchase price; when they tried to raise the rest by taxing the Cypriots they had driven the people into rebellion. They willingly recouped their losses by selling the island to Guy for 40,000 bezants. The Lusignan family ruled the island for nearly three centuries, with Guy as the first king. This was his second throne in a decade, a substantial achievement for a lowly Poitevin knight of limited ability who had arrived in the Holy Land only twelve years before.

There now occurred one of the most controversial events of the entire crusading period, and one for which Richard has unjustifiably carried the blame: the assassination of Conrad of Montferrat by followers of the "Old Man of the Mountain." When Henry of Champagne arrived at Tyre with the news for which Conrad had been waiting ever since his fortuitous arrival at Tyre five years before, he sank to his knees and swore a great oath: he prayed that he should not be crowned king unless he was worthy of it. Cynics later remembered these words and wondered whether hubris had not contributed to Conrad's undoing. His task completed, Henry set off to prepare for the coronation at Acre.

Conrad now fell victim to an unbelievably trivial series of events that led up to his death. Even great men were not immune from the fate of the commonest of their vassals. On the evening of April 28, 1192, Conrad had expected to dine with his wife, but she took so long in her bath that the hungry husband despaired of having a meal unless he sought it elsewhere. He therefore set out alone to dine with his friend the Bishop of Beauvais, only to discover that the bishop's table was being cleared. Shrugging and reflecting that at least the walk would work up his appetite, he set off for home in the hope that his wife would be ready to eat by the time of his return. On turning a corner, he virtually collided with two cowled monks who claimed to have a letter for him. As he leaned forward to take the letter the monks plunged daggers into him, killing him where he fell. The two murderers were followers of the famous Muslim sect of Rashid al-Din Sinan, more commonly known as the "Old Man of the Mountain," the same order of assassins as those who had tried to kill Saladin in the 1170s.

Only weeks before it would have seemed that Richard was the man to benefit most from Conrad's death; many indeed accounted him the main suspect. However, his recent volte-face had changed the circumstances. The situation in England and France had forced him to reach an accommodation with Conrad and he had even dealt peaceably with the redundant "king" Guy of Lusignan. However much Richard may have resented Conrad's treacherous behavior during the crusade, Richard's own knights and barons had been adamant that it was Conrad not Guy that they wanted as their leader should Richard return to Europe. Having settled the leadership question, Richard had more strategic sense than to throw it in confusion by killing the very man who could unite the crusaders in the event of his own departure. Saladin had far more to gain than Richard from Conrad's death. After all, next only to Richard, Conrad was the man whom the Muslims most feared in the Christian ranks. Moreover, once he had reached a settlement with Richard, Conrad was no longer a useful diplomatic weapon for Saladin in his struggle with the King of England. Yet, for two obvious reasons, Saladin could not have arranged the death of Conrad. In the first place, given the speed of the settlement between Richard and Conrad, Saladin would not have had time. Secondly, Saladin was a bitter enemy of the "Old Man of the Mountain" and his assassins, and would have chosen a different way, even had he stooped to political assassination. The truth was far simpler than this. Conrad had, in fact, fallen afoul of Sinan by carrying out an act of piracy, during which some of Sinan's followers had been robbed and then drowned. The tale of Richard's involvement in the plot had been hatched by the assassins with the specific intention of protecting the two murderers. Saladin heard and apparently believed the cover story, which also spread to Europe, doing the King of England untold harm in the long run.

The murder of Conrad threw the whole crusader cause into confusion. Having been satisfied with his arrangements for Conrad and Guy, Richard now found that instead of two candidates for the throne of Jerusalem there were none. Furthermore, if he did return to England, there was no longer a suitable commander to take his place. Hugh, Duke of Burgundy, uncertain whether Conrad's murder was attributable to Richard as a means of reuniting the crusade, decided that his own safety was best guaranteed by the French seizing Tyre. When he tried to do so, however, Conrad's wife, Isabella, showed good judgment in occupying the citadel and telling the duke that she would not admit the French. She would pass on the keys only to King Richard or to the next "king" of Jerusalem, whoever that might be.

Richard decided that swift action was needed. Isabella was, in fact, the "key" to the kingdom herself, and he decided that it would be best if she were to be married to a new claimant, his nephew Henry of Champagne. Just a week after Conrad's death, Isabella, although pregnant, was married to the Count of Champagne, who thereby became the new King of Jerusalem. No sooner had he been crowned than Henry promised to set out with his knights to join Richard, who was planning to strike even deeper into Egyptian territory by attacking the coastal town of Darum.

Richard was enduring the torments of inaction. On May 14 he packed his siege equipment aboard his transport ships while he set off overland down the coast to Darum. He took with him only a small force of his own knights, leaving the bulk of his army in and around Ascalon to wait for Henry of Champagne's forces. When Richard arrived at Darum, his soldiers were astonished at how great a fortress they were expected to capture with such a small force. The Turkish garrison was similarly astonished and immediately rode out to challenge the crusaders to battle, but Richard refused the challenge and stayed by the beach awaiting the arrival of his siege engines. The Turks then saw how both the king and his prominent nobles stripped off their finery and worked like laborers, carrying and wheeling the heavy equipment across the sands and into position to strike at the walls of their city. Richard took personal responsibility for loading and firing one of the machines, concentrating on battering the keep, while his engineers undermined the city walls. Accompanying Richard's soldiers there were specialist siege experts from Aleppo, whom he had hired at Acre and whose help was required again here. These men, some of them Muslims, fought for pay rather than for their religion, and respected Richard as a worthy and reliable paymaster. After four days Darum fell, with Richard refusing the garrison terms of surrender and calling on them to fight like men. Sixty of them died in the assault and a further 300 were enslaved along with their wives and children. Richard was delighted to free some forty Christian prisoners, who returned with him in triumph to Ascalon. On the way they met Henry of Champagne riding up with a large force of knights. Richard took further pleasure in handing over the last Muslim coastal fortress to his nephew.

The ever-restless Richard did not immediately return to Ascalon but made a detour via the Valley of the Wells, where one of Saladin's emirs had fortified the Castle of the Figtrees and held it with a force of 1,000 men. Richard, ever eager to fight the Turks, called out the whole army from Ascalon to support him, only to find that when he closed in on the castle it was empty and its garrison had fled. The chroniclers relate that the crusaders were next struck by a plague of biblical proportions: for three days they traveled through a swarm of minute flies that stung every piece of exposed flesh until they all resembled lepers.

Aware of the difficulties in England, Richard was torn by conflicting pressures. One day his chaplain, William of Poitiers, walked up and down outside his tent weeping. The king demanded to know what was wrong, and the chaplain's reply is recorded at some length in the chronicles: Richard had been the chosen instrument of God to free the Holy Land; for that purpose he had survived wounds and sickness that had killed others; William wept because Richard, preeminent among all kings and warriors, could think of forsaking the Christian cause. Richard did not reply at first and indeed for a further twenty-four hours. However, the next day he had a message proclaimed throughout the army that he would not leave the Holy Land until the following Easter and that every man should prepare himself for an immediate advance on Jerusalem.

Richard's decision galvanized the crusaders into action. Henry of Champagne returned to Acre to call the French back to duty, as well as to round up the adherents of the late Conrad of Montferrat, and agreed to meet Richard at Beit Nuba by the middle of June. Saladin, meanwhile, was aware that the moment of decision was at hand: the Christians were about to besiege the holy city. He therefore divided his army, half remaining within Jerusalem and half going outside to harass the crusaders and, if possible, to force them into a series of expensive skirmishes. During the three weeks that Richard spent at Beit Nuba there were many minor clashes, some brought on by Muslim raids, others by Richard's own aggressive reconnaissances. Everyone, whether Christian or Muslim, was on edge waiting for the arrival of Henry of Champagne and his army. Some crusaders, particularly the French nobles, urged Richard not to wait for his nephew but to attack Jerusalem straightaway. Showing his usual strategic mastery, Richard refused to be tempted into a rash decision that might enable Saladin to cut him off from both his fleet and the rest of the army moving down from Acre. The chroniclers, no doubt as bored as the rest of the waiting crusaders, introduced legends to fill the gaps in their narratives. One, in particular, has added a tragic flavor to Richard's predicament at this moment. During one of his reconnaissances Richard rode to the top of the hill that the crusaders of a hundred years before had named Montjoie, from which they had first seen Jerusalem. Struck by the coincidence, Richard put up his shield to block out the sight of the holy city and, according to Joinville, said, "Lord God, I pray thee not to let me see thy Holy City, if so be that I may not deliver it out of the hands of thy enemies."

While Richard continued to wait for Henry of Champagne's reinforcements, he heard that a great Muslim caravan from Egypt, accompanied by thousands of Egyptian soldiers, was moving up from Bilbeis to Jerusalem. On June 21 three of his spies came into his camp and bade him ride back with them straightaway if he wished to ambush the caravan. Richard asked for help from the Duke of Burgundy, who agreed on condition that the French kept a third of the spoils. Five hundred Christian knights and sergeants rode from Blanchegarde southward. Saladin, of course, had his own spies and these reported that the crusaders were riding to intercept the caravan, whereupon the sultan sent 500 of his own men under the emir Aslam to warn the caravan and reinforce it. The Muslims, riding faster than Richard's force, reached the caravan first at a place known as the Round Cistern. Aslam argued with the Egyptian commander, Felek-ed-Din, insisting that he should allow him to lead the caravan by night toward Hebron. The Egyptian simply refused, claiming that in the darkness the caravan would break up and fall an easy prey to the Christians at first light. Felek-ed-Din had his way and camped by the Round Cistern, where Richard's scouts found them and rode back to tell their master. Richard formed up his troops and rode toward the caravan, determined to strike it at dawn. The Muslims were soon aware that Richard's crusaders were about to attack them; while some formed up in defensive formation in the hills, many of their best horsemen fled, abandoning the infantry to their fate. Aslam, disgusted that his advice had been rejected, took his horsemen into the hills, hoping to be able to swoop on the crusaders as they looted the caravan. This in fact happened, but with little success: the morale of the Turks was poor and most relied on the speed of their mounts to save them from the Christian soldiers.

Of all Richard's victories over the Turks this was the most complete for him and the most disgraceful for the Muslims. Outnumbering the Christians by three or four to one was not enough to prevent many of the Turks from fleeing rather than engaging in battle. The victorious crusaders could hardly believe their good fortune. The booty they took from this caravan was far greater than they would have had from the fall of a great city. Four thousand camels were taken, many laden with precious materials, including "gold, silver, silks and purple cloths, grain and flour, sugar and spices, tents, hides and weapons of all kinds." In addition, there were also thousands of horses and mules. Perhaps best of all, at least as far as Richard was concerned, Saladin lost the service of more than 2,000 Egyptian troops. It was an unparalleled defeat for Saladin, achieved at the cost of a mere handful of Christian casualties. As one of the chronicles put it, "No tidings ever dealt a more grievous wound to the heart of the Sultan than those which were brought to him at the close of that day." To the crusaders it seemed that their superiority over the enemy was assured; to the Turks that safety in flight was the only option left to them.

Saladin had reached his lowest point. Convinced that Richard would now advance on Jerusalem without delay, he set about positioning his troops on the ramparts and sending out parties to poison the water nearby so that the crusaders could find none for a lengthy siege. Dissension was rife in the Muslim camp, with Kurds, Turks, and Egyptians at odds with each other. Saladin appealed unsuccessfully for Muslim unity, but the emirs demanded a meeting to discuss what should be done. Clearly they were terrified that the relentless King of England might massacre the garrison if he captured Jerusalem, and they felt it was foolish to concentrate the only "fighting force and stay of Islam" in a single place, where they would be unable to use their superior skills and mobility in the event of defeat. Saladin offered to stay within Jerusalem if necessary, but his friends would not allow it. On the other hand, most emirs refused to take orders from anyone but him. Baha al-Din advised his master to leave any decision to a higher power. Saladin's prayer was evidently answered. Muslim scouts watching the Christian camp reported that a great meeting had taken place, after which the whole crusader army had begun to retreat.

What had happened was that on June 29 Henry of Champagne had arrived at Beit Nuba with his army and the crusade was more united than it had been at any time since the siege of Acre two years before. But nothing had really changed. Richard's success against the caravan was only temporary. It was a victory out of all context to the main purpose of the crusade, to preserve Christian faith. It was ridiculous to watch men from Winchester or Chartres or Pisa squabbling over oriental chessboards or silken cloth, or to hear the sounds of misplayed Muslim musical instruments or the cawing of parrots and other exotic birds.

Richard again tested opinion among the enlarged host. Once more the local knights argued against the march to Jerusalem, pointing out that it was known that Saladin had poisoned the water supplies on which they must depend as they approached the holy city. Some of them had been on the terrible march to Tiberias five years before and had no wish to see all their victories lost in a single day of miscalculation. They also reiterated that they were still heavily outnumbered and that divisions among the crusaders remained rife. The French, under Hugh of Burgundy, having benefited from the spoils of the caravan, were now financially independent for the first time in several years and were no longer likely to follow the orders of either Richard or, indeed, of the man they saw as his puppet, Henry of Champagne, the new King of Jerusalem. To demonstrate their independence, the French camped apart from the other crusaders and quarrels often arose. Matters were made worse when

Hugh arranged for a song ridiculing Richard to be written; it was sung by French soldiers about the camp. Richard apparently retaliated by composing a song that poked fun at the French.

Richard went to elaborate lengths in order to ensure that he did not bear the blame for the final decision concerning Jerusalem. First, from among the nobles and knights 300 men were appointed; these were then requested to vote for twelve adjudicators who would decide whether to march on Jerusalem or not. Their decision was to be final and there would be no appeal.

In spite of the fact that both Muslims and Christians used spies widely, it is surprising that neither Saladin nor Richard really understood how seriously each side had been damaged by the struggle so far. It is the current view of modern historians that Richard would have achieved an easy and swift conquest of Jerusalem. The morale of the Muslims was so low that, as the subsequent battle of Jaffa was to show, they would have been unable to resist Richard's crusaders in battle. However, so much depended on the presence of Richard himself that had he been absent from any fight the Muslims would have gained strength while the Christians would have been sapped. The Muslim emirs drew similar strength from Saladin's presence; if he were not in Jerusalem in person, it is doubtful whether the Turks would have offered stiff resistance. While the Muslims were divided against themselves, they were united in their confidence in Saladin's leadership. On the other hand, Richard was himself the cause of divisions within the Christian army, notably between himself and the French. Indeed it is surprising that Philip Augustus' remaining troops had served their Angevin enemies even as well as they did. Only by the capture of Jerusalem could Richard have maintained the support of the French, who had no intention of following the King of England on his proposed adventures in Egypt. The longer he failed to take Jerusalem, or even attempt to do so, the less they were willing to accept his orders as commander in chief. And when he handed over the decision about the march on Jerusalem to twelve adjudicators, they were the first to begin the march back to the coast. As far as they were concerned, the crusade was over and Richard of England had betrayed them.

Richard now fell back on his usual policy when matters turned against him: he tried to negotiate a settlement with Saladin. How serious the negotiators were this time remains uncertain. Saladin definitely took precautions in case Richard changed his mind and turned back to attack Jerusalem, but it seems likely that the French defection was the final straw for Richard. Probably he had known for some time that the crusade was doomed to fail if Jerusalem was to be its only target. Egypt was a possible alternative, provided he maintained control of the sea with the help of the Pisans and the Genoese. Jerusalem, however, was strategically an impossible target, while he was greatly outnumbered by the Turks and while the level of local Christian manpower was still so heavily reduced. Only a massive influx of new settlers into Outremer could, in the long run, ensure that Jerusalem could be held against future Muslim leaders after Saladin. In the meantime, Richard was prepared to share the land with Saladin, as long as he held the coast and, particularly, the city of Ascalon, which would give him a grip on Egypt. His assessment was clearly a valid one, for Saladin was prepared to grant him almost everything except Ascalon.

Richard now drew back to Jaffa, dismantling the fortress at Darum and placing 300 Templars and Hospitallers as a garrison in Ascalon. On July 22, the bulk of the army withdrew to Acre, accompanied by the fleet. The assumption in both Christian and Muslim circles was that Richard was preparing to sail home once he arrived at the temporary capital. However, in this everyone had misjudged Richard's character. He had no intention of leaving any of the coast in Muslim hands, and at that time, Beirut was still held for Saladin. Although far less important than the southern ports, Beirut was still a prize that would cap the crusade with an easy victory. As a result, as soon as he arrived in Acre he sent seven galleys to prepare a plan for the capture of the city. He prepared to follow on the next day and would have done so had not serious news arrived from the south. Saladin, in the absence of his rival, had recovered his nerve.

Hearing from his spies that Richard was at Acre, Saladin assaulted Jaffa on July 27. For four days the garrison resisted him, but then on July 31 a breach was made and the Muslims broke into the town, with the remaining Christian soldiers retreating to the citadel. These negotiated a surrender with Saladin on condition that they were not rescued by three o'clock the following afternoon. Saladin was content with this arrangement, believing that even Richard could not arrive in time to rescue them. But as usual they were wrong: Richard never wasted time contemplating failure. He had received a message from the garrison, sent on the day they had first espied the Muslim army, and had already summoned his army to ride with him to Jaffa. Many Templars, Hospitallers, and Syrian knights set off to the rescue, but the French contingent absolutely refused "to stir a foot with him." Richard, facing the inevitability of being outnumbered many times over, assembled some of his English and Angevin knights along with some Italian seamen and set off for Jaffa by galley. The knights traveling by land were held up at Caesarea. Little did Richard know that he was sailing virtually alone to lift the siege of Jaffa and challenge the full strength of Saladin's army.

Contrary winds held up Richard's seven ships, so that when he eventually arrived off Jaffa, there were just two galleys left with him. Saladin's nerves were fraying. He had just heard that Richard was on his way to Jaffa, so that a long negotiation with the garrison over their surrender was not worth risking. Saladin therefore addressed his troops, who were surly and exhausted from the intense fighting, and ordered them to take the citadel by force of arms. As he went to bed in his tent he had every reason to believe that this time Richard would arrive too late. However, he was awoken at dawn by a trumpet call announcing the arrival of the King of England in his red ship. Panicking, Saladin ordered Baha al-Din to lead troops into the town and call on the garrison to surrender at once. The chronicler did as he was bidden and the crusaders promised to surrender once they had assembled their possessions. However, they had already seen Richard's ships offshore and they moved with deliberate slowness. Out to sea, Richard and his men were scanning the shore, which was packed with Muslim soldiers, and trying to see any evidence that the Christians still held the fortress. The grim stonework told no tales and Richard was preparing to abandon his efforts, assuming that this time he had arrived too late, when a priest leaped from the battlements into the sea and swam out to the king's ship. "Gentle king," said this heroic cleric, "the people who await you here are lost, unless God and you have compassion on them." Richard was astonished to hear that there were crusaders still in Jaffa and asked the priest where they were. "Before the tower," said the man, "awaiting their death." Richard needed no further encouragement. Waving his sword above his head, he clambered over the side of the galley into water at least waist deep, followed by knights in heavy armor and barefoot seamen. The crusaders began to stumble and wade toward the shore, all the time under fire from the massed Turks there.

Meanwhile, the remaining forty-nine men of the garrison were in the process of surrendering on the landward side of the town, each paying his ransom fee as he passed through a line of Turks. Suddenly, those at the back of the queue saw that men were landing from the ships. They quickly donned their armor, took up their weapons again, and swept Baha al-Din and his men out of the main gate. Saladin, meanwhile, was in his tent receiving the surrender of the Patriarch of Jerusalem, who was in Jaffa at the time entirely by chance. Baha al-Din slipped round to the back of the sultan's tent and drew his attention with some coughs and throat-clearing. Saladin was rendered almost speechless. Matters became farcical when, just as the patriarch was about to put pen to parchment, the sultan's tent was almost tipped over by fleeing Turks. Saladin promptly ordered his guards to drag the patriach with them while he told his whole army to retreat to Yazur.

Richard and his companions had, meanwhile, cleared the beach and had set up a barricade alongside the city wall made up of driftwood and old barrels. The king then assembled his men behind this impromptu fortification, while more and more crusaders waded ashore from the fleet. By now more galleys had come up in support of the king's red ship. In spite of vastly outnumbering the crusaders, Saladin's troops had once more shown that they had no stomach for a fight. Richard, having broken into Jaffa by a side entrance through the house of the Templars, found Turks still looting and killed some of them before raising his banner on the battlements. He then found a loose horse in a stable and charged out after the fleeing Turks. Aware that this horse was one of just three available to his army in the whole of Jaffa, he rode it quietly back to the camp that he set up on the ground that Saladin had abandoned only minutes before.

Richard was in fine form when a group of Turkish emirs rode into the Christian camp, asking to speak with him. He gently taunted them that Saladin, the greatest leader of Islam, had run away when he, Richard, had not even come to fight and had no armor on his legs and wore only his boating sandals. Richard was, in fact, more ready for peace than ever. His manpower was growing more limited all the time, and few of his knights could now be certain of fighting mounted. Yet he would not sacrifice Ascalon, and it became clear that Saladin would not concede him this city. The war must go on. In desperation, the ever-imaginative Richard offered Saladin his own knight-service for Ascalon if the Turkish leader would enfeoff him, but Saladin wanted no "overmighty" subjects to add to his problems.

As usual Richard was as casual in the protection of his own life as he was protective of the lives of his vassals. While helping to repair the fortifications at Jaffa, he chose to pitch his tent outside the walls in a small camp, guarded by a mere handful of his men. Saladin, apprised by his spies that Richard was virtually unprotected in his tent and could be easily captured, moved his whole army to surround the camp in darkness, so that at first light they would sweep down and take Richard prisoner. The plan would probably have worked except that one insomniac crusader overheard the Muslims and warned the king. Richard was in his nightclothes and just managed to pull a mail shirt on before leaping, bare-legged, onto a horse. With a handful of knights, similarly unarmored, he prepared his army for battle. While he did so, the Turks forced their way into Jaffa once again, thereby cutting Richard off from any salvation behind walls. Improvising, Richard assembled another wooden barrier, like the one he had built on the beach only days before, so that his minuscule force could shelter behind it. Then, with perhaps sixty knights on foot and no more than six mounted men, and with a "hardy and valiant" German named Henry carrying his banner, he charged into Jaffa and routed the Turks who had forced their way in. Having summoned the garrison from within the citadel and ordered them to defend the town, he returned to the barricade with what reinforcements he could and prepared for the most desperate encounter of his life.

Saladin now had an opportunity to win the military solution that had so far eluded him. His great enemy, the man on whom all Western hopes rested, had placed himself in an impossible position. The strength of the crusaders rested surely in their armored knights and their irresistible charge, but now Richard had hardly a dozen mounted knights to face the thousands of Mamelukes that Saladin was about to unleash. However, Saladin had once again misinterpreted the strength of the Christian strategy which rested, in defensive battles, on the coordination of the armored knights and the crossbowmen. And at Jaffa a full fifth of Richard's 2,000 men were equipped with crossbows. Moreover, Richard's organization of his army was masterful. He arranged his foot soldiers in two lines, the front consisting of men kneeling with their spears fixed in the sand and pointing diagonally up at the breasts of the horses, the second of crossbowmen standing in the gaps between two soldiers. Behind them stood men reloading the crossbows and handing them to the man in front to fire. All that was necessary was for the infantry to show a firm discipline, which, under Richard's leadership, they did. Warning them all that if a man fled he would personally cut off his head, Richard and his few mounted knights stayed out of the initial combat so that they could launch miniature charges against knots of enemy horse.

This medieval combat has something in common with the early stages of the battle of Balaclava (1854), in which Sir Colin Campbell's "thin red line" held the Russian cavalry at bay. At Jaffa Richard's similarly thin line held thousands of Turkish horsemen back, saving not only the king's life but his hold on Jaffa. The Turks continued the battle for several hours, suffering heavy casualties both in men and horses. As the Muslim charges weakened, Richard and his few horsemen charged the Turks and sent them fleeing. Saladin, beside himself with fury, threatened to crucify some of the cowards who had fled. When he called upon his horsemen to charge again, only one man was willing to go. Faced with mutiny, Saladin decided to withdraw rather than remain on the field impotently viewing Richard's tiny force. The Muslim chroniclers relate that at this moment Richard seized his lance and rode up and down the full length of the Muslim army, challenging any man there to come out and fight him. Nobody dared. It was a psychological victory almost unparalleled in military history. After this debacle it was obvious to the Muslims that peace would have to be made. Saladin could no longer rely on his soldiers to fight for him or even for their faith.

Legends abound of this battle to such an extent that it is difficult to separate fact from fiction. What is certain, however, is that the chroniclers present on both sides acknowledged that Richard the Lionheart's personal contribution could not be overestimated. One referred to his return to camp "with arrows sticking out all over him like the bristles of a hedgehog, and with his horse in the same plight." Another wrote:

The king was a giant in the battle and everywhere in the field, now here, now there, wherever the attacks of the Turks raged most fiercely. On that day his sword shone like lightning and many of the Turks felt its edge. Some were cloven in two from their helmet to their teeth; others lost their heads, arms and other limbs, lopped off at a single blow. He mowed down men as reapers mow down corn with their sickles. Whoever felt one of his blows had no need of a second. He was an Achilles, an Alexander, a Roland.

At the height of the battle Richard rescued one of his closest companions, Robert, Earl of Leicester, whose lion emblem had convinced the Turks that they were fighting the king himself. They soon discovered their mistake when the king rode up, dealing death on all sides, and freed his courageous companion. It was in this battle that one of the most famous legends associated with Richard supposedly took place. The view from the Muslim camp made it seem impossible that any of the crusaders would survive the battle, least of all Richard, who was always in the thick of the fighting. At one point, it is alleged, Richard fell from his steed and was assaulted by crowds of Turks, intent on taking him dead or alive back to their sultan. At this moment Safadin sent a rider to take a fresh mount to the English king, so that he could return to the fray on equal terms. It is difficult to credit such an action by an enemy. Perhaps the incident was apocryphal, but even so, it epitomizes the aspects of chivalry that transcended national or religious conflict.

The incredible victory at Jaffa was Richard's culminating achievement in the crusade. The nervous exhaustion and physical collapse that followed was said at the time to have been caused by the Turks having mixed pig carcasses with human remains to pollute the air and spread disease, but the king's malady could more simply be attributed to stress. Close to death as Richard clearly was, he sent defiant messages to Saladin asking for peace but threatening war. Saladin did not react but waited until more reinforcements arrived from Egypt. Richard's next request was more conciliatory: he asked Saladin to send him fruit and snow for his fever. Meanwhile, divisions within the Christian camp continued to plague him. He called on the Templars and Hospitallers to take over the garrisons at Ascalon and Jaffa so that he might retire to recuperate at Acre; the response was that they would do so only if he remained with them as their leader. This seemed to break his resolve. In despair, he summoned Saladin's envoy, Abu Bekr, and sent Saladin a new proposal: the Turks could keep Ascalon provided they paid Richard for his expenses in refortifying it. It was the proposal of a profoundly sick man.

While Saladin considered Richard's latest offer some of the most important leaders of the crusade, including Hubert Walter, Bishop of Salisbury, began negotiations with Badr al–Din Dildirim, an emir with whom the king had established good relations. The bishop told the emir that as Ascalon was now the only sticking point between the two sides, Richard would concede it unconditionally. Saladin was cautious at first, so much having turned on the king's mood and physical condition in the past. But Dildirim reported that he had heard the words from Richard himself and taken his hand. Saladin, reassured, now assembled his emirs to discuss a truce. While these discussions were in progress, Saladin continued to probe the Christian defenses at Jaffa, still hoping for a miraculous victory. His spies brought news that pleased his heart. There were just 300 mounted men in Jaffa, most riding nothing more than mules. Yet when he discussed his plans with Baha al–Din, the chronicler emphasized that the Muslim soldiers "were weakened and wearied and longing for their homes"; they might mutiny and refuse to fight the crusaders at all. A further defeat, like that at Jaffa, might even encourage Richard to continue the fight in the hope of ultimate victory.

The truce that was drawn up was to last for three years. The Christians were to evacuate Ascalon, but were to be recompensed with Ramla and Lydda, to add to the cities of Tyre, Acre, Cayphas, Arsuf, and Caesarea, which they already held. Richard was too ill to read the document, but it was confirmed by Henry of Champagne and other leaders, who swore the oath to ratify the treaty on Richard's behalf. Richard could not resist roaring at least one more time in Saladin's direction, warning that he had agreed to a truce only so that he might visit his own lands, put all to rights, and return with a new army. Then, he went on, he would wrest from Saladin the whole of the "Land of Jerusalem." Saladin, interpreting the roar as no more than the meow of a weakened kitten, replied elegantly that if he had to lose Jerusalem he would rather lose it to Richard than to any other prince he had ever known.

And so the Third Crusade came to an end. While Ascalon was demolished by combined parties of Christians and Muslims, the armies mingled and the crusaders began to demand to be allowed to complete their pilgrimage to Jerusalem. Richard, though urged to go there by his men, refused to visit the holy places. As he said, he would not take as a gift from a heathen ruler what had been denied him by God. Spiritual leaders now came to the fore: the Bishop of Salisbury led the pilgrims to the holy places, which Saladin allowed on the grounds that once they had done so they would be less likely to return with any future crusade. As

[211]

the pilgrims traveled through Muslim territory, many Turks begged their leaders for permission to fall upon them and avenge their own losses, but Saladin ordered Safadin to ensure the safety of the Christians, and he was delighted when the crusaders returned to Acre rejoicing in his honor.

Richard, meanly though understandably, asked Saladin to refuse access to the holy places to the French crusaders, who had caused him so much trouble. Saladin, however, refused to take sides in a Christian dispute. As he put it, "There are men here who have come from afar to visit the Holy Places, and our law forbids us to hinder them." Christians of all nations eventually had the chance to visit the holy city.

Saladin showed great courtesy to the Bishop of Salisbury, escorting him to the holy places and offering him accommodation in Jerusalem, but the bishop preferred to sleep on the ground with his fellow pilgrims. Saladin met Hubert Walter in his tent and they had long discussions, particularly on the subject of Richard. Flattery and a good dinner prompted Saladin to offer the bishop any gift that he would name; after due consideration, he asked to be allowed to place two Latin priests and two Latin deacons at the Holy Sepulchre in Jerusalem, along with Latin priests at Bethlehem and Nazareth. When Saladin agreed, the bishop was overjoyed, because he had not liked the Syrian services held in Jerusalem.

Richard had, meanwhile, moved on to Acre, where he had begun to recover his health. While the fleet was prepared Richard's mind turned to what had been one of the bravest gestures by any of his knights during the crusade, namely William of Préaux sacrificing his freedom to save the king from capture. Richard had already made tentative inquiries about freeing William, but the Muslims placed an enormous price on this. Only when the king offered ten of his noblest Turkish prisoners in exchange were the Turks prepared to release the brave knight. As a man of honor Richard felt he could do no less, and William was allowed to leave the Holy Land with the rest of the crusaders. On September 29 Berengaria and Joanna went aboard a dromon at Acre and set sail for Cyprus, followed ten days later by the king himself. As Richard left the Holy Land behind him, his thoughts appeared heavy to one of the chroniclers: "O Holy Land, to God do I entrust thee. May He, of his mercy, only grant me such space of life that, by his good will, I may bring thee aid. For it is my hope and intention to aid thee at some future time."

Richard was not destined to return to Palestine or to send further aid to the Christians there. His reputation, however, lived long with the Muslims, and in that respect he remained in the Holy Land at least in spirit. For many years afterward Muslim women quietened their fractious children with the words "Be quiet! The King of England is coming." And a rider would call to his restless horse, "Is the King of England in front of us, then?" While Richard lived on, if only as an addition to Turkish folklore, Saladin died without being able to enjoy the fruits of peace. Exhausted by six years of intense fighting, he had seen the triumphs of 1187, of Hattin and Jerusalem, lead to the disasters of Acre, Arsuf, and Jaffa. He had seen men whom he had trusted to ride with him through every danger turn in panic and flee from the very idea of a man who had become like the angel of death to the Muslims.

12

|◆|◆|◆|

The End of a Legend 1192–1193

LIKE AN OLD GUARD DOG Saladin remained on duty in Jerusalem until he received irrefutable evidence that Richard had sailed from Acre. At last he allowed himself to relax and seek solace in his religion. He was fifty-four years old and had long wanted to undertake a pilgrimage to Mecca. For the first time in seven years he was free of war. But even though his own fears had subsided, those of the many Muslims who relied on him had not. Much as his emirs wished Saladin health and long life, they feared that if their leader were to disappear even temporarily into the deserts of Arabia the Franks might return, particularly the dreaded "Melec Rik," to overthrow all they had achieved. By making himself indispensable Saladin had become a prisoner of the fears of his own followers, who would not set him free. He had become a legend in his own lifetime, and believers in legends must be free to invoke them whenever they perceive the need. While Richard had given his blood in battle for those who needed him, Saladin had allowed his followers to drain his very life force. Even with the enemy gone, Saladin was not allowed any rest.

Saladin's doctors were concerned at the way he had abused his always fragile health and realized that he was unlikely to live to a comfortable old age. They tried to combat his rigid adherence to religious fasting, but their efforts were often in vain, for Saladin seemed to sense his own mortality. The longed-for pilgrimage was postponed while he carried out tasks that could have been left to his brother al-Adil or his sons, notably

[214]

his heir al-Afdal. But probably he knew that, without himself at the head, the empire he had created would shatter and disintegrate, not from the pressure of Frankish invaders—in fact, the crusaders had served as cement to unite the Ayyubid lands—but from the quarrels and greed of the sons he left behind. It was a bitter pill to swallow, the thought that what the father had fought and struggled his whole life to create his sons would waste in a matter of years. The shades of Henry II of England might have nodded at the irony of Saladin's position.

In October 1192 Saladin was back in the saddle, riding out of Jerusalem and beginning a tour of frontier fortifications. The crusaders had gone and for him it was business as usual, administering justice and giving rewards to those who had deserved it in the hard-fought wars. Before Richard the Lionheart had left Acre, he had made a chivalrous if ultimately empty threat to return at the end of their three-year truce and recover Jerusalem. In reality, both men must have known that if the battle must go on it would be under new leaders, yet Saladin's emirs insisted on taking the King of England's words literally and so warlike preparations continued. While, unknown to them, Richard was heading toward an Austrian dungeon, Saladin was himself being driven toward death. Both men were victims of their friends, Richard of the enemies he had made of them, Saladin of the way he had made them dependent on him.

On October 19 Saladin arrived at Tiberias in stormy weather. Despite the state of his health, he was undeterred by the heavy rain and muddy paths and rode on with his party, visiting all the fortresses between Tiberias and the coastal city of Beirut. It was a punishing schedule. At Beirut he held a splendid reception for the Christian Prince of Antioch, Bohemond III, who paid homage to Saladin and recognized him as his overlord. Saladin responded in appropriate style, awarding Bohemond a robe of honor and 15,000 gold pieces. It was the completion of his northern journey, and Saladin returned to Damascus to spend the winter there. He had not been able to spend much time with his wives and younger children, and the thought of this must have given him pleasure. His entrance into Damascus was a memorable occasion, accompanied by displays of affection from the crowds not only for a successful warrior but for a genuinely good man and a hero of Islam.

Free for a while of the burdens of state, Saladin joined his brother al-Adil, who had traveled from Jezireh to see him. During the day they enjoyed some gazelle hunting, while at night they reminisced about their times in Egypt, a land that meant much to both of them but that Saladin was fated never to see again. Sadly, Saladin had grown distrustful of his loyal brother, aware that his ambitions must be at the expense of Saladin's own sons. Would they receive al-Adil's loyalty when he himself had gone? Saladin knew that his heir, al-Afdal, was no match for al-Adil. None of his sons had inherited Saladin's statesmanlike qualities, and it was with bitter thoughts that the great man went to his grave. Without an overlord to enforce obedience, his sons and their uncle would compete for his lands and civil war was the inevitable outcome.

The return of the pilgrims to Damascus from Mecca took place in February 1193 and must have stirred in Saladin a deep longing to be with the next party that left Syria. Amid the general rejoicing Saladin rode out with his people to welcome the returning hadjis and stayed out in the heavy rain, occasionally shivering, as Baha al-Din observed. The chronicler also noticed that his master had forgotten to don the padded doublet that he always wore in the winter: "He seemed like a man waking out of a dream and asked for the garment, but the master of the wardrobe could not find it." At the end of the ceremonial return of the pilgrims Saladin complained that he felt unwell and he was soon running a fever. Death had found Saladin unprepared. None of the mail tunics that had preserved him from harm in numberless battles could help him now. The cold and damp had given him a chill, and this mild ailment would usher him to Paradise.

In his last days, Saladin was blessed by the company of two of his greatest friends and colleagues, Baha al-Din and his wise mentor al-Fadil, but the third presence, his son and heir al-Afdal, must have filled him with foreboding. Al-Afdal proved to be one of the least of his numerous offspring, matching neither his father's political skills nor his generous nature. In the week before Saladin's death al-Afdal revealed features of his personality that showed he would make a poor successor to his father.

In his last illness Saladin displayed almost saintly characteristics. Baha al-Din records several anecdotes concerning Saladin's treatment of servants. In one Saladin was awaiting his bath, which was too hot, and when the servant brought cold water he tripped and tipped the jug all over his master. Chilled as he was, Saladin simply responded: "My dear fellow, if you aim to kill me, give me due warning." On another occasion, the sixth day of his final illness, he called for warm water to drink after his medicine. The first cup was too hot and the second far too cold. Instead of chiding the servant, he mused: "Dear God, can no one produce water of the right temperature?" At this, Baha al-Din left the room in tears, reflecting to al-Fadil, "What a spirit Islam is about to lose. By God. Any other man would have thrown the cup at the head of the servant."

By the ninth day it was clear that Saladin was not going to recover, and rumors spread in the streets of Damascus. The people, fearing a disputed succession on the great man's death, began to clear their property from the market stalls and barricade their houses. Each time al-Fadil or Baha al-Din visited the palace they were followed by crowds anxious to know the latest details of Saladin's condition. Once al-Afdal heard that the doctors had abandoned hope, he summoned the leading emirs of Damascus and called upon them to swear an oath of allegiance to him to ensure a peaceful transition of power. Some of them were unwilling to do so, and it was necessary for the machinery of Saladin's state to continue operating even in the last moments of Saladin's life by enforcing penalties on those who refused. In the end it was al-Afdal, not the emirs, who challenged the natural succession, by dismissing his father's most important ministers, including Baha al-Din and al-Fadil.

After the morning prayer on March 4, 1193, with the priest having spoken the words "There is no other God but he, and in him is my trust," Saladin was seen to smile and cease breathing. Baha al-Din had just entered the room at the moment of death and observed his master "pass into the bosom of divine grace." A thousand miles away, in the German castle of Triffels, high in the Swabian mountains, Richard of England sat alone in a dark dungeon, guarded by the German emperor's toughest soldiers, all with swords drawn at every moment of night and day. As Richard peered up at the barred windows above his head, he might have seen a single bird fly upward at that moment, free as his great adversary was now free, while he languished in the prison of those who had been his allies and fellow crusaders. Saladin had been his enemy, not by choice but by circumstance. There had been no hatred between them, only the hostility of men who found themselves on opposite sides of a great divide. They had grown to respect each other, not just as fellow commanders but as fellow men. Had Richard heard of Saladin's death that day he might have shed tears as genuine as any he had shed for his father and brothers. Had Saladin, in his final illness, heard of Richard's imprisonment, he would have mourned for a great man betrayed by those he had served well, of a lion brought down by jackals.

When news of Saladin's death spread, there were scenes of lamentation and great grief in the streets of Damascus. It was apparent that unlike many powerful rulers whose followers had to orchestrate public mourning, Saladin needed no such propaganda. True, his sons went out from the palace and joined the mourning in the streets, but they acted spontaneously and were greeted with pity by the people as having lost a father and a friend. Uniquely for a sultan, Saladin died in total poverty. It was even necessary for al-Fadil to pay for the shroud and the drape for the coffin. Saladin was buried in the west pavilion of the palace garden at the hour of evening prayer. Even his enemies found it impossible to accuse Saladin of the greed generally associated with successful conquerors and generals. One of his bitterest foes conceded, "In a word, he was the marvel of his time, a man rich in fine qualities marked by his fine actions and by the great campaigns he led against the Infidel, as his conquests proved."

13

┤◆│◆│◆├

The Lionheart Caged 1192–1194

RICHARD'S JOURNEY TO THE Holy Land had involved him in a close encounter with death in an Italian peasant village, the siege and capture of the Sicilian port of Messina and the conquest of Cyprus. His return to England was not as peaceful and untroubled as the passage back to France of his great rival, Philip Augustus. The drama that Richard seemed to attract was with him once more as he sailed from Cyprus bound for his European lands. Common sense must have suggested that the return journey should be by sea, at least as far as Marseilles, and probably all the way to England. He had many enemies in continental Europe, notably in France and Germany, and would be risking his freedom and possibly even his life if he were to take a landward route home. Yet Richard seldom allowed common sense to rule his actions. The greatest soldier of his age was not a good sailor and he suffered from seasickness, so he was keen to keep his time aboard ship to a minimum. Thus, when word reached him that Count Raymond of Toulouse was planning to seize him when he landed at Marseilles, he was left with a choice: he could either continue the voyage all the way to England, a dreadful prospect for a poor sailor; or he could land in Italy and travel through Germany. Convinced that Raymond of Toulouse was in league with Philip Augustus, he decided to take the warning seriously and opt for the German route. Even this, he must have realized, would involve considerable risk.

Once Richard's mind was made up there was no changing it. He ordered his fleet to change course and make a stop at the island of Corfu, where he had spotted three pirate galleys. The chronicles relate that Richard approached the pirates in a small ship and attempted to hail them. Initially they attacked his apparently helpless craft, but the fighting soon subsided when they realized that the strangers in the boat were interested in doing business with them. Richard offered the pirate captain 200 silver marks to take him and some twenty companions secretly up the coast to the Byzantine city of Ragusa. This unlikely scene placed the most famous ruler in Europe in the hands of a band of cutthroats of questionable reliability and allegiance. If it is true, it exemplifies Richard's authority over the numerous powerful and intelligent clerics and noblemen who were with the English fleet. Once again, Richard was prepared to risk his life and the welfare of all those under his command, whether with the fleet, in England, or in Normandy, on the assumption that he would be able to travel incognito through much of Western Europe. While their king, disguised as a traveling pilgrim, sailed northward with the pirates, the English fleet made its own way back to England.

After an eventful journey up the Dalmatian coast, during which the pirates proved that navigation of rocky coasts was not their strong point, Richard and his companions were put ashore near Ragusa. After his conquest of Cyprus, also Byzantine, this was not a sensible destination, especially as he had a guard of only twenty men. Furthermore, his skills at disguise and impersonating servants were proving limited. Discovery was almost certain, particularly as it became generally known that he was returning to England overland.

Richard certainly entered into the spirit of the charade, for that was all it was; but while most charades end in laughter, this one ended in bitterness and disaster, both for the King and for the English people. Neither a beard nor the garments of a poor pilgrim could disguise the tall, burly, straight-backed warrior, who spent too freely and was clearly accustomed to being a dominating presence. Richard had vowed that once he was on dry land again he would thank God for his safety by making a donation to the cathedral at Ragusa. He was as good as his word, but the local clergy were unaccustomed to receiving such munificence from traveling pilgrims and were soon suspicious of his identity.

Richard hastily continued his journey by sea, leaving Ragusa only hours before the local officials decided to find out who this rich pilgrim might be. Not to be spared further storms, he and his companions were washed up on the coast of Istria, not far from Venice, their ship having been wrecked. Richard now adopted the disguise of a traveling merchant named Hugh, who was in the party of a well-known crusader, Baldwin of Béthune, who was returning from the Holy Land. This latest deception was sheer folly. The rumor that the King of England was traveling in Italy or Germany in disguise was widespread. Richard next compounded the folly by sending a messenger to the local nobleman, the Count of Goritz, informing him that Baldwin of Béthune was passing through his lands and requested safe passage. The count suspected that Richard was disguised either as Baldwin himself or as one of his servants. Word was sent ahead to Frederick of Betesov, who planned to intercept the crusaders at Freisach, in Carinthia. He employed a Norman knight, Roger of Argentan, who was staying with him and claimed to know Richard by sight. The Count of Goritz already had it in mind to take Richard prisoner and hold him for ransom. The Norman knight easily detected the king's disguise, but, although he was himself married to the count's daughter, he felt strong ties of loyalty to Richard as Duke of Normandy. This led him to try to help Richard escape. He devised a plan whereby Baldwin and Richard split up, with Baldwin remaining for four days and spending money lavishly while Richard rode on, with one companion and a German-speaking boy servant. The plan worked at first in that local officials arrested Baldwin and questioned him and his companions. However, it did not take them long to realize that Richard had gotten away and was now virtually alone. Richard, however, had covered 145 miles in just three days, arriving at Vienna in midwinter. Vienna was probably second only to Paris as the most unwise place for Richard to visit. His treatment of Leopold of Austria during the recent crusade had turned the duke into his most bitter enemy. To make matters worse, the Count of Goritz, no doubt hoping to make some profit out of the information now that Richard had escaped from his lands, sent a message to warn Leopold that Richard was in his territory.

Richard and his companions took lodgings outside Vienna. The king and his knight stayed hidden while the servant was sent on errands. The boy, pardonably in view of his age, was no better at concealment than the king. When he went to the city market to buy provisions, he used Byzantine gold coins. People soon became suspicious and the boy was questioned by the duke's officers. Not surprisingly, he was unable to answer sensibly, claiming that his master was a rich merchant who had had a debt paid to him in Byzantine coinage. The officers asked to meet this merchant, but the boy said he was not currently at home. The duke's men let him go, presumably intending to follow him, but the boy escaped by running off through the snow. Back at the lodgings, he warned the king that he should flee at once, but in the bad weather Richard decided to postpone his departure by one more day. Again he sent the boy out to buy food. It was now so cold that the boy borrowed a pair of gloves that the king gave him. This proved the last straw. The Viennese market holders wanted to know where the boy had found such opulent gloves. The boy got no chance to lie, for this time he was beaten and interrogated, confessing that his master was the King of England.

Once Leopold was informed, he had the lodging surrounded by troops, who were heavily armed in view of Richard's reputation as a fighter. Even Richard realized that resistance was useless and offered to surrender to Leopold's officers, but only if the duke came in person to accept his sword. It was another example of his arrogance. He had believed himself invincible and yet, through his own stupidity, had placed himself in the hands of one of the two men who hated him most. Leopold must have been willing to walk through the fires of hell rather than the snows of Vienna for such a prize. Soon he arrived and pushed through the crowds of inquisitive Viennese who had now surrounded the house, wondering what they would see when the Lionheart was taken away by the soldiers. In the end they were probably not disappointed, for, humiliated as he must have felt to be taken prisoner by a man for whom he felt only contempt, Richard knew how to fill the part of the captured hero, straight-backed and every inch a king, marching willingly with the guards and the duke following him like jackals.

Two days after his capture, Richard was taken from Vienna to the castle of Dürenstein, built high above the Danube and sufficiently remote to challenge any would-be rescuers. So alarming was the prospect of imprisoning a man of Richard's reputation that Leopold had him guarded night and day by soldiers carrying their swords unsheathed. It was as well that Leopold made the most of Richard's captivity in Austria, for more powerful predators than he had plans for the King of England, including Leopold's overlord, Emperor Henry VI of Germany. Henry had problems of his own, inside Germany and in other parts of his domain, for which the captive King of England might provide the solution. Not only was the emperor eager to take control of Southern Italy and Sicily, where Richard's new ally Tancred held the crown, but he hoped to subdue his Welf opponents in Germany, for example Henry the Lion, who had familial and political links with Richard. For the leader of the Christian armies in the crusade, Richard seemed to have made a lot of enemies among the Christian kings of Europe. While Henry made his own plans to exploit the capture of Richard, he was quick and eager to send the good news to Philip Augustus of France that the hated Lionheart was no longer free to foment trouble. Soon it seemed that much of Europe was celebrating the news that the champion of Christendom had been taken prisoner on his journey home from the crusade.

The political "horse-trading" now began for control of the King of England. It was a cynical exercise in view of the fact that the life and liberty of all crusaders was sacrosanct, yet, significantly, only Pope Celestine III complained at Richard's treatment. Emperor Henry summoned his vassal, Leopold of Austria, to bring the captive king to the court at Regensburg. Leopold obeyed, though he was not willing to surrender his prize until he had negotiated a suitable settlement. It took six weeks of hard bargaining, during which time Richard was returned to Dürenstein before Leopold was willing to hand him over to the emperor. The settlement was that Richard would have to pay a ransom of 100,000 marks to the emperor, half of which would be paid to Leopold, who would use it as a dowry for his son's marriage to Eleanor of Brittany. Furthermore, the two decided to exploit Richard's undoubted military ability. Their agreement committed Richard to supplying the emperor with a fleet of fifty galleys and 100 knights for his proposed campaign against Tancred of Sicily, as well as requiring Richard to attend in person with a further 100 knights under his own command. The English king must also supply 200 hostages to ensure that he met the stringent requirements, as well as agreeing to release Isaac Comnenus and his daughter. Should Richard fail to agree to these terms he would immediately be returned to captivity at Dürenstein, in Leopold's custody.

Philip Augustus, delighted as he had been to hear of Richard's misfortunes, was not content to see them resolved too quickly. He had his own agenda, which involved Richard's brother John, so when he heard details of the settlement, he informed Leopold and Henry that he was prepared to pay a larger figure to keep the Lionheart imprisoned in Germany than Richard could pay to gain his freedom. In a diplomatic power struggle of this kind, such bribery, far removed from the principles that had supposedly inspired the crusaders, was relatively common. If Richard was in prison in Germany, he could not molest his neighbors and threaten to take their lands. On the other hand, neither could he defend his lands from those, like the King of France, who might try to seize them. The rights and wrongs of European warfare might be debated by learned clerics of the time, but for the feudal lords who held the land, success needed no justification. For half his life Richard had lived by this rule, and once free he would live by it again. Neither morality nor filial duty had ever stopped him from making war on his father or his brothers. With this in mind it is difficult to stand in judgment of Philip Augustus when he joined John in declaring war on Richard and invading his Duchy of Normandy, taking the castles of Gisors, Neaufles, Châteauneuf, Gournay, Aumale, and Eu. Only Rouen stood out against the French attacks, although Philip Augustus used twenty-three siege engines to besiege the city. The defense of Normandy's ducal capital was helped by the fortuitous arrival of one of Richard's greatest crusaders, Robert, Earl of Leicester, who stiffened the garrison. At one stage the gates were opened and Philip Augustus was invited to enter to discuss terms. The cautious Frenchman declined the offer. Prince John tried to arrange an invasion of England with Flemish troops, but his mother raised levies along the south coast and the invasion did not take place. John next garrisoned Windsor Castle with mercenaries, announcing himself as king on the grounds that Richard was dead. Nobody of consequence believed him.

Fortunately, Walter of Coutances did not panic. He had none of the information that his enemies had. Instead, he had to rely on rumors and the reports of spies. He was fortunate to see a copy of Henry VI's letter to Philip Augustus, and this revealed to him for the first time the full implications of Richard's situation. He responded by seeking contact with Henry, and this was achieved through one of the emperor's distant relatives, Saveric of Bohun, Bishop of Bath. While these initial exchanges were taking place, two abbots were sent to Germany to try to locate Richard and possibly speak to him. Although legendary accounts give the laurels to the minstrel Blondel, it was the abbots who eventually tracked the Lionheart down in the castle of Ochsenfurt, on the Main.

They managed to meet Richard and found him in surprisingly good spirits. When they told him of the part that his brother John had played, in alliance with the King of France, Richard just laughed. "My brother, John, is not the man to subjugate a country, if there is a person able to make the slighest resistance to his attempts."

Only gradually did Richard piece together the story that had so turned the emperor against him. When he had an audience with Henry he found that a long list of grievances against him had been presented, notably by French crusaders who had left the Holy Land before him and had done their best to blacken his reputation wherever they could. Foremost among these had been Philip Augustus's kinsman Philip, Bishop of Beauvais, who had so twisted the details of the crusade that he had convinced the emperor that Richard had betrayed Christianity by making peace with Saladin and had, furthermore, been the man responsible for arranging the assassination of Conrad of Montferrat. Once he heard these accusations Richard presented so redoubtable a defense that in a matter of hours Henry was convinced of his innocence. The two monarchs even began to discuss conditions for Richard's release, though when Richard heard the terms of the emperor's agreement with the Duke of Austria he absolutely refused to accept them, stating that he would prefer to die than suffer such dishonor. However, Richard did agree to pay the 100,000 marks, on condition that Henry try to pacify Philip Augustus, which the emperor agreed to attempt.

Richard was now moved to Speyer, and from here he began to send letters to church and lay figures in England, instructing them to begin raising the enormous sum for his ransom. He wrote a particularly long account of his "adventures" in Germany to his mother, thanking her for her sterling work in protecting England from John's machinations and urging her to place her confidence in Hubert Walter, Bishop of Salisbury, who was just arriving in England on his return from Outremer. He urged Eleanor to support Hubert's candidacy for the vacant see of Canterbury, thereby showing his loyalty to those of his companions who had most deserved it. While he was in the castle of Hagenau he was visited by his ex–Chief Justiciar, William Longchamp, to whom he was able to relate that the emperor was prepared to release him once 70,000 marks had been paid. He asked Longchamp to list how much each of his nobles paid and also to issue pledges of repayment for all the gold and silver church ornaments that were confiscated and melted down. Raising the great sum required for Richard's ransom was an enormous task, requiring a national effort.

Richard's meetings with Henry VI had given him the impression that he could trust the emperor to keep his word. However, the Lionheart was not always a very good judge of men, and while the ransom was being raised in England he began to hear rumors of French schemes to keep him prisoner indefinitely. He had already heard that Philip Augustus was prepared to pay more for his imprisonment than Richard was for his own freedom. Henry and Philip now arranged a meeting to be held on June 25 between the cities of Vaucouleurs and Toul to discuss this very point. Fortunately for the imprisoned Lionheart, affairs in Germany were instrumental in winning him the emperor's support and breaking the proposed agreement with the French.

In November 1192, the murder had occurred of the Bishop of Liège and suspicion had fallen on the emperor, who seemed to have most to gain from the crime. The German church had been outraged and had lined up with the deceased's relatives to avenge his death, by force if necessary. In the early months of 1193 Henry's domains teetered on the brink of civil war. Richard, through his Welf relations, had an understanding of German affairs and, through the sort of subtle diplomacy with which he is not usually associated, he was able to bring the two sides together, placating the supporters of the murdered bishop and satisfying his family by getting Henry to swear an oath that he was not involved in the crime. Richard's triumph over this issue won him the affection of the emperor, who canceled his meeting with Philip Augustus and agreed that the ransom terms should remain unchanged.

While Richard was fighting a successful defensive campaign from a prison cell in Germany, his justiciars in England were conducting a more aggressive one to raise the money for his ransom. Their difficulties were understandable. Only four years before Richard had raised taxation to unprecedented levels in order to fund his crusade, and now, before most Englishmen had been able to make good their losses, they were being asked for further massive contributions. The sum of 100,000 marks was so enormous, even for a national treasury, that a new direct taxation had to be levied. The justiciars decreed that all the king's subjects would have to pay a quarter of all their revenue for 1193 into the Exchequer. As mentioned above, all church vessels of gold and silver would be melted down and used to swell the fund, while knight's fiefs were all assessed at

20 shillings each; monks who rejected earthly wealth and therefore had no gold and silver vessels paid in kind, from their wool sales for the year.

The collection, counting, and delivery of the ransom required a major effort of those running the country in Richard's absence. His mother, Queen Eleanor, headed the operation, assisted by the new Archbishop of Canterbury, Hubert Walter, the earls of Arundel and Warrenne, and the Mayor of London. The money when collected was to be packed in huge locked chests, sealed with the dowager's seal, and kept in St. Paul's Cathedral under the heaviest guard. Final negotiations were to be carried out in Germany by William Longchamp, accompanied by numerous senior clerics and noblemen. Hostages were required, but when Longchamp, a notorious homosexual, called on the nobles to send their sons with him, many refused, offering instead their daughters. In the event, Longchamp took no hostages with him. He did, however, finalize the arrangements with the emperor at Worms, whereby German officials would visit England to weigh the treasure at St. Paul's in the presence of witnesses. The ransom would then be taken to Germany under guard and at Richard's risk until it reached the imperial frontier, after which the emperor would accept responsibility.

These final obstacles to Richard's freedom were now mere formalities, and his enemies were depressed at how swiftly the ransom issue had been agreed. Philip Augustus contacted Prince John, warning him, "The devil is now let loose." He also hurried to make peace with Richard before the Lionheart could begin to settle some old scores. On July 9, 1193, he met William Longchamp at Mantes and gained a suspiciously favorable settlement, in which he was left in control of much of what he had conquered. Negotiating for John, the French king also got a guarantee that the prince could still keep the lands he held when Richard had first left for the crusade. Hearing of the Lionheart's imminent release, other men who had attacked his lands in his absence hurried to enjoy the apparent generosity of this "changed" Lionheart. They should all have known better. Richard had not changed, for better or worse. It was simply that on the point of gaining his freedom he was in no mood to threaten anyone who might delay the process by even a day, particularly not the King of France. There would be time enough to pay back those who had mistreated him with the same coin.

In England the collection of the ransom comprised the main business of the government and occupied the summer and autumn of 1193. The problem was that nobody could judge how much money the direct tax of 25 percent would actually bring in. In some cases there was genuine overassessment; there were also instances of theft and corruption, in which underpaid collectors would help themselves to a cut. Eventually, the coffers in St. Paul's were filled and the emperor's representatives arrived to weigh and measure the ransom. Once satisfied, Henry wrote to inform Eleanor that he proposed to release her son in January 1194. The queen did not receive the letter, as she and the Archbishop of Rouen were already on their way to Germany, where they spent Christmas 1193 with the still-imprisoned Lionheart at Speyer.

Even at the last moment John and Philip Augustus tried to persuade the emperor to keep Richard imprisoned. In January 1194 they made a counteroffer that delayed the Lionheart's release for a further two weeks. By this time, however, Henry felt bound not only by his oath to Richard but by their growing friendship. On February 4, 1194, in a curious ceremony, the emperor released his prisoner into his mother's hands. Before that moment Richard was required to surrender a cap symbolizing the English crown to Henry, who then returned it to him on condition that England become a fief of the empire; Richard must pay homage to the emperor and an annual sum of £5,000. Even more extraordinarily, the regalia of the English crown were surrendered to Henry so that he could invest future English kings as his vassals. (This arrangement did not last long: after Henry's death in 1198, his successor, Otto of Brunswick, returned the royal regalia to England.)

Free at last, after an imprisonment of one year and six weeks, Richard now viewed his enemies with a predatory eye more typical of an eagle than a lion. He immediately wrote to Philip Augustus, warning him that he should prepare to surrender the castles and lands he had seized and informing him that as a vassal of the empire he, Richard, was entitled to the emperor's assistance in recovering his property. He also wrote to his nephew, Henry of Jerusalem, promising him renewed aid, though this was wishful thinking for he had more than enough to keep him fully occupied at home. Accompanied by his mother and William Longchamp, Richard passed through the lands of friendly rulers, meeting part of his own fleet at Antwerp and crossing the Channel on March 13, to land in England at Sandwich.

So much of his father's work in England and the Angevin lands in France had been undone during Richard's time on crusade that he found himself confronted with the sort of challenge that a new ruler might have faced after a prolonged civil war. Not only was the realm bankrupted after the enormous financial efforts of 1190 and 1193, but because of his brother's disruptions, there were many dissidents who did not welcome his return to the throne.

Richard started his comeback at Canterbury Cathedral, where he offered thanks for his safe return from the Holy Land and from Germany at St. Thomas's tomb, before setting off for London. His entry into his capital had to be stage-managed, and crowds, both willing and unwilling, came to welcome the return of their king who had fought for his faith in the Holy Land, humbled the great Saladin, alienated his fellow crusaders, humbled the kings and princes of the Mediterranean, bankrupted his English subjects, and ultimately been humbled in his turn in Germany. The multitude cheered as he rode into London like a conqueror returning, but they searched in vain for the coins in their pockets to drink his health.

14

┤◆│◆│◆├

The Lionheart Rampant 1194–1199

Richard i has always been viewed as one of the worst kings of England. Many accounts of his reign have referred to the time he spent on crusade being longer than the time he spent in his own kingdom, as if this in itself was a sign of failed majesty. Yet this is entirely misleading. Medieval kings were not governed by concerns for the welfare of their subjects. It is anachronisitic to expect a man of Richard's upbringing and experience to have been much concerned with the common folk. He was a feudal monarch, obliged to protect the land over which he ruled and the vassals who owed allegiance to him. The nature of such protection entitled him to extend his territory by falling upon that of his neighbors or, should this prove impossible, by marrying his sons and daughters so that they could acquire land for him in dowry settlements. Richard was no better and no worse than dozens of his royal contemporaries. And, along with such predecessors as Heraclius, Charlemagne, and Godfrey of Bouillon, he was one of the paladins of medieval Christianity.

The first requirement Richard faced in reestablishing his rule in England was money, and this he would employ not directly in England's interest but to win back the land he had lost in France. Civil war in England, which might have occurred under a more able man than his brother John, was avoided as Richard had predicted it would be, because the justiciars he had left in charge while he was on crusade had proved too strong for John's band of desperate mercenaries. By the time Richard returned to England the country was not teetering on the brink of civil war, as most Hollywood versions of *Robin Hood* seem to indicate. True, John's cronies held Nottingham Castle, but it did not need any "merry men" to wrest it from his control. It is said that the mere news that Richard had been released from imprisonment caused the constable of St. Michael's Mount in Cornwall, a supporter of Prince John, to drop dead from fright or apoplexy.

Richard arrived at the epicenter of the "revolt," Nottingham, on March 25, 1194, and found that Prince John's supporters amounted to little more than an assembly of local lords discontented by the heavy taxation. He had assembled a large army as a symbolic gesture rather than to threaten the liberties of his subjects. He realized that the size of his following would subdue the enemy without recourse to much fighting. Unfortunately for them, the defenders of Nottingham Castle would not believe that Richard had come in person to besiege them, and as they offered resistance, they enraged the Lionheart, who ordered his carpenters to build gallows in sight of the castle walls and soon had some of John's followers swinging from the end of ropes. This had the desired effect: as soon as the defenders saw the king, they surrendered the castle without further ado. With Nottingham gone, the rebels surrendered Tickhill forthwith and the "rebellion" collapsed. Richard paid a lightning visit to Sherwood Forest, presumably to establish some local legends, before returning to the business of state. All but seven sheriffs of the realm were removed from office and were replaced by more trustworthy men, who combined reliability with a willingness to buy their new posts and help to repair the shattered royal treasury.

Richard now went south to Winchester, where he underwent a second "coronation" on April 17. This ceremony was considered wise in case his curious crowning by the German emperor in some way appeared to diminish his right to the throne. On this occasion, therefore, he assembled at the cathedral a strong team of clerics to sanctify the occasion, including the new Archbishop of Canterbury, Hubert Walter, the Archbishop of Dublin, and eleven other bishops. Unlike his coronation in London, this time Richard had the support of the distaff side, with his mother and the greatest ladies of the realm packing the cathedral, though curiously his wife Berengaria was not present. No expense was spared at the celebrations that followed, which were obviously designed to convey the message both to his subjects and to the world in general that it was "business as usual." Yet Richard was chafing at the bit, eager to be back in France confronting the enemy who had done more than anyone to undermine him: Philip Augustus.

After his second coronation Richard stayed just a further three weeks in England, during which he indulged in a mass of administrative work designed to restore the country to a condition in which it could once again finance his wars on the continent. On April 24 Richard was at Portsmouth, fretting at the inclement weather that prevented him from crossing the Channel. News from France had been bad, and his patience was growing so thin that eventually he decided against further delay. The fleet set sail into a storm that drove it straight back into Portsmouth. Another week passed until the advent of fine weather at last allowed him to sail on May 12.

Once in Normandy, Richard rode hard for Lisieux, where his mother had arranged a meeting with John. It is not known how much pressure their mother had to apply to persuade her favorite son to forgive John. Suffice it to say that when at last the two brothers did meet Richard was surprisingly gentle in his treatment of his aberrant brother, apparently welcoming him with the words "Don't be afraid, John, you are a child. You have had bad companions and your counselors shall pay." The "bad companion" Richard was referring to was, of course, the King of France. Richard was determined to locate his enemy and punish him for his treachery to a crusader. Richard's anger against Philip Augustus had been smoldering throughout his imprisonment in Germany, and now that he was free to give vent to it, it rose to the surface and almost choked him. He rode madly from one town to another, killing horses under him but always arriving just after the French forces had withdrawn. During this period of frantic activity Richard found that the concept of loyalty was not entirely dead. His marriage alliance with Sancho the Strong of Navarre had stood firm, in spite of his own curious treatment of Sancho's daughter, Berengaria. During the Lionheart's incarceration in Germany, Sancho had not only intervened twice in Aquitaine to drive out Richard's enemies but had sent his own son as one of the hostages needed to ensure the Lionheart's release.

For the next five years Richard was at war with Philip Augustus, despite occasional truces, almost continuously. By the end he had regained most of the territory he had lost during the crusade and his imprisonment in Germany. It was a bitter war, fought mainly by mercenaries, and Richard employed ruthless men like Mercadier to lead his armies. His experiences at the hands of Henry VI, Philip, and his own brother seemed to have embittered him in a way that his great struggle with Saladin never did.

Richard's fury began to abate when on July 3, 1194, he caught up with the French rearguard as it was moving away from Vendôme and captured the royal baggage train at Fréteval. He had killed few French in the attack but had gained incriminating evidence in the form of charters issued by Philip Augustus to nobles in Normandy who had renounced their allegiance to Richard in favor of France. As during the crusades, Richard had ridden at the head of his knights. He sped forward, hoping to capture the French king and hold him for ransom. However, as Richard huffed and puffed, Philip Augustus had taken refuge in a nearby church and was hearing mass at the very moment that Richard was vowing to cut him into small pieces. Philip completed his devotions, rejoined his army, and rode back into his own territory. Richard's first meeting with Philip since they had gone their separate ways at Acre was not on the battlefield but at Tillières on July 23, where they negotiated one of their several truces. However, hardly was the wax dry before Richard had broken its terms. Eventually, at the Peace of Gaillon in January 1196, Richard regained all the territory he had lost during his imprisonment in Germany except Gisors and the Vexin.

Nevertheless, during 1197 fighting broke out again and Richard gained revenge on one of his greatest enemies, the man who played the most significant part in blackening the Lionheart's name in the period after the crusade, Philip of Dreux, Bishop of Beauvais. This cousin of Philip Augustus had continually harassed Richard's lands in the Vexin until Richard's captain, Mercadier, invaded the Beauvaisis, captured the bishop, and imprisoned him for three years, first at Rouen and later at Chinon. Despite the fact that he was a bishop by title, Philip of Beauvais had never been anything other than a military man, fighting as a knight and loving the life of a warrior. When he appealed to Pope Celestine III for help, he received a flat refusal and the comment: "Into the pit you have made you have deservedly fallen. You have worn the hauberk and the alb, the helmet and the miter." After Richard's death his brother John released the old man in 1200, probably earlier than the Lionheart would have wanted.

Richard's clerics would, no doubt, have seen the hand of God in the events that occurred in Germany after the release of their master. After all, Richard had been a crusader returning from service in the Holy Land when he was captured and held for ransom, which was an absolute violation of church law. The fate of Leopold of Austria was therefore a stark warning to those who violated God's law on earth. Leopold had been excommunicated by Celestine III for laying hands on a crusader. Furthermore, he had refused to return the ransom received for Richard's release on the grounds that little of it had arrived, and he was still waiting for the dowry from the marriage of his son to one of Richard's nieces. As neither the young lady nor the money had arrived, he threatened to kill the English hostages who had been demanded when Richard was released. In order to arrange this, one of the hostages, Baldwin of Béthune, was sent back to England in December 1194, escorting Queen Eleanor and the wretched daughter of Isaac Comnenus. Before Baldwin and Eleanor could carry their message to Richard the hand of God was laid upon Leopold. On December 26 his horse fell on him, crushing his foot. The foot turned black and amputation was deemed necessary, but neither his surgeons nor even his son and heir had the courage to risk the operation. Eventually Leopold had to hold an ax to his ankle and order a servant to strike it with a mallet; the foot was severed after three agonizing blows, but the gangrene had already spread. Leopold died, having promised to restore the ransom money to Richard and, in his eyes at least, having made his peace with the church. But the pope pursued him beyond the grave, insisting that Leopold could not be buried in sanctified ground until the English hostages were released. The first of Richard's German foes had felt the wrath of God.

While Leopold's revenge had been the initial reason for Richard's incarceration in Germany, it was Henry VI who had exploited the captivity and made it so costly. Henry had tried to clear his conscience and to gain Richard's forgiveness by sending an offer to refund the ransom. Repentance came too late. He died in September 1197, before his offer had been delivered. Like Leopold, Henry had been excommunicated and was denied a Christian burial. As a deeply religious man, Richard may have taken satisfaction from the fate of the emperor who had treated him badly, but as a pragmatic ruler he looked to the next generation. Just before his death Henry's wife had given birth to a boy, named Frederick, who became a ward of the pope and was destined to rule Sicily. However, Richard was determined to play a significant role in the future of Germany, so he turned his support to Otto of Brunswick. Otto was a close kinsman of the Angevins and had been brought up at Richard's court in Poitou, eventually becoming Richard's agent in the province as Count of Poitou. Richard put all his considerable weight behind Otto's candidacy as German emperor, aware that there was a powerful rival in Philip of Swabia, the late emperor's younger brother. Then there was an unexpected turn of events; Pope Celestine III died in January 1198 and was succeeded by Innocent III, a man who favored Otto of Brunswick and was, incidentally, at odds with Philip Augustus over his repudiation of his wife Ingeborg of Denmark; the new pope was therefore a welcome ally for Richard.

Richard was quick to exploit this new alliance and appealed to Innocent III to redress his grievances against the late Leopold of Austria. Having investigated Richard's claims and ruled in his favor, the pope not only instructed Leopold's son to refund the ransom money but made the same demand of Philip of Swabia, as heir to his brother's estate. Innocent then told an ecstatic Lionheart that he was pursuing all and any who had benefited from Richard's imprisonment in Germany. And when Richard heard just a few weeks later that Otto had been chosen as King of the Romans and emperor-elect by the German electors in session at Aachen, his cup seemed to run over. Otto was crowned emperor on July 12, 1198, consolidating the closest-ever ties between England and Germany. Richard could view himself not only as a kingmaker but as probably the most powerful monarch in Europe.

But triumph and disaster were always close bedfellows for Richard, and he still had the biggest score of all to settle with Philip Augustus. For that he would have to wait. Having lost Gisors to the King of France, Richard had decided to build a splendid new castle to defend his Duchy of Normandy. The expense was enormous, at least £11,500, and the building took two years to complete, 1196–8. Built to Richard's own design at Les Andelys, Chateau Gaillard was the most advanced castle in the world.

Not until September 1198 did Richard at last come face-to-face with his enemy in battle, though not quite as either had expected. On this occasion Richard, accompanied by his trusty mercenary captain Mercadier and a small group of knights, rode into a strong force of 300 French knights, commanded by Philip Augustus, traveling in the direction of Gisors. Richard did not hesitate but charged straight at the French knights, who fled toward Gisors with Philip somewhere in their midst.

As they approached the gates of Gisors, the reverberation of so many horses caused the bridge over the river Epte to collapse, tipping many French knights into the water, among them the king himself. Richard reined back his horse and laughed uproariously at the sight, for, as he later reported, "The French king had to drink of the river." Philip nearly drowned in the incident, and was dragged out by one leg. Twenty French knights did indeed drown, while a further one hundred were captured by Richard and another thirty by Mercadier. It was a minor victory but one dear to Richard's heart, in that it heaped personal ignominy on a man Richard could not regard with the respect due an enemy warrior.

Richard's death, when it came, was literally like a bolt from the blue, altering the balance of power in Western Europe in a moment. The facts of what happened are not in dispute, but his motives in besieging the unimportant castle of Chalûs, near Limoges, garrisoned by just two knights and a rabble of peasants, have been misunderstood. Did greed really lead the Lionheart to his death?

The story of Richard's end passed down by contemporary chronicles concerns a treasure, either of antique coins or of a Roman relic in gold, which was dug up by peasants plowing on the land of Achard of Chalûs, a vassal of Aimar of Limoges, who was in turn a vassal of Richard. Aimar had, apparently, demanded it from Archard and part of the treasure was sent to him. When Richard heard of this he, in turn, demanded the rest of the treasure from Achard, who fled to Limoges for protection, having—or so Richard believed—hidden it in the castle of Chalûs. Although chroniclers relate that it was mercenary greed that drove Richard to descend on Chalûs, modern research suggests that his motives were far more likely to have been political. Aimar of Angoulême and Aimar of Limoges were, in fact, part of a rebellion against him, and the treasure of Chalûs gave Richard an excuse to assert his authority in an area he had not visited for more than three years.

The main explanation for Richard's anger against Aimar of Limoges must lie in his hostility to the wretched garrison of Chalûs; the Lionheart would not have applied a hammer as heavy as this to crack a nut as small as the treasure. He could have left the siege to the redoubtable Mercadier rather than organize it himself, but it was almost as if he felt personally challenged by the situation. Even though, after a three-day siege, the garrison offered to surrender to save their lives, Richard refused, telling them that he would hang them all. Absentmindedly he would occasionally test his own skill with the crossbow, shooting down figures who appeared on the battlements. When he did this he disdained to don his defensive armor, relying instead on ducking behind a shield held before him. It was as if it was all part of a game, a view enhanced by his sight of a young man on the battlements armed with a crossbow in one hand and a frying pan as shield in the other. As the man knocked away arrows with his kitchen utensil, Richard laughed aloud at his skill and even applauded. He took one chance too many. As he ducked behind his shield to avoid one of the darts, he was too slow and the missile hit him at the base of his neck, where it joined his left shoulder.

Instructing Mercadier to take the castle by assault and hang all the garrison except the "knight of the frying pan," he rode back to his tent, not yet unduly worried by his wound. Taking his fate in his own hands for the last time, he tried to pull out the arrow but succeeded only in breaking the shaft, leaving the barbed point deep within the wound. Matters had now taken a serious turn. Only the extraction of the complete missile could have saved him, for it must have driven strands of dirty material from his clothing deep into his body, and these were likely to cause infection. The extraction of the barb, without disinfectant, might also spread disease and make gangrene a strong possibility. One of Mercadier's soldiers, who claimed to be a surgeon, took on the unenviable task and the operation, conducted by torchlight, involved a great deal of mangling of Richard's flesh. The main problem was that, now in his forty-second year, Richard had grown fat and the excess flesh made it difficult to find the steel point. A second surgeon joined the operation, but so much damage had been done during the extraction that infection was now certain. The wound would not heal, swelled, and became discolored. Soon it had become gangrenous and Richard knew that he was dying.

Richard wrote to his mother, and she rushed to Châlus from nearby Fontevrault to be with him in his last hours. He also prepared a will and called on his four most trusted lieutenants to swear an oath of fealty to his brother John as his successor. Unlike Saladin, who died a pauper, Richard was still a rich man, but in donating a quarter of his wealth to the poor he did as much as was conventional in Christian Europe. The rest went to John, except for all his jewels, which were bequeathed to his nephew, Emperor Otto of Germany.

Mercadier, meanwhile, had captured the castle, hanged the garrison, and dragged the bowman who had shot Richard into the dying king's presence. Their conversation has become famous as yet another of the legends that surround this monarch. Roger of Howden begins with a bizarre question from the king, in view of the fact that he was besieging a castle and threatening to hang all the garrison. "What evil have I done to thee? Why hast thou slain me?" asked Richard, to which the cross-bowman replied, "Thou didst slay my father and my two brothers with thine own hand; thou wouldst have slain me likewise." The dying king then made the kind of magnanimous gesture that was more typical of Saladin than himself, though one must remember how he said much the same to William Marshal, after Henry II's death. "I forgive thee my death," he said to the bowman, ordering that he should be released, with a hundred shillings. But Mercadier, full of hatred for the murderer of his great patron, waited for Richard to breathe his last before having the young bowman flayed alive. It was an end more in keeping with the most ferocious warrior of his age.

Queen Eleanor was with her son when he died, and she recorded that at the last he "placed all his trust, after God, in her, that she would make provision for his soul's welfare with motherly care to the utmost of her power." She also commented: 'I have lost the staff of my age, the light of my eyes.' Richard had always been the love of her life. Eleanor carried out his final wishes that his brain and internal organs should be buried in the Poitevin abbey of Charroux, his heart at Rouen, and the embalmed corpse at his father's feet in the abbey church of Fontevrault.

The final words on Richard the Lionheart should, perhaps, be left to those who suffered most from the "lion" but appreciated the honesty of Richard's "heart": his adversaries in the holy war. Ibn al-Athir wrote, "Richard's courage, shrewdness, energy, and patience made him the most remarkable ruler of his times."

Select Bibliography

Primary Sources

LATIN AND FRENCH HISTORIANS

Ambroise, *L'Estoire de la guerre sainte*. Edited and translated by Gaston Paris (Collection de documents inedits sur l'histoire de France: Paris, 1897); translated by M. J. Hubert and J. La Monte as *The Crusade of Richard Lion-heart* (New York, 1941)

Ernoul, *Chronique d'Ernoul et de Bernard le Tresorier*. Edited by L. de Mas-Latrie (Paris, 1971)

L'Estoire d'Eracles empereur et la conqueste de la terre d'outremer: La continuation de l'estoire de Guillaume arcevesque de Sur, Recueil des Historiens des Croisades: Historiens Occidentaux, vols. 1–2 (Paris, 1859)

De expugnatione terrae sanctae per Saladinum Libellus. Edited by William Stubbs (London, 1875)

Fulcher of Chartres, *Historia Hierosolymitana: Gesta Francorum Iherusalem Peregrinantium*, ed. H. Hagenmeyer (Heidelberg, 1913)

Gesta Regis Henrici II and *Gesta Regis Richardi I*. Edited by William Stubbs, Rolls Series 49, 2 vols. (London, 1867)

L'Histoire de Guillaume le Marechal. Edited and translated by P. Meyer, 3 vols. (Paris, 1891–1901)

Itinerarium peregrinorum et gesta regis Ricardi. Edited by William Stubbs, Rolls Series 34: I (London, 1864)

Jacques de Vitry, *History of Jerusalem*. Translated by A. Stewart (London, 1896)

Joinville, *Histoire de Saint Louis*. Edited by N. de Wailly (Paris, 1883)

Raymond of Aguilers, *Historia Francorum qui ceperunt Jerusalem*, Recueil des Historiens des Croisades: Historiens Occidentaux, vol. 3 (Paris, 1866)

Roger of Howden, *Chronica*. Edited by William Stubbs, Rolls Series 51, 4 vols. (London, 1868–71)

William of Tyre, *Historia rerum in partibus transmarinis gestarum*, Recueil des Historiens des Croisades: Historiens Occidentaux, vol. I (Paris, 1844)

ORIENTAL HISTORIANS

Abu Shama ['Abd al-Rahman ibn Ishma'il], *Kitab al-raudatain*, vols. 1–2 (Cairo, 1956–62); vols. 4–5 in Recueil des Historiens des Croisades: Historiens Occidentaux (Paris, 1898 and 1906)

Baha al-Din [ibn Shaddad], *Sirat Salah al-Din*. Edited by J. al-Shayyal (Cairo, 1962)

Ibn al-Athir, *Al-kamil fi'l-tarikh,* 12 vols. (Beirut, 1965)

Ibn Jubair, *The Travels of Ibn Jubayr [sic]* Edited by W. Wright, Gibb Memorial Series (Leiden, 1907)

Imad al-Din al-Isfahani, *Al-barq al-shami*. Sec 3; MS, Bruce II, Sec 5; MS, Marsh 425 (Bodleian Library, Oxford)

—, *Sana al-barq al-shami*. Abridged by al-Bundari, Fath b. Ali, pt. I; edited by R. Sesen (Beirut, 1971)

—, *Kitab al-fath al-qussi fi'l-fath al-Qudsi*. Edited by Landsberg (Leiden, 1888)

Usamah ibn Munqidh, *Memoirs*. Edited and translated by P. K. Hitti as *Memoirs of an Arab-Syrian Gentleman* (Khayats: Beirut, 1964)

Secondary Sources

A. S. Atiya, *Crusade, Commerce and Culture* (Bloomington: London, 1962)

P. Aube, *Badouin IV de Jérusalem* (Tallandier: Paris, 1981)

J. W. Baldwin, *The Government of Philip Augustus* (University of California Press, Berkeley, CA 1986)

M. W. Baldwin, *Raymond III of Tripolis and the Fall of Jerusalem: 1140–1187* (Princeton University Press: Princeton, NJ, 1936)

J. H. Beeler, *Warfare in Feudal Europe: 730–1200* (Cornell University Press: London, 1972)

M. Benvenisti, *The Crusaders in the Holy Land* (Macmillan: New York and London, 1970)

M. Bloch, *Feudal Society*. Translated by L. A. Manyon (Routledge & Kegan Paul: London, 1961)

T. S. R. Boase, *Kingdoms and Strongholds of the Crusaders* (Thames & Hudson: London, 1971)

J. Bradbury, *Philip Augustus* (Longman: London, 1998)

C. M. Brand, "The Byzantines and Saladin, 1185–1192: Opponents of the Third Crusade": *Speculum*, xxxvii (1962), pp. 167–81

—, *Byzantium Confronts the West 1180–1204* (Harvard University Press: Cambridge, MA, 1968)

A. Bridge, *The Crusades* (Granada: London, 1980)

J. A. Brundage, *The Crusades: A Documentary Survey* (Marquette University Press: Milwaukee, 1962)

J. A. Brundage, *Richard Lionheart* (Scribner's: New York, 1973)

P. Contamine, *War in the Middle Ages*. Translated by M. Jones (Blackwell: Oxford, 1984)

N. Daniel, *The Arabs and Medieval Europe* (Longman: Beirut, 1975)

H. Delbruck, *Geschichte des Kriegskunst im Rahmen der Politische Geschichte*, vol. 3 (Berlin, 2/1923)

P. Deschamps, *Au Temps des Croisades* (Hachette: Paris, 1972)

P. W. Edbury and J. G. Rowe, "William of Tyre and the Patriarchal Election of 1180," *English Historical Review*, ccclxvi (1978), pp. 1–25

A. S. Ehrenkreutz, *Saladin* (New York University Press: New York, 1972)

F. Gabrieli, *Arab Historians of the Crusades* (Routledge & Kegan Paul: London, 1969)

H. A. R. Gibb, "The Arab Sources for the Life of Saladin," *Speculum*, xxv (1950), pp. 58–72

—, *Studies on the Civilization of Islam* (Princeton University Press: Princeton, NJ, 1962)

—, *The Life of Saladin from the Works of Imad ad-Din and Baha ad-Din* (Clarendon Press: Oxford, 1971)

J. Gillingham, *Richard the Lionheart* (Weidenfeld & Nicolson: London, 2/1989)

J. Gillingham, *Richard Coeur de Lion* (Hambledon Press: London, 1994)

J. Gray, *A History of Jerusalem* (Robert Hale: London, 1969)

F. Groh, *Der Zusammenbruch des Reiches Jerusalem: 1187–89* (Jena, 1909)

R. Grousset, *Histoire des Croisades et du Royaume franc de Jérusalem*, 3 vols. (Plon: Paris, 1934)

B. Hamilton, "The Titular Nobility of the Latin East: The Case of Agnes of Courtenay," *Crusade and Settlement*, ed. P. W. Edbury (University College Cardiff Press: Cardiff, 1985), pp. 197–201

I. Heath, *Armies and Enemies of the Crusades: 1096–1291* (Wargames Research Group: London, 1978)

—, *A Wargamers' Guide to the Crusades* (Patrick Stephens: Cambridge, 1980)

P. Herde, "Die Kampfe bei den Hornern von Hittin und der Untergang des

Kreuzritterheeres (3. und 4. Juli 1187)," *Römische Quartalschrift fur Christliche Alterumskunde und Kirtschengeschichte*, lxi (1966)

G. F. Hill, *A History of Cyprus*, 4 vols. (Cambridge University Press: Cambridge, 1940–52)

G. Hindley, *Saladin* (Constable: London, 1976)

J. E. Hult, *Bohemond III: Prince of Antioch* (unpublished thesis, New York University, 1974)

G. Jeffery, *Cyprus under an English King* (Zeno: London, 1973)

B. Z. Kedar, "The General Tax of 1183 in the Crusading Kingdom of Jerusalem: Innovation or Adaption?," *English Historical Review*, lxxxix (1974), pp. 339–45

—, "The Patriarch Eraclius," *Outremer: Studies in the History of the Crusading Kingdom of Jerusalem*, ed. B. Z. Kedar, H. E. Mayer and R. C. Smail (Yad Izhak Ben Zvi Institute: Jerusalem, 1982), pp. 177–204

J. E. King, *The Knights Hospitallers in the Holy Land* (Methuen: London, 1931)

A. Krey, "William of Tyre: The Making of an Historian in the Middle Ages," *Speculum*, xvi (1941), pp. 149–66

J. L. La Monte, *Feudal Monarchy in the Latin Kingdom of Jerusalem: 1100–1291* (Medieval Academy of America: Cambridge, MA, 1932)

S. Lane-Poole, *Saladin and the Fall of the Kingdom of Jerusalem* (Khayats: Beirut, 1964)

T. E. Lawrence, *Crusader Castles*, 2 vols. (Golden Cockerel Press: London, 1936)

F. Lot, *L'Arte Militaire au Moyen Age en Europe et dans le Proche Orient*, 2 vols. (Paris, 1946)

M. C. Lyons and J. Riley-Smith, *Saladin: The Politics of the Holy War* (Cambridge University Press: Cambridge, 1982)

A. Maalouf, *The Crusades through Arab Eyes*. Translated by J. Rothschild (Al Saqi: London, 1984)

H. E. Mayer, *The Crusades*. Translated by J. Gillingham (Oxford University Press: Oxford, 1972)

—, "Henry II and the Holy Land," *English Historical Review*, ccclxxxv (1982), pp. 721–39

M. Meade, *Eleanor of Aquitaine* (Muller: London, 1978)

J. F. Michaud, *Bibliothèque des Croisades*, 4 vols (Ducollet: Paris, 1829)

W. Muller-Weiner, *Castles of the Crusaders* (McGraw-Hill: New York, 1966)

D. C. Munro, *The Kingdom of the Crusaders* (Kennikat Press: Port Washington, 1966)

P. H. Newby, *Saladin in his Time* (Faber: London, 1983)

R. L. Nicholson, *Joscelyn III and the Fall of the Crusader States: 1134–1199* (Brill: Leiden, 1973)

K. Norgate, *Richard the Lionheart* (Macmillan: London, 1924)

J. J. Norwich, *The Kingdom in the Sun* (Macmillan: London, 1970)

Z. Oldenbourg, *The Crusades.* Translated by A. Carter (Weidenfeld & Nicolson: London, 1966)

C. W. C. Oman, *A History of the Art of Warfare in the Middle Ages,* vol. 1 (Methuen: London, 1924)

G. Ostrogorsky, *History of the Byzantine State* (Blackwell: Oxford, 1956)

R. Payne, *The Dream and the Tomb: A History of the Crusades* (Robert Hale: London, 1986)

R. Pernoud, *The Crusaders.* Translated by E. Grant (Oliver & Boyd: London, 1963)

J. Prawer, *Histoire du Royaume Latin de Jerusalem* (Editions du Centre National de la Recherche Scientifique: Paris, 1969)

—, *The Crusaders' Kingdom* (Praeger: New York, 1972)

—, *The World of the Crusaders* (Weidenfeld & Nicolson: London, 1972)

—, *Crusader Institutions* (Clarendon Press: Oxford, 1980)

—, "The Jerusalem the Crusaders Captured: A Contribution to the Medieval Topography of the City," *Crusade and Settlement,* ed. P. W. Edbury (University College Cardiff Press: Cardiff, 1985)

J. Richard, *Le Royaume Latin de Jerusalem* (Presses Universitaires de France: Paris, 1953)

J. Riley-Smith, *The Feudal Nobility and the Kingdom of Jerusalem: 1174–1277* (Shoe String Press: Hamden, CT, 1973)

R. Rogers, *Latin Siege Warfare in the Twelfth Century* (Oxford University Press: Oxford, 1992)

R. Rohricht, *Geschichte des Königsreichs Jerusalem* (Innsbruck, 1898)

—, ed., *Regesta Regni Hierosolymitania* (Innsbruck, 1893–1904)

C. J. Rosebault, *Saladin: Prince of Chivalry* (Cassell: London, 1930)

S. Runciman, *A History of the Crusades,* 3 vols. (Cambridge University Press: Cambridge, 1951–4)

—, *The Families of Outremer: The Feudal Nobility of the Crusader Kingdom of Jerusalem* (London, 1959)

H. Russell Robinson, *Oriental Armour* (H. Jenkins: London, 1967)

G. Schlumberger, *Campagnes du Roi Amaurey 1er de Jerusalem* (Plon: Paris, 1905)

—, *Renaud de Châtillon: Prince d'Antioche* (Plon: Paris, 1923)

K. M. Setton, ed., *A History of the Crusades,* 4 vols. (University of Wisconsin Press: Madison, 1969)

D. Seward, *The Monks of War: The Military Religious Orders* (Eyre Methuen: London, 1972)

E. Simon, *The Piebald Standard: A Biography of the Knights Templars* (Cassell: London, 1959)

R. C. Smail, *Crusading Warfare: 1097–1193* (Cambridge University Press: Cambridge, 1956)

—, *The Crusaders in Syria and the Holy Land* (Praeger: New York, 1973)

—, "The Predicaments of Guy of Lusignan, 1183–1187," *Outremer: Studies in the History of the Crusading Kingdom of Jerusalem*, ed. B. Z. Kedar, H. E. Mayer and R. C. Smail (Yad Izhak Ben Zvi Institute: Jerusalem, 1982), pp. 157–76

W. B. Stevenson, *The Crusaders in the East* (Cambridge University Press: Cambridge, 1907)

L. A. M. Sumberg, "The Tafurs and the First Crusade," *Medieval Studies*, xxi (1959), pp. 224ff

C. Thubron, *Jerusalem* (Heinemann: London, 1969)

A. A. Vasiliev, *A History of the Byzantine Empire* (University of Wisconsin Press: Madison, 1961)

J. F. Verbruggen, *The Art of Warfare in Western Europe during the Middle Ages* (Amsterdam and New York, 1976)

W. M. Watt, "Islamic Conceptions of the Holy War," *The Holy War*, ed. T. P. Murphy (Ohio State University Press: Columbus, OH, 1976)

T. Wise, *Armies of the Crusades* (Osprey: London, 1978)

—, *The Knights of Christ* (Osprey: London, 1984)

Index